BLACKWELL/MARYLAND LECTURES

The Development of Language

The Development of Language
Acquisition, Change, and Evolution

David Lightfoot

University of Maryland

First published 1999

2 4 6 8 10 9 7 5 3 1

Blackwell Publishers Inc.
350 Main Street
Malden, Massachusetts 02148
USA

Blackwell Publishers Ltd
108 Cowley Road
Oxford OX4 1JF
UK

Library of Congress Cataloging-in-Publication Data

Lightfoot, David.
The development of language : acquisition, change, and evolution /
David Lightfoot.
p. cm. — (Blackwell/Maryland lectures in language and
cognition ; 1)
Includes bibliographical references and index.
ISBN 0–631–21059–8 (acid-free paper). — ISBN 0–631–21060–1 (pbk.)
1. Linguistic change. 2. Language acquisition. 3. Grammar,
Comparative and general. 4. Language and languages—Origin.
I. Title. II. Series.
P142.L54 1998
401'.93—dc21 98–28674
CIP

British Library Cataloguing in Publication Data

A CIP catalogue record for this book is available from the
British Library

Typeset in 10 on 12½ pt Sabon
by Graphicraft Limited, Hong Kong
Printed in Great Britain by M.P.G. Books, Bodmin, Cornwall

This book is printed on acid-free paper

Contents

This book is dedicated to Homer, who knew that the journey is the thing, and to Heraclitus, who taught us that everything is always traveling.

Foreword

Homer understood that we can learn much about people by seeing how they change in the face of changing circumstances. Odysseus wanders aimlessly for long periods, lies with Circe for five years, and then faces cataclysmic events which change him: shipwrecks, the rage of the Cyclops, a trip through the netherworld, his crew devouring the cattle of the Sun. Through these events, Odysseus changes, and we come to understand more about the man and about humankind and about life. So with languages. Individual languages are on their own odyssey through time, and they are liable to change, sometimes dramatically; some of those changes reveal something about the nature of the language or about language in general.

To switch our Greeks, Heraclitus believed that everything is in flux, and consequently that we can never step into the same river twice, because things are always different. Now we may adjust our metaphor and think of a language's odyssey as flowing water. Water has intrinsic properties of its own, but it flows chaotically, not exactly the same from minute to minute. Sometimes water flows down a riverbed through rapids, over weirs and waterfalls; the Greeks called these things *catastrophes*.

Language is used chaotically, and no two people say and hear the same things. In particular, no two *children* step into the same river in the same way, and they do not hear the same things. Often this makes no real difference, because there is flexibility in the system. Children differ in their early experience, but they may nonetheless grow up with essentially the same mature capacity. It is true that no two people speak exactly the same way; we often know in a split second who is on the other end of the telephone, because a person's language is as distinctive as their thumbprint. But people raised in the same speech community often end up talking pretty much the same way.

Not always, however. Sometimes children turn into adults who have linguistic capacities which are very different from their parents', and this may be a function of quite minor differences in early experience – what chaos theoreticians call "sensitive dependence on initial conditions." This is grammatical change, and I call these discontinuities "catastrophes"; they reveal much about the nature of people's linguistic capacities.

This book is about language change and what that tells us about intrinsic human properties. People have long been fascinated by this topic, and modern linguistics has its origins in work on language change. There is a continuous tradition of systematic work on language, beginning in the early nineteenth century and continuing to the present day. Initially that tradition was concerned entirely with language change; then in this century, linguists broadened the scope of their analyses. People continue to work on language change – indeed, this work has flourished – but they work alongside colleagues who study different dimensions of language: how it is acquired by young children, how it is understood on-line, how it can be modeled on a computer, and so on.

The study of language is still in its infancy, and many of our ideas are quite crude. Yet certain things are now understood well, better than in the nineteenth century. Other things are within range of being understood, and we can gain more insight; and other intriguing things cannot be thought about very usefully at present and are now beyond our reach.

There was a significant shift in linguistic thought in the 1950s, when some old ideas were reactivated and began to reshape the way that people thought about language: our language capacity manifests biological properties of the organism. We have been slow to assimilate the effects of that shift, but it changes how we study language change. Over the last several years, many people have studied linguistic change in the light of this shift. The DIGS (Diachronic Generative Syntax) meetings have become a forum for this work, flipping from one side of the Atlantic to the other every two years. At this point, we have substantial results which show that students of language change have much to gain from the conceptual shift that Noam Chomsky brought about.

If we take on board Chomsky's conceptual shift, then thinking in terms of individual grammars represented in people's brains enables us to circumvent some of the earlier problems in explaining why and how languages change. We can make progress in understanding change. That progress, in turn, has consequences for the way we think about language acquisition: it shows that the way in which Chomsky's shift has been applied to the study of language acquisition needs to be rethought. Any theory of grammar and any theory of acquisition need to be compatible with the fact that languages change, but some current theories fail in this regard and give no understanding of why changes happen in the way they do.

I shall develop some ideas about how language acquisition takes place, which differ from those in much of the formal learnability literature. I shall offer explanations for change in grammars without invoking any *theory* of change, and I shall account for language acquisition without invoking any learning algorithms. In that sense, my analyses are more "minimalist" than those which use these extra devices. Two big ideas drive the analyses. One is that language acquisition is "cue-based": children scan their linguistic environment for certain pre-specified abstract cues, and they pay no attention to the set of sentences that their emerging grammars may generate. The second is that change, like the life of Odysseus, is highly contingent, dependent on particular circumstances; we should not expect to find deterministic explanations for long-term changes, of the kind that have long enchanted students of language change. Neither of these ideas is novel; each can be found in the work of others, even in very early work. But I shall weave the ideas together in a particular way.

Science is the most cooperative of enterprises, and nothing is entirely new. Indeed, several aspects of what we think of as the Chomskyan shift were anticipated by nineteenth-century writers. As you read the book, you will see whose shoulders I stand on. There are certain shoulders that I stand on in an immediate sense, which requires acknowledgement. The ideas that I explore here have been changed and improved by discussions with many colleagues and with audiences who have listened to presentations of one kind or another. I think particularly of lively exchanges with audiences at the University of Texas, Yale University, the City University of New York, Tsing Hua University in Taiwan, the Istituto Veneto di Scienze, Lettere ed Arti in Venice, and the Scuola Normale Superiore in Pisa. I owe a great deal to ongoing discussions over many years with Stephen Crain, Norbert Hornstein, and Juan Uriagereka in my own department at the University of Maryland, and with Elan Dresher, Tony Kroch, Ian Roberts, and Anthony Warner on distant islands.

Some people who are not professional linguists have taken the trouble to read drafts of some chapters with their nonspecialist spectacles: Sari Hornstein, Richard Price, Felice Sacks, and Elizabeth Wallace. Their comments have been important to me, because, while I am writing in part for my seasoned peers, this is not a monograph, and I have also tried to make our work accessible to beginning graduate students and to historians, biologists, and physicists who have thought a little about language, perhaps having read Steven Pinker's *The Language Instinct* or some other introductory text. The central ideas, I believe, can be understood without the need for much technology. At some points, things are more complex, and I explore technicalities which are there for the dedicated linguists and which some readers will want to skip, and sometimes I discuss fundamental matters which the experts will want to skip. When I cut corners in the interest of accessibility, I hope that the nonspecialists will thank me and the historical linguists forgive me. Since I have tried to write at two levels, I have adapted a useful idea from Kip Thorne's book *Black Holes and Time Warps* and have shaded those passages written only for dedicated linguists.

I owe special thanks to the energy and insight of Stephen Anderson, Noam Chomsky, Mark Hale, Norbert Hornstein, April McMahon, Robert McMahon, Nigel Vincent, and Anthony Warner, who gave me helpful, substantive feedback on the manuscript. Charles Rutherford helped with some translations. I am indebted to my university for a Distinguished Faculty Research Fellowship, which provided time for my own odyssey, without the distractions of teaching. My colleagues in the Linguistics Department generously invited me to give the first Blackwell/Maryland Lectures on Language and Cognition; this book is the written report of those lectures. I have long enjoyed Philip Carpenter's cocktail of creativity, common sense, and commercial nous; he was the compleat publisher and the ideal respondent when Norbert came up with the idea of this lecture series.

Now on to Homer's wine-dark sea, under the care of bright-eyed Athena, urbane goddess of practical rationality:

> Sing to me of the man, Muse, the man of twists and turns
> Driven time and again off course . . .

1

Introduction

Anybody who has attended a performance of *Othello* or read the King James version of the Bible knows that English has changed over the last 400 years. Shakespeare's sentence structures were not like today's, but when we read a speech by Othello, we believe that it is English, and often *1610* we understand it more or less straightforwardly.

> How may the duke be therewith satisfied,
> Whose messengers are here about my side,
> Upon some present business of the state,
> To bring me to him?

Sometimes we do not understand.

> If I do prove her haggard,
> Though that her jesses were my dear heart-strings,
> I'd whistle her off, and let her down the wind,
> To prey at fortune.

In this case, we need to know some falconry: *haggard* referred to an adult hawk caught in the wild; *jesses* were short leather straps attached to a hawk's legs, usually with a ring on the end; a hawk flying with a following wind generally did not return. For Shakespeare, the conjunction *though* was typically followed by *that*, unlike in modern speech. Nonetheless, if we abstract away from the cultural factors and knowledge of falconry, the *1410* language itself is familiar, and we continue to assume that we hear English. *1380*

From Shakespeare, go back another 200 years and listen to Chaucer's wife of Bath report the woes of marriage. She had credentials, having married five times since she was twelve, each time to a man who was worthy in his own way. The language is a good deal less familiar.

> Experience, though noon auctoritee
> Were in this world, were right y-nough to me
> To speke of wo that is in mariage;
> For, lordinges, sith I twelf yeer was of age,
> Thonked be god that is eterne on lyve,
> Housbondes at chirche-dore I have had fyve;
> For I so oft have y-wedded be;
> And alle were worthy men in hir degree.

Travel back a few more centuries to the Old English translation of Bede's *Ecclesiastical History of the English People*, and one may as well be reading a foreign language.

> Ða wæs þy æfteran geare, cwom sum monn in Norðanhymbra mægðe; wæs his noma Eomær. Wæs he sended from Westseaxna cyninge, se wæs haten Cwichelm, þæt he scolde Eadwine þone cyning somed ge rice ge life beneoman.
>
> Then was there come in the following year a certain man into the country of the Northumbrians; his name was Eomær. He had been sent from the king of the West Saxons, who was called Cwichelm, so that he should deprive Eadwine the King of rule and life together.

Not only do sentence structures change in the course of time, but so do the meanings of words, their form, and their pronunciation. Shakespeare could rhyme *convert* and *depart*, and if he were revived and read Othello's speech in his usual way, a modern listener would understand very little. Chaucer would pronounce the vowel of *ripe* like modern *reap*, and *rout* like modern *root*, and his language might sound about as foreign to our ears as Dutch does today.

There is nothing better or worse about any of these forms of English. Anything that one can say in one form of English, one can say in another form. The techniques and the grammatical devices may vary, and certainly the pronunciation varies. Old English had a rich system of case endings attached to nouns, indicating their function in the sentence. Present-day English speakers do not use such cases outside of the pronoun system (which distinguishes *they*, *them*, *their*, depending on whether the pronoun is a subject, a direct object, or a possessor). Instead, we make more extensive use of prepositions and have a more rigid word order. No better, no worse, just different.

The linguist's job is to describe properties of some stage of some language and to offer explanations for why they should be the way they are. Historical linguists provide descriptions for two or more stages and, where

If language foundation is biological, what is the basis? Change? Cultural?

→ Old English artifacts, etc.

Introduction 3

possible, offer explanations for why things changed. They try to provide accurate descriptions, showing how people actually spoke in the past or speak at the present time, and they provide explanations for why structural changes took place.

1.1 Progress or Degeneration?

The goal of accurate description is at odds with a popular, pessimistic attitude which sees pervasive degeneration, wishes to stop it, and seeks to prescribe how people *should* speak. In 1755, Samuel Johnson wrote in the preface to his dictionary that "Tongues, like governments, have a natural tendency to degeneration," and he encouraged his readers to "retard what we cannot repel, that we palliate what we cannot cure."[1] Around this time in England, there was an active political movement to establish an academy to regulate language use, in the fashion of the Académie Française, and to protect English against further rot and decay. This attitude was particularly vigorous in London in the eighteenth century, but it is found frequently in many places. Otto Jespersen (1922: 42) reported that Jacob Grimm in the mid-nineteenth century bemoaned the idea that "six hundred years ago every rustic knew, that is to say practised daily, perfections and niceties in the German language of which the best grammarians nowadays do not even dream." Certainly since the eighteenth century, there has been no shortage of people who set themselves up as language experts, mavens, pontificating on the decline of public speech, and no shortage of people willing to read their complaints and join their lamentations. Every Saturday *The Washington Post* publishes a column of letters decrying linguistic usage found in the papers of the previous week.

For a linguist, this is as senseless as an ethologist telling us that a sparrow doesn't fly as well as it might, or that a bulldog doesn't run as well as a greyhound. The ethologist describes the sparrow's flight and the bulldog's gait, and the scientist studying language describes the way people use English or Hungarian these days. We describe how people use the adverb *hopefully* without urging them not to use it with sentential scope, the way they use *supposedly* or *evidently*; we may note that many people use *data* as a singular noun, uninfluenced by the word's etymology as a Latin plural, and so on. Prescriptions about not using dangling participles or not ending a sentence with a preposition (that is a rule up with which Winston Churchill famously said he would not put) are of no more interest to a linguist than parents' criteria for judging their children's haircuts are to a biologist interested in hair. These prescriptions relate to peripheral

"I'll technology"

Split infinitive

aspects of language use, to decorative details; parents who say *snuck* are upset with children who say *sneaked*, and vice versa. Nobody has to tell children or delinquent adults not to say **The lion seems sleeping*, or **Who did you visit Kim and?*, or **visited Kim London?* (* indicates a form which does not occur). These phenomena reflect core structural properties, and they brook no variation.[2] *except w~ long time*

Optimists may also make value judgments about change, but they take the opposite view: they hold that change means progress, and that time allows languages to become better in some way. Charles Darwin, citing the linguist Max Müller, believed that in language change "the better, the shorter, the easier forms are constantly gaining the upper hand, and they owe their success to their inherent virtue" (1874: 88). This belief in the progress of languages comes in a package with ideas about changes having a general direction to them; we shall discuss these ideas at various points, in chapters 2, 4, 8, and 10, and show that they have little merit.

It is matters of language use that exercise the mavens, and these are very different from issues of literacy. Society may have legitimate goals for changing usage in the domain of literacy. Literacy is an adult skill which relates to people's ability to write language and to interpret written records.

 This is a skill which is taught, and it may be taught differently at different times and in different places, and it may be taught more or less success-fully. To that extent it is a skill like playing chess. Literacy skill, like chess-playing skills, may vary from time to time and may need to be extended to meet some social goal.

A person's speech is different. The ability to use speech grows naturally in children under normal childhood conditions and is more closely ana-logous to the sparrow's flight than to human chess-playing skills. Of course, a person's speech may be amended through conscious choice in maturity, and people may choose to adopt a certain kind of accent or to use a certain kind of vocabulary, in the same way that they may choose to paint their fingernails or to dye or shave their hair. Linguists are most interested in the natural growth of linguistic ability in ordinary people under ordin-ary conditions, abstracting away from this kind of adult contrivance. There is plenty there to wonder at and to puzzle scientists, as we shall see in chapter 3. For example, in a sentence like *Jim is taller than Kim is*, the first *is* is often reduced to *'s* in colloquial speech, but the second is not; one would not say **Jim's taller than Kim's* in normal conversation. We don't need the mavens to tell us this, nor an Academy of the English Language. It is simply a fact about English speakers – a fact which needs to be explained. Why should *is* be reducible in one context but not in another, and how did English speakers come to behave like this?

aunt, double negative (handwritten annotation)

The grammatical mavens are often way behind the curve. A hallmark of their laments is that they fight battles which have already been lost. Consider indirect passives like those in (1) below, where an indirect object serves as the subject of the passive verb. (1a) corresponds to the active sentence *I gave Kim the book*, where *the book* is the direct object and *Kim* the indirect object.

1 (a) Kim was given the book.
   (b) Kim was bequeathed the estate.
   (c) Kim was loaned the money.

These forms are unusual, and there are no real analogues in French, Dutch, German, Italian, and many other languages. Nor did they occur in early English. They began to appear in the fifteenth century. At this time they occurred with the verbs *allow, learn* (= "teach"), *offer, proffer, teach, pay, bring, yield, leave, grant, give, allow,* and *ask*. Some examples from the fifteenth century are shown in (2).

2 (a) All my shepe ar gone, I am not left one. (ca. 1460, *Townley Pl.* ci 24)
   (b) He was gyvyn the gre be my lorde kynge Arthure. (ca. 1470, Malory, *Works* (Vinaver), 699)
   (c) If Sir Thomas thynk that he shuld be alowyd mor, he shal be. (1422–1509, *Paston Letters* (Gairdner), vol. 1, 252)
   (d) I was offered iiij marcs to lese my tytle in the said tythes. (ca. 1479, *Stonor Letters* (Camden), no. 245, 83)

In the sixteenth century the construction became more common and was attested with more verbs: *say, threaten, adjudge, foretell,* and *show*.

These are some facts about the early occurrences of indirect passives. Contemporary grammarians, however, seem to have been oblivious to these forms. Grammarians before Henry Sweet in the late nineteenth century usually did not even mention the indirect passive; then, when they did become aware of it, they decried it as another instance of degeneration. As recently as 60 years ago, Stokoe commented that "it is strictly speaking wrong to make the Indirect Object of the Active idiom the Subject in the Passive idiom" (1937: 78). In 1957 Kirschner provided a list of verbs occurring in the indirect passive, calling several of them "Americanisms": *accredit, adjudge, administer, appoint, apportion, assure, attribute, bequeath, cable, concede, envy, furnish, land, loan, mail, phone, provide, restore, sell, stand, supply, tender, vote, wire, wish, write*. Several of these verbs appear in Visser's lists of indirect passives, attributed to British authors as early as Shakespeare and Goldsmith – much too early to be influenced by "Americanisms." This is an innovation which affected English, first in the fifteenth century, and led to the language having a construction which is unusual among the world's languages. Our goal is to describe it and explain it (chapter 5), but there is no useful value judgment to be made, and no reason to follow Samuel Johnson's advice and seek to "retard" it.

Modern prescriptivists tell us that it is wrong to end sentences with prepositions, that double negatives are a hallmark of inferior speech, and so on. In recent months, there has been much consternation in the press about "Ebonics," a form of English which uses double negatives, as in *I didn't meet nobody*, which is equivalent to *I didn't meet anybody* in the speech of the President of Harvard.[3] Yet great writers have used double negatives prolifically for hundreds of years. For example, in the prologue to the *Canterbury Tales*, Chaucer piles negative upon negative in describing a knight who was a perfect gentleman and who never yet said a rude word in all his life to any man:

> He nevere yet no vileyne ne sayde
> In all his lyf unto no maner wight.

Double, triple, and quadruple negatives are not generally used in modern "standard" English, but they are used commonly in other languages. French, the world's most "logical" language according to some mavens, routinely uses double negatives; there are two negative forms, *ne* and *personne*, in *Je n'ai vu personne*, "I have seen nobody." There is nothing inherently inferior or "illogical" about double negatives, and they were common in Chaucer's English.

Another change – a favorite of mine and interesting for issues of "correctness" – concerns the meaning of verbs such as *like, ail*, and *repent*. These verbs used to mean, respectively, "to cause pleasure/pain/regret for," and they have undergone a switch and come to mean "to derive pleasure/pain/regret from." In early English, apples might like me, shingles might ail me, and my sins might repent me; but in modern English, I like apples, I may be ailing from a bad cold, and it is up to me to repent of my sins. (*What ails you?* is a frozen relic of the past, used as a question or an indefinite relative clause.) So these and about 30 other verbs underwent a kind of switch in their meaning, and all at about the same time: the noun phrases which used to occur as subjects have come to be objects, and vice versa.

A lot of energy has been devoted to figuring out why this change took place, why it happened at the particular time it did, and why it affected just these verbs. We shall discuss this in section 5.3. One element of some explanations that have been offered is that these verbs could occur in an unusual order, object–verb–subject, which ceased to be possible from the fifteenth century onwards. This means that a simple sentence like *The king likes the queen* would be analyzed by speakers with the old system as (3a), and by speakers with the new system as (3b). In (3a) the syntax is object–verb–subject, and *like* means "cause pleasure for"; in (3b) the syntax is subject–verb–object, and *like* means "derive pleasure from."

3 (a) object[the king] verb[causes pleasure for] subject[the queen].
   (b) subject[the king] verb[derives pleasure from] object[the queen].

Speakers would be blissfully unaware of any change. Each generation would interpret the sentence to mean that the king was happy and that the queen was the reason for his happiness. However, speakers with the old system would also produce sentences like (4); in each instance, the first noun is a direct object and the second the subject of the verb, and *like* has its old meaning. We know this because the first noun is in the accusative case insofar as we can tell (4a), the second noun has nominative case (4c), and the verb agrees in number with the second noun (4b, c). None of the forms of (4) would be generated by the new system, but instead one would find forms like (5), where the first noun is the subject of the sentence, and the verb has its new meaning. As a result, (4a) had the same meaning as (5a), (4b) as (5b), and (4c) as (5c).

4 (a) Him likes the queen.
   (b) The king like the princesses.
   (c) The princes likes she.

5 (a) He likes the queen.
   (b) The king likes the princesses.
   (c) The princes like her.

This is the way that change may take place: it may be covert, and people are often unaware of changes as they happen. But it is likely that there would have been some disorder and recrimination around the dinner table. Parents with the old system would not have known that their children were analyzing *The king likes the queen* differently; but they would have noticed the novel forms of (5), and they would have encouraged their children to "speak properly" and use forms like those of (4). This would probably have been translated into issues of "correctness." We can be sure that William Safire, the self-styled "language maven", who writes a weekly column "On language" for *The New York Times*, would have written a column berating young people who produced forms like (5) for contributing to the decline of English, if *The New York Times* had been around in the fifteenth century.[4]

Parents would have been upset at children using forms like those of (5), but they would have been unaware of the structural change taking place in the language. Changes like this may upset people as they happen; but linguists are interested in describing them and, if possible, explaining why they happen. They are facts of the life of languages, and intriguing. They are a historical linguist's subject matter, and they constitute the twists and turns of a language's odyssey.

1.2   The Records, our Witnesses

Facts like these raise a prior question: how can we know how people spoke in the fifteenth century or, harder, in classical Rome? All we have are marks on a page, and those marks have often been edited and changed. Worse, they tell us nothing about certain things. There is a big difference between the rhythm of a South African's speech and that of a Texan, between a Yorkshireman and an English-speaking Indian; but there is no way you could tell from the letters they write – the written word makes them all sound the same. The question of how we may legitimately interpret our records is an enormous one, the topic of many books, most recently one by Roger Lass (1997).

Lass (1997: 19) offers a simple example. What is the last line of the prologue to Chaucer's *Canterbury Tales*? Any recent standard edition ends thus:

> And he bigan with right a myrie chere
> His tale anon, and seyde as ye may heere.

But some editions give the last line as

> His tale anon, and seyde in this manere.

We do not have the manuscript that Chaucer wrote, only later copies; and the oldest of those copies give both versions. This example shows how

much scribes and editors are willing to change a text deliberately, in order ①
to meet some self-imposed standard. Then, of course, there may be acci- ②
dental errors in copying. So it is not obvious what Chaucer wrote. Nor is
it obvious exactly how Chaucer himself would have pronounced what is
written. Masses of truly fascinating detective work has been devoted to
questions like these. The texts are witnesses to the past, but, as always, the *cf.*
testimony of witnesses cannot be taken at face value and must be evalu- *New testament greek etc.*
ated carefully. *Copies etc*

Sometimes skillful detective work allows us to interpret the apparent
messiness of a text as revealing a change in progress. Lass (1997: 67)
considers some texts by William Caxton which show the oblique third
person plural form as *them* 62 percent of the time and *hem* 38 percent.
Further analysis shows that the alternation is different in different contexts: 81 percent *them* and 19 percent *hem* as a direct object, and 57 percent *them* and 43 percent *hem* after a preposition. This shows that the
substitution of *them* for *hem* started earlier with direct objects than with
prepositional objects. This kind of revealing variation is often eliminated
by editors concerned with uniformity and consistency in texts. The different versions of Chaucer's prologue show how ruthless editors can be.

There are, of course, general questions about the proper way to interpret
historical records, and particular issues arise in the context of particular
analyses. I do not plan to tackle these questions here. Suffice it to say that
they arise differently for different instances. The question of how Cicero
and other Latin speakers in pre-imperial Rome pronounced *quinque* "five"
is very different from the question of how Chaucer ended his prologue.
To take another example, if we find forms like *Doth he speak of Malory?*
in a particular writer in the sixteenth century, while contemporaries have
Speaketh he of Malory?, and if those forms are relatively frequent in his
writings, then it is reasonable to conclude that he would *say* that kind of
thing. It is not always the case, of course, that we can take written texts
as indications of the way that people spoke. There are writing conventions
which lead us to write things that we would not say in quite that way,
and, in the case of printed texts, editors may have amended the text, in the
way that my editors sometimes rephrase what I write. Words like *however*,
notwithstanding, and *whom* are familiar in modern written texts, but much
less common in the speech of most people. Similarly there may be construction types, some perhaps borrowed from Latin at a time when Latin
carried prestige, which were favored in writing but were not the kind of
thing that people would say.

In this book we shall be focusing on syntactic changes, changes in the
structure of utterances, viewing them as manifestations of changes in

individual grammars. For us, a grammar is part of human biology; it is a
mental entity, represented in a person's mind/brain and encoding that person's linguistic capacity. This is not the lay sense of *grammar*, and we shall
discuss grammars in detail in chapter 3. There is no question that people's
grammars used to have the verb *like* meaning "cause pleasure for" and did
not generate structures with indirect passives like *Kim was given the book*.
Many details are important, as we shall see; but we may confidently draw
the broad conclusion without too much concern about what occurs in individual texts. What one finds in individual texts, and how that manifests
the properties of people's grammars, becomes important as we consider
the way in which the change took place. We shall discuss this matter
generally in chapter 4, and in the context of specific case studies in chapters
5–7, particularly in the context of the loss of case endings (section 5.3).
So when we find indirect passives showing up profusely in written texts,
it is reasonable to assume that many people of the time spoke that way. If
we ask questions about major structural shifts which are manifested by a
variety of surface forms that we may expect to find in written texts, we are
less likely to be confounded by the distorting effects of writing conventions.
On the other hand, if our major focus were on more peripheral matters
like the use of *however* in spoken language, it would be harder to get
round the writing conventions and establish its spoken usage.

Before we proceed to the body of the book, it will help orient us if I
give some general information about the major divisions of the history of
English. Historians generally distinguish certain periods. Old English covers
the period from the earliest records, dating from about 700, up until 1150.
Towards the end of the ninth century King Alfred developed a written
standard form based on the West Saxon dialect. This standard was extended
a century or so later through the prolific work of Ælfric. From 1066,
Norman-French became the language of power and administration, up until
about 1400. Little English has survived from 1066 to 1200, when records
were generally kept in Latin. There are some translations of earlier homilies, and for original work we have the continuations of the *Anglo-Saxon
Chronicle* (the last entry is for 1154), although the scribes for the later
periods seem not to have been fully literate in English.

Old English is similar to modern Dutch and German in many ways.
It has four case endings, adjectives have strong and weak forms, and
they agree with nouns in number, gender, and case. Verbs have distinctive
subjunctive forms. And word order is object–verb quite consistently in
embedded clauses.

The Middle English period, usually taken to be 1150–1500, is very
different. Surviving records change substantially at the end of the period.

From 1415 Henry V and his court began to correspond in English, and *X* much government, court, and Parliamentary business was conducted in English. The "King's English" became a basic standard language of administration, which was promoted by the introduction of printing in 1476, first in Westminster, the seat of government. And the language changed. By the beginning of the fourteenth century, case endings on nouns and adjectives had pretty much disappeared, prepositions became more widely used, nominative subjects became obligatory, and word order was standardized to the modern verb–object in all clause types.

The most important external influence on English came from the *Viking* Scandinavian invasions and settlements, which began in the 700s and continued until the Norman Conquest in the eleventh century. The Scandinavian invaders had more effect on English structure than did the French invaders somewhat later, although the French had a greater influence on *French* the lexicon, the words of the language. The th- pronouns (*they, them, their*) were originally Scandinavian and replaced the native forms, first in the north, where the settlements were, and eventually spreading south. Scandinavian influence may also have contributed to the loss of nominal and verbal inflections.

This was the big development of Middle English; the loss of inflections had profound effects on the language, and we shall discuss some of them in chapter 5. The usual view is that the loss of case endings was a particular instance of the collapse of unstressed vowels, whereby such vowels all came to be pronounced the same way, as a central vowel; this process had begun before the arrival of the Scandinavians. Frisian, the closest relative of English, underwent a similar development and lost its case system, despite having no Scandinavian influence.

The usual view may be all that is needed, but it is also possible that the development was facilitated by the mixture of languages. There were many bilingual households, with Anglo-Saxon mothers and Scandinavian fathers providing input for children. Both languages had word-final case endings and verbal inflections, and both languages stressed initial syllables. One gets a taste of this by comparing the forms of the word for "stone" in Old English and Old Norse.

Case	Old English		Old Norse	
	singular	plural	singular	plural
nominative	*stān*	*stānas*	*steinn*	*steinar*
accusative	*stān*	*stānas*	*stein*	*steina*
genitive	*stānes*	*stāna*	*steins*	*steina*
dative	*stāne*	*stānum*	*steini*	*steinum*

Many children would have been exposed to forms from both languages. It is possible that they grew up bilingual, with two distinct systems coexisting, as often happens; in that event, Scandinavian influence was irrelevant to the loss of case endings in English. However, it is also possible that the loss of the inflectional system reflects a scenario in which children ignored the different endings on words that they perceived as the same in their parents' speech and converged on a single grammar in this regard, in a kind of creolization. So *stān-* and *stein*-forms would have been perceived as equivalent, regardless of the second syllable, triggering the growth of a single, invariant item; the second syllable would have varied a great deal in the parents' speech, but would have been dropped in the children's system (O'Neil 1978).

Whatever their source, these morphological changes show up first in the written record of the thirteenth century, when scribes trained in French and not necessarily literate in English were responsible for many of the records which have survived. This may be another coincidence, or perhaps a contributing factor.

1.3   Lack of Change and Historical Explanation

So languages may change in the way that I have indicated, and we shall devote our energy in later chapters to explaining why various changes took place. It is also worth bearing in mind that sometimes languages do not change and show odd properties which can be explained historically, as relics of some past form. This is a different kind of historical explanation; here we are not explaining change so much as using history to explain peculiar properties of some language. This is not what we are going to do in this book, but let me briefly sketch what I have in mind.

In general, simple adjectives occur in front of the noun they modify in modern English (*the tall girl*, etc.); but some forms occur post-nominally: *alive, asleep, afire, afloat*, etc. So one finds sentences like *A student asleep makes no contribution to seminars* and *No professor alive is cited so often*, not **An asleep student* or **No alive professor*. These words are adjectives: like adjectives, they have comparative and superlative forms (*more alive, most afire*), they may be modified by *so* (*The students were so alive that they took over the seminar*), and they mean the same or the opposite as other clear cases of adjectives (*dead, sleepy*). So why do they not occur in the expected pre-nominal position?

The answer is that they are etymologically descended from preposition phrases, which, from Middle English onwards, have always occurred after the noun they modify: *Students* ₚₚ*[of linguistics], Woman* ₚₚ*[from Chicago]*, not *$_{pp}$[Of linguistics students], *$_{pp}$[From Chicago woman]. A was a preposition, according to the Oxford English Dictionary, a "worn-down proclitic" variant of on, and a preposition phrase consisting of a preposition a and a noun, $_{PP}$[a noun], became reanalyzed as an adjective consisting of a prefix a and a noun, $_A$[a-noun]. Alive etc. behave like preposition phrases in terms of word order, because they used to be preposition phrases. This, in turn, suggests that languages are influenced quite directly and specifically by their histories, and that we should not draw too rigid a demarcation between synchronic and diachronic analyses (the study of a language at a single point in time versus in its evolutionary stages).

We shall look to history – sometimes to the history of the English language and sometimes to cultural history – to understand quirks of the modern language. History will tell us why singers sing but hammers don't ham and fingers don't fing, why teachers taught but preachers never praught, why there is no apple or pine in pineapple, why boxing rings are square, why you can make amends but not one amend, why in the USA we park on driveways and drive on parkways, and why a slim chance and a fat chance are the same.

Ed Keenan (1994) offers a more intricate, more illuminating illustration of the same kind of phenomenon, of English showing an oddity which may best be understood historically. Consider a passage from the Book of Genesis (3: 7–10) as it appears in the King James version of the Bible, written in the early seventeenth century (1611):

And the eyes of them both were opened, and they knew that they were naked; and they sewed fig leaves together, and made themselves aprons.

And they heard the voice of the Lord God walking in the garden in the cool of the day: and Adam and his wife hid themselves from the presence of the Lord God amongst the trees of the garden.

And the Lord God called unto Adam, and said unto him, Where art thou?

And he said, I heard thy voice in the garden, and I was afraid, because I was naked; and I hid myself.

This language may be slightly unfamiliar to modern ears, but it is easy enough to understand. It is quite different from the same passage as it appears in the version of the monk Ælfric, written some 600 years earlier, at the beginning of the eleventh century:

& heora begra eagan wurdon geopenode; hi oncneowon ða ðæt hi nacode wæron, & sywodon him ficleaf, & worhton him wædbrec.

Eft ða ða God com, & hi gehyrdon his stemme ðær he eode on neorxnawange ofer midne dæg, ða behydde Adam hine, & his wif eac swa dyde, fram godes gesihðe on middan ðam treowe neorxnanwonges.

God clypode ða Adam, & cwæð: Adam, hwær eart ðu?
He cwæð: ðine stemne ic gehire, leof, on neorxnawange, & ic ondræde me
for ðam ðe ic eom nacod, & ic behyde me.

Keenan focuses our attention on the fact that Old English used ordinary
pronouns where the modern language uses special reflexive pronouns like
themselves, myself. So the first sentence in Ælfric's version ends *& worhton
him wædbrec*, "and made themselves aprons," and the whole passage ends
& ic behyde me, "and I hid myself." This means that in Old English
pronouns could be locally bound (i.e. have the same referent as another
phrase in the same clause, indicated here by co-indexing), which led to
structures which are not possible in present-day English (6). Present-day
English, instead, uses special reflexive pronouns, which were unavailable in
Old English (7a, b). These reflexive pronouns in modern English, which
are marked by -*self*, always have a local antecedent; compare (7a–c),
where the antecedent is local, to the nonoccurring (7d–e), where it is not.

6   (a)   *I hid me.
    (b)   *They$_i$ hurt them$_i$.

7   (a)   I hid myself.
    (b)   They$_i$ hurt themselves$_i$.
    (c)   [their mother]$_i$ hurt herself$_i$.
    (d)   *I said that John hurt myself.
    (e)   *[their$_i$ mother] hurt themselves$_i$.

Keenan follows Visser (1963: vol. 1, 420–39), Quirk and Wrenn (1955),
Mitchell (1985: 189), Levinson (1991), and others, and explains the change
from Old English usage by showing that the modern reflexives are, in fact,
reanalyzed relics of another Old English construction.

In present-day English, reflexive pronouns are nouns, but they do not
occur everywhere that nouns occur, and they have an odd distribution. For
example, they do not occur as subjects (8).

8   (a)   *Himself laughed.
    (b)   *He said that himself laughed.
    (c)   *He said that he self laughed.

They do not occur as genitives (9b).

9   (a)   Kim lost her (own) key.
    (b)   *Kim lost herself's key.

They mark person, number, and gender: *myself, yourself, himself, herself, itself, ourselves, themselves.* They occur as nouns within inherently contrastive phrases (10), but here they may have nonlocal antecedents (indexed):

10   (a)   Each student$_i$ thought that no one but himself$_i$ would flunk.
     (b)   John$_i$ tackled a problem that neither himself$_i$ nor the teacher could solve.
     (c)   No one$_i$ thought that anyone smarter than himself$_i$ would apply for the job.
     (d)   John$_i$ thinks that it is only himself$_{i,j}$ that the teacher$_j$ will criticize.

They occur as nonarguments, modifying full phrases and indicating contrast or comparison (11).

11   (a)   The judge himself did it.
     (b)   The judge did it himself.

Reflexives may be specifically selected by verbs, and in such cases they may not be replaced by referential nouns (12). These verbs generally do not occur with direct objects, but they do allow reflexive pronouns.

12   (a)   John perjured/behaved himself.
     (b)   *John perjured/behaved Mary.

So much for the oddities of present-day English. Keenan then turns to Old English and shows that Old English *self* was not a reflexive but modified full phrases, agreeing in number, gender, and case, and had a contrastive effect, like the nonargument uses of *himself* in present-day English (11). At this time *self* was an independent word in these contexts, carrying stress and counting for alliteration in poetry (Old English poetry was predominantly alliterative rather than rhyming). Keenan also shows that late Old English made extensive use of "pleonastic" pronouns, which occurred in the predicate in the dative case, agreed with the subject in number and gender, and served to emphasize the role of the subject: *The king went him to London.*

These two construction types might co-occur, and pleonastic pronouns might occur with the emphatic *self*, as in a sentence like *He com him sylf æfter,* "He came himself later." Here *him* and *self* are independent items, each of which can be omitted, and *sylf* modifies the subject (we know this, because it has the nominative form *sylf*; if it modified the dative *him*,

*[handwritten margin notes: grammatical change * independent of culture change?]*

it would have had its dative form, *sylfum*). In the eleventh century these pronoun + dative *self* + nominative forms, occurring inside predicates, came to be interpreted as a unit, meaning something like "identify the referent of the subject, emphasize and contrast it." At this stage, local binding is still expressed only by the personal pronouns (*me, him,* etc.), but, like other definite nouns, these forms may be emphasized and contrasted by *self.* So in an Old English sentence like *John washed him sylf, John washed him* would mean "John washed himself," and *sylf* would emphasize *him*; the meaning of the sentence would be something like "It was himself that John washed."

Then in the thirteenth century came the reanalysis: each *him sylf* form came to be treated as a single phonological word. "Independent *self* basically dies out as a contraster; single words like *himself* remain, inheriting the involvement/contrast interpretation contributed by each part separately" (Keenan 1994: 5). This development was almost certainly facilitated by the loss of case endings, which occurred at the same time; as a result, *self* was no longer perceived as distinctly nominative. Now *himself* takes local antecedents: a sentence like *John hurt himself* contains *himself* as a single unit, which refers back to the subject *John. Himself* may now function as a reflexive, and the distinctive reflexive form ending in *-self* comes to be the standard way of expressing local anaphora. In the sixteenth century pleonastic pronouns cease to occur, leaving a majority of local bindings expressed by *-self* forms. By 1600 local bindings are expressed by *-self* forms 75 percent of the time, and this figure rises steadily to 99 percent by the mid-eighteenth century, by which time we have the present-day system.

Keenan's paper is rich in details and argument, and it allows us to understand the modern reflexive pronouns as reanalyzed versions of earlier emphatic forms, explaining their odd distribution. Those forms were reanalyzed in a minor way in early Middle English, such that *himself* etc. came to be viewed as one word referring back to the subject. This enabled such a form to take on the function of a local, reflexive anaphor referring back to the subject, and to supplant the function of an ordinary pronoun like *me, him,* etc. As a result, the language looks very different, as we saw in the two versions of the passage from the Book of Genesis; but the grammar has changed only in a minor way. We understand its modern properties in the light of its history.

I have worked through these two examples to show how modern systems may reflect their histories and how we can get historical explanations for modern phenomena. My goal in this book, however, is somewhat different: I shall ask not so much how history explains the shape of modern English, but rather how we can explain the structural changes which have affected the grammars of English speakers. In this context, we seek to explain why that thirteenth-century reanalysis took place and what drove people to analyze *him sylf* as a single unit – a very different matter.

1.4   Our Odyssey

very late

Serious work on language change began in the nineteenth century, and that is where our odyssey must start. Nineteenth-century scholars made immense contributions in comparing languages, mostly of the Indo-European family, and in postulating historical relationships. The linguists were fully integrated in the intellectual life of that century, whose dominant figures include Darwin and Marx, two men preoccupied with matters of history and change. I call it "the century of history." The enormous success of the linguists made them obligatory reading for biologists and historians concerned with evolutionary and political change, and it meant that their ideas came to dominate linguistic thinking long after linguists had broadened their interests to include nonhistorical matters. Our nineteenth-century predecessors continue to influence modern linguists, even as we approach the twenty-first century. So it is important to understand their work and their influence, and we shall begin with them.

At the risk of oversimplifying, I have two beefs: like many of their contemporaries in other disciplines, nineteenth-century linguists tended towards too deterministic a view of history, and they had an incomplete view of language.

First, under a deterministic view of history, given a good description of some synchronic state, a theory of change would predict future outcomes, often far into the future. The goal was to find "inexorable laws of history," which would provide linear predictions.

Second, they saw language as a collection of phenomena, inventories of words and sounds. And they were concerned with how these inventories changed over the course of time. Words change their form, as one can see by comparing Latin *pater* with French *père* and Spanish *padre*, all meaning "father". These linguists focused on the products of the language capacity; they knew that there was more to a language than this, but they paid much less attention to the abstract system which must be involved. They were able to get away with this by focusing on changes in sound, but one cannot think about syntactic change productively without dealing with the abstract system, the grammars which generate the products. So we begin by considering this enormously resilient nineteenth-century work on language in chapter 2, and then proceed to consider the modern work on abstract, biological grammars and their acquisition in chapter 3. Here we shall leave talk of "languages" behind us, and I shall argue that there is an individual entity which develops in a person's mind/brain, which embodies the system of linguistic knowledge that a person has; we call these entities *grammars*.

In chapter 4 we consider the consequences of the shift in perspective away from languages and toward biological grammars, dealing with some old questions about the nature of change: in what sense is it gradual, and in what sense is it sudden and "catastrophic"? If we focus on change in the products of grammars as seen in the surviving texts, then change seems to be gradual and piecemeal; if we focus on change in the grammars themselves, then structural change may occur abruptly and spread rapidly through a speech community. This clears the decks for some case studies, which will show that understanding changes in grammars is a key component in understanding changes in language.

Chapters 5–7 make up the analytical core of the book and involve somewhat more technology than the other chapters. There I develop an approach to language acquisition which differs from that of the standard formal models of learnability. I call it a "cue-based" model and argue that children attain their grammars by scanning for cues, elements of grammar found in the mental representations which result from understanding and "parsing" utterances. As children find these cues, so they acquire their grammars. If the distribution of those cues shifts somewhat – and that may happen for a variety of reasons – then structural change takes place. This model of acquisition provides far more contingent explanations of change than are common in the literature, explanations which differ from those of the nineteenth century and from those of many of my contemporaries. The model is based on and illustrated by a series of case studies, mostly from the history of English.

I develop a view of change which is similar in some ways to the "punctuated equilibrium" model of evolution of Eldredge and Gould (1972): evolution is not steady, gradual change, but takes place in fits and starts, in short bursts of dramatic speciation against a background of stasis and equilibrium. Similarly, as Roger Lass puts it, "languages may vary all the time, but they change in bursts" (1997: 305). I shall explain these dramatic changes in terms of the nature of language acquisition. The details of the model are new, but the emphasis on child language acquisition as a major source of structural change echoes nineteenth-century thinking: "the main occasion of sound change consists in the transmission of sounds to new individuals" (Paul 1891: 53–4); "all the major changes in pronunciation ... originate in child speech" (Passy 1891: 231); "[i]f languages were learnt perfectly by the children of each generation, then language would not change: English children would still speak a language as old at least as "Anglo-Saxon," and there would be no such languages as French and Italian" (Sweet 1899: 75). Our predecessors dealt with language acquisition differently, but they knew that it was an important factor in language change.

Two big ideas emerge from our case studies: language acquisition is cue-based, and grammatical change is more contingent than is often thought. Chapter 8 focuses on the nature of the explanations offered in the earlier chapters, contrasting them with the more deterministic, nineteenth-century-style accounts which have generally been favored. Here I ask whether it is possible to explain the kind of long-term, large-scale changes that have been postulated in the literature. I am skeptical, but, perhaps surprisingly, I raise the possibility of a positive answer, based on properties of the acquisition system, not on historical laws.

In chapter 9 I explore the consequences of this approach to grammars and change for questions of how the language faculty might have evolved in the species, a topic which has become fashionable in recent years and has led to an outpouring of work of doubtful value. Again, I offer an account which is very different from what is in the literature, by focusing on elements of the faculty which seem to be maladaptive and which therefore cannot be explained by natural selection.

When we finally sail home to Ithaca, we shall have work on grammar change integrated with work on variation and acquisition. We shall have a different way of thinking about language acquisition: children's linguistic development results from their finding certain abstract structures in their chaotic environment, in much the same way that the development of their visual system results from exposure to very specific, abstract, visual stimuli like edges and horizontal lines. This is pretty much what one would expect of selective learning quite generally. One line of argument for this cue-based approach to acquisition is that it permits the right kind of contingent explanation for structural changes which may take place as one generation of speakers comes to converge on a grammar which is structurally distinct from grammars of earlier generations. That's not all there is to change, of course; but it's a central, substantial part, and it results from taking a better view of language acquisition than one usually finds. There is a science of historical change in all this, but a science more familiar to modern chaos theoreticians than to unreconstructed Newtonians.

Notes

1 This passage is often quoted by people like me when they decry popular tendencies to prescribe "correct" speech; but, in fact, Johnson was well aware of the
  need for description and the futility of prescriptivist urgings to "put a stop to
  those alterations which time and chance have hitherto been suffered to make."
  Elsewhere in his preface he says that

> now [I] begin to fear that I have indulged expectations which neither reason
> nor experience can justify. When we see men grow old and die at a certain
> time one after another, from century to century, we laugh at the elixir that
> promises to prolong life to a thousand years; and with equal justice may the
> lexicographer be derided, who being able to produce no example of a nation
> that has preserved their words and phrases from mutability, shall imagine
> that his dictionary can embalm his language, and secure it from corruption
> and decay, that it is in his power to change sublunary nature, and clear the
> world at once from folly, vanity, and affectation.

2 Pinker 1994: ch. 12 offers a perceptive, often hilarious discussion of these
  language mavens.
3 In 1996 the School Board of Oakland, California, concerned about shockingly
  low test scores among its black students, acknowledged that many of these
  students were brought up to use a distinct form of English which the board
  called "Ebonics." The board reasoned that acknowledging the existence of this
  language distinction might help teachers improve students' use of standard
  English, and thus help their test scores in a number of areas. This led to an
  extraordinary and fundamentally wrong-headed outburst decrying the inferior-
  ity of Ebonics or Black English and the actions of the School Board.
4 I first discussed this change in Lightfoot 1979: §5.1, offering a different analysis
  in Lightfoot 1991: §6.1.

2

The Nineteenth: Century of History

It is said, grandly, that the twentieth-century mind has been shaped by Darwin, Marx, and Freud. Certainly Darwin and Marx had a view of history which has been very influential in the past century, a view which involves *principles of history*. Contemporary linguists were intimately involved in this distinctive, nineteenth-century approach, influencing Darwin and Marx and being influenced by them. And those linguists have shaped the way in which their twentieth-century grandchildren and great grandchildren have thought about language change. Their influence will spill over into the twenty-first century, and we can profit from understanding what work they did, what their influence has been, which of their ideas should be preserved, and which should be discarded.

I am interested here in one particular line of thought, dealing with principles of history. I do not suggest that our predecessors walked in lockstep; indeed, they often sought particular causes for particular changes in the actual analyses that they offered, taking a more contingent approach. Nonetheless, many nineteenth-century linguists invoked historical principles to some degree, and "historicism" was an important ingredient in nineteenth-century thinking. It has influenced us all, and it needs to be understood. In order to understand the kind of explanation that our predecessors sought, we must first investigate the nature of their enterprise and the kinds of things that they wanted to explain.[1]

2.1 Historical Relationships

It is no accident that the words for "father" are so similar in the Romance languages: *père* in French, *padre* in Spanish, *padre* in Italian, *patre* in Sardinian, *pare* in Catalan, *pai* in Portuguese. These forms are all transmogrified versions of Latin *pater*, and we know that French, Spanish, Italian, Sardinian, Catalan, and Portuguese are historically related to each other, in the sense that they are all descended from Latin. That is, they share many words which are *cognate* and have a common, Latin ancestor.

We can have a lot of fun searching for etymologies, the historical origins of words, many of which are far from self-evident. English *pal* and *brother* are etymologically related: both words are descended from the ancient word for "brother", which occurs as Sanskrit *bʰrātā*, Greek *pʰrátēr*, Latin *frater*. But they come by different routes: *pal* is a borrowing from Romani.

Russian
brat
Latvian
bralis

In the town where I was raised, just across the Cornish border, there is an area called Pennycomequick. The locals had all kinds of fanciful explanations involving penny tolls or pennies rolling down hills, but in fact there was once a farm there called in Cornish *pen-y-cwm-gwik*, "the valley at the head of the creek," and Pennycomequick was an anglicization of the farm's name. Etymologies and the changes in individual words over the course of time reveal more general sound changes.

Words are transmitted from one generation to the next, and they may change their form over time. As a result of examining "correspondences," as in the Romance words for "father", linguists have postulated that languages are historically related to each other to greater or lesser degrees, and that they cluster in "families." There are parent and daughter languages and sister languages, and sometimes one gets the impression that for historical linguists everything is relatives. English and Dutch have more cognate words, and the cognate words are more similar to each other, than English and Spanish, so English and Dutch are more closely related, even though they have plenty of words which are not cognate: English *bicycle* and Dutch *fiets* refer to the same object but do not have a common origin.

because
peculiar
or similar
different

The word for "father" in the Germanic languages is different from what we find in the Romance languages, but not *very* different: Gothic *fadar*, English *father*, Dutch *vader*, German *Vater*, Danish *fader*. As with most of the Romance words for "father", we have a two-syllable word, and the initial segment is a labial consonant (/p/ in Romance, /f/ in Germanic), followed by an open vowel and an alveolar consonant, then some kind of vocalic *r*. Compare the very different words for "father" in other languages, where the words do not have a common ancestor (as far as we can tell): Chinese *fuqin*, Japanese *titi-oya*, Basque *aita*, Finnish *isä*, and Korean *apeci*. The degree of similarity between the Germanic and Romance forms and the degree of difference reflect the fact that the Germanic languages are historically related to each other and are also historically related to the Romance languages, though less directly. English is related historically to Dutch, Spanish, and Armenian, but most closely to Dutch and least closely to Armenian.

We believe that languages change over the course of time. We also believe that modern French, Italian, and Rumanian evolved from some form of Latin, and that Hindi and Urdu evolved from some form of Sanskrit, even if Hindi and Urdu hardly differ from each other and are labeled as distinct languages mostly because they are spoken in two (often warring) countries and have different writing systems. We suppose that Latin and Sanskrit evolved from some common source for which we have no records, and we call that source "Proto-Indo-European."

This idea that languages are historically related to one another is not very old. It is found in the writings of Dante but was not generally accepted until the late eighteenth century. The idea began to be worked out in detail only in the nineteenth century, a century that saw intellectual developments in several fields focusing on the nature of historical change, with the study of language change a central component of that more general phenomenon. I'll focus on nineteenth-century thought in this chapter, because this is where the ground was prepared for subsequent work on change. Nineteenth-century linguists made valuable contributions, and they influenced scientists in other domains, so it is important to be clear about what we can now, a century later, take to be their real contributions.

It is now commonplace to think of languages as historically related, and these relationships are often expressed in cladistic models (figure 2.1). These models were introduced by August Schleicher in 1861. Schleicher had a *Stammbaumtheorie*, or genealogical tree model, which reflects the methods of botanical classification by species and genera in the Linnaean system. In fact, the trees are quite similar to the cladograms of modern biologists, which is why I refer to Schleicher's trees as cladistic models; these cladograms express the varying degrees to which species are related, depending on the number of *shared derived characters* ("synapomorphies"). Schleicher regarded himself as a natural scientist and language as a natural organism; he wrote a short book on Darwinian theory and linguistics, *Die darwinische Theorie und die Sprachwissenschaft* (1863).

One hundred years later, Henry Hoenigswald (1963) noted that the tree model may also have been inspired by the comparative method of reconstructing the genealogy of manuscripts developed by one of Schleicher's teachers, F. Ritschl. We have nothing written in the hand of Thucydides or of Chaucer, just manuscripts written by later scribes. Those manuscripts differ from each other in many ways, and much ingenious detective work goes into figuring out what Thucydides or Chaucer must have written, based on these indirect records. If manuscripts B and C have common peculiarities, then an intermediate manuscript that no longer exists is hypothesized.

Figure 2.1 Schleicher's tree.

In these cladistic models, languages are grouped together in subfamilies – Romance, Celtic, Germanic, Indic, etc. – according to the distinctive elements they share. For each subfamily, a parent *Grundsprache* (common language) is postulated, like some form of spoken Latin as the source of the Romance languages, or a language which is not recorded. The common ancestor of all the Indo-European languages, Proto-Indo-European (PIE), is not recorded and has been reconstructed by comparing the corresponding forms in the various subfamilies.

Figure 2.1 is the tree for the earliest stages of the Indo-European languages proposed by Schleicher in his *Compendium der vergleichenden Grammatik der indogermanischen Sprachen* (1861–2). I have anglicized and modernized some of his labels. The tree is incomplete, of course: many languages that I have not specified fall under Germanic, and Celtic was subdivided into two groups, Brythonic and Goidelic, the former consisting of Cornish (which died out in the eighteenth century), Breton, and Welsh, the latter embracing Manx (which died out in the nineteenth century), Irish, and Scots Gaelic. The tree expresses the idea that, say, the Celtic languages are more closely related to the Latin-derived "Italic" languages (which we now call "Romance": Italian, French, Sardinian, Spanish, Galician, Catalan, Rumanian, etc.) than the Slavic languages (Polish, Russian, etc.) are to either; and that the Baltic languages (Latvian, Lithuanian) are more closely related to Germanic than to Celtic, but not as closely related to Germanic as they are to the Slavic languages. And so on. This was the first tree proposed for the Indo-European languages. We have no direct records for most of the *Grundsprachen* postulated, Aryan-Greek-Italo-Celtic, Balto-Slavic, etc., and we now doubt that Albanian and Greek represent any kind of unity. Cal Watkins maintains that Italo-Celtic was not a unit. On the other hand, some features of Schleicher's tree remain undisputed today, and many relationships not specified in Schleicher's tree have come to be established convincingly.

A great deal of work by many linguists over many generations has been devoted to articulating the details of the Indo-European family relationships. Cladograms like those of figure 2.1 are a somewhat misleading shorthand for something more complex. To say that two languages are historically related means that they share similarities which are not due to chance, borrowing, or universal features of all languages. Words may be cognate: spelling out the parent form of the word and the changes which produced the forms in the daughter languages constitutes the precise relationship between the languages. The cladograms are a very rough quantification of such correspondences.

Varying amounts of attention have been devoted to other families. I was intrigued to learn that there is a lively dispute about whether Japanese, or, as some say, the various Japanese languages, are historically related to the Korean languages, and if so, how.[2] There has also been a vigorous dispute about how many language families there are in Africa and among the indigenous, native American communities; much of this has been triggered by the ambitious work of Joseph Greenberg, who has tried to establish very ancient historical relationships. Others argue for superfamilies like the famous Nostratic, which covers most of the languages of Europe, Africa, India, Asia, and, in some versions, even some North American languages.

Nostratic has captured the popular imagination and has been the subject of long articles in *The New York Times*, the *Atlantic Monthly*, and other papers. The term is due to Holger Pedersen (1931: ch. 8), but the idea of a superfamily goes back to the nineteenth century. Henry Sweet (1900) argued that the Indo-European family came from the same source as "Ugrian" (Finno-Ugric), "Altaic" (which included Turkic, Mongolian, Tungusic, and Japanese), and Sumerian. Nostratic has grown and changed over the years. A recent taxonomy (Bomhard 1990) includes Indo-European, Kartvelian (south Caucasus), Afro-Asiatic, Uralic-Yukaghir, Elamo-Dravidian, and perhaps Sumerian. Others have added a Korean-Japanese family and a new Chukchi-Eskimo group. From there it is a fairly small step to "Proto-World," which has also been advocated by some of my more imaginative colleagues. Proponents of Proto-World assume monogenesis for all the languages of the world and assume that it can be demonstrated through the surviving properties of recorded languages.

There is much that is speculative in our reconstruction of the parent forms of Proto-Indo-European. The further back we go, the greater the speculativeness. It is possible that the Indo-European and Semitic languages descended ultimately from some common source, which predated Proto-Indo-European, but it is difficult to have much confidence in what the words for "father", "mother", etc. were. Indeed, Ringe (1995) has argued that the resemblances between the language families on which the Nostratic hypothesis is based seem not to be greater than chance. It is perfectly possible that human language evolved just once, and that all the languages of the world derive from that single evolutionary step and are historically related, but trying to reconstruct "Nostratic" strikes many of us as an idle fantasy. Some of the reasoning is based on the ethnic affinities of speakers: so, in terms of physical anthropology, south Indians are closely affiliated with certain African groups. But this tells us nothing about the languages, because linguistic affiliation has no necessary connection with biological affiliation. English remains a northwest European language, even though it is spoken by people from southeast Asia and Australia; and it would remain a northwest European language even if some cataclysm were to eliminate all English-speaking communities outside southeast Asia and Australia.

Perhaps it is best to treat hypotheses about Nostratic and Proto-World in the same way as a report in today's newspaper: some British scientists have argued that one of the factors leading to the extinction of *Tyrannosaurus Rex* was that the species suffered from gout. It could be true, but it will be hard to demonstrate.

The fact is that there is only one kind of scientific evidence involved here: analyses resulting from the comparative method. Using the comparative method, one postulates a common source for corresponding forms in different languages; the corresponding forms are then said to be *derived* from the common source by sound changes. If the postulated sound changes are general and phonetically plausible, one has a productive account; if they are *ad hoc* and phonetically implausible, one has an *ad hoc* account. If a relationship cannot be demonstrated by the comparative method, there is simply no basis for asserting it as a matter of science. Because the comparative method involves comparison of words and morphology, and because these things change and are somewhat evanescent, there is an unavoidable temporal horizon. Any linguistic relationship that implies a time-scale of more than 7,000–10,000 years has to be conjectural. So, as Stephen Anderson writes to me, Nostratic (and much more so, Proto-World) doesn't just require us to work harder and longer, because such relationships are intrinsically unprovable by the only existing scientific method available. This point is important to understand, because the Nostraticists and the Greenbergians portray themselves in popular magazines and elsewhere as innocent targets of malicious reactionaries. Those of us who take issue with them may be conservative, but we have our reasons.

Whatever the scale of our ambitions, we may think of language relationships in the way shown in figure 2.1, but we should recognize some of the idealizations involved. Trees of this kind idealize away from the fact that *rght!*

languages do not split sharply at some specific point and suddenly emerge
in their full individuality. The splitting process is more gradual and is
initiated by relatively minor divergences. We shall see in chapter 3 that languages are not, in fact, organic entities: there is no linguistic distinction
between a dialect and a language, so there is some arbitrariness in what we
call a distinct language. We might say that the first change which affected,
say, Latin and not any of the other languages is the bifurcation point, the
point at which Latin suddenly splits away. But that is not enough. Saying
that French and Italian are descended from Latin glosses over the fact that
they descended from different forms of Latin, and that *Latin* is a cover
term for many different forms of speech. As a result, the conventional tree
models of historical linguists would require vast elaboration to be equivalent to modern, biological cladograms, which are usually based strictly on
the molecular structure of organisms.

In addition, languages used in areas which are geographically adjacent
sometimes influence each other in one way or another, even if they are not
closely related historically. This kind of contact influence was recognized
in the nineteenth century, and the *Stammbaumtheorie* was supplemented
by the *Wellentheorie*, a theory of waves of changes which might spread
over a geographical area through linguistic contact. So there may be common innovations which have nothing to do with a common history. To take
a trivial example, many historically unrelated languages have a word for
"television" which sounds pretty much like the English *television*. During
the period of the Scandinavian settlements, English drew many common
words directly from the language of the settlers: *bait, bull, egg, fellow,
give, hit, husband, law, low, loose, meek, oar, sister, skin, sky, take, wrong.*
English drew much from French during the period of the Norman occupa-
tion, musical terms from Italian, *pundit, thug,* and *calico* from India, and
moccasin, toboggan, and *tomahawk* from American Indian languages. This
kind of commonality, due to factors other than a common history, is not
expressed by cladograms, linguistic or biological.

*Arabic
is.
Persian*

The cladograms of evolutionary biologists deal with branching order
alone and exclude any other kind of similarity, such as similarity of form,
function, or biological role. The lungfish and the coelacanth are vertebrates
with scales and fins – fish to you and me. However, genealogically, they
are more closely related to creatures which crawled onto land to become
amphibians, reptiles, mammals, and birds. The cladogram ignores the fact
that the coelacanth looks and acts like a fish, and puts it in a sister group
with birds and mammals.

Biologists recognize two very different reasons for similarities between
organisms: similarities may arise because organisms inherited the same

features from a common ancestor (homologies), or because they evolved the features independently, in response to life in similar environments (analogies). So humans share hair and a warm-blooded physiology with chimpanzees and mice as a result of evolutionary history, or homology. Birds and bats both fly by analogy; they have a very different evolutionary history, bats being mammals. Similarly, languages may share features because of a common ancestry or because of common developments. Distinguishing common ancestral features from common developments is often tricky, for both biologists and linguists;[3] but the linguists' tree models and the biologists' cladograms are historical models only and determine relatedness only on the basis of homologies.

The fact is that we now view languages as historically related to each other in this way, but this wasn't always the case. The old roads of Europe are dotted with milestones, even though there is an infinite number of ways to measure miles on those roads. They represent a very partial account of geographical reality; but linguists of all stripes point to a milestone which, they say, marks the beginning of scientific efforts to understand language: a 1786 publication by Sir William Jones.

The study of language goes back to classical antiquity, to Greece and India in the pre-Christian era. Much of that work was very productive. Pāṇini's grammar, the Aṣṭādhyāyī, formulated more than 2,500 years ago, contains some 4,000 sutras, formal rules for the word forms of Sanskrit, and remains "one of the greatest monuments of human intelligence" (Bloomfield 1933: 11). The study of language was often closely linked with the study of mind, taking language to be a "mirror of the mind" and assuming that the study of language would give special insight into human thought. Not much of the early work on language dealt with change and historical relationships, but some did. An unknown Icelandic scholar of the twelfth century, held up now as the "First Grammarian," postulated a historical relationship between Icelandic and English. He was interested primarily in spelling reform, and his *Treatise* was published only in 1818, and even then remained largely unknown outside Scandinavia. Dante in his *De vulgari eloquentia* divided the Romance languages and dialects into three groups: each language was descended historically from one of three vernaculars, which in turn were descended from Latin. Other writers had alternative models of the historical relationships among languages, often deriving modern languages from favored religious languages, usually Hebrew, Latin, or Sanskrit.

These people did not have the impact of Jones and were not petrified as milestones. Jones, by contrast, is the marker. He was a British judge who served with the East India Company and worked in Calcutta. He

william
Jones
1786

wrote a great deal, producing all kinds of speculations, some of which are nonsense. However, he hit the intellectual jackpot in an after-dinner speech in which he suggested that Greek, Latin, and Sanskrit were similar in ways which indicated that they had descended historically from some common source, which might no longer exist.[4] In the same speech, he made many unsustainable claims about language relatedness, and he did no systematic research on the matter. The key idea was that the origin of particular languages should not necessarily be sought in other, currently observable languages like Hebrew or Sanskrit, but it may be found in a hypothetical language for which we have no records. This insight had a profound effect and initiated an enormous outpouring of philological work; it gave birth to an independent discipline which we now call "linguistics," although it was left to Franz Bopp to get the real work going.

It was clear that God did not place the languages of the modern world where they are now spoken, but the historical record shows that they evolved from earlier forms. For some reason, this view, articulated clearly in the eighteenth century, has never attracted the attention of the "creationists," who have engaged the evolutionary biologists. People thought that we might be able to find out precisely how languages developed from one another. A central idea was that if we can understand the sound changes which transform words as they are transmitted from generation to generation, so we may understand the historical relationships among languages and how a language may have descended from some earlier language. The upshot was a century of research, which discovered much about sound changes affecting the Indo-European languages.

2.2   Sound Change

Linguistics began as a *historical* science, and it turned out to be tremendously influential in the nineteenth century – in many ways at the center of intellectual life of the time. Linguists, biologists, and historians talked to each other and read each other. The work of linguists had a marked effect on developments in biology and in history, outstandingly through the work of Charles Darwin and Karl Marx. And those nineteenth-century ideas have continued to influence the work of linguists at the very end of the twentieth century – for better and for worse.

The ideas, we can now see, were in some ways right, in some ways wrong; and in some respects they can be understood more deeply now than was possible a century ago. We have a lot to learn from the early stages of work on language change, both positively and negatively. Reexamining nineteenth-century ideas has consequences for the way in which modern linguists go about their work and the ways in which biologists and historians understand their enterprises and the history of those enterprises. I look at this work, of course, not just on its own terms, but through the eyes of a late-twentieth-century linguist, more interested in learning something useful for current work on language change than in avoiding backward-looking anachronisms. The true historian would try to interpret the past simply in its own terms, but that is not my goal here.

There are many questions one can ask about language: how it is acquired by children, how it is used by poets, how it varies sociologically, and so on. The central research question for the nineteenth century was: How did a language get to be the way it is? As far as Hermann Paul was concerned, this was the only possible question: "It has been objected that there is another view of language possible besides the historical. I must contradict this" (1891: xlvi). Whether other views were possible or not, this historical question first became central in Germany, and it grew not only out of Sir William Jones's insight but also from a general intellectual movement of the late eighteenth to mid-nineteenth century that we refer to today as "Romanticism." The Romantics focused on ethnic and cultural origins of various phenomena. Since race, language, and culture were seen as closely related, the reconstruction of the prehistory of Germanic was attractive to the Romantic temperament. These links were quite clear in the work of the linguists Herder and Grimm. Jones's publication also coincided with a new interest in Near Eastern and Indian studies by European scholars.

As the nineteenth century progressed, linguists formulated historical "laws" with ever greater precision. They studied the similarities among cognate words, words derived from the same historical source; this was the basis for establishing historical relationships, and then for establishing the sound changes which derived one form from another historically. To get a flavor of the general enterprise, it will be useful to track one matter in some detail: the shift in the Germanic consonant system, which has become famous as "Grimm's Law."

Early in the century, the great Dane, Rasmus Rask, postulated general correspondences between the consonants of German and the ancient Indo-European languages, usually Greek, Latin, and Sanskrit. He compared words in different languages which seemed to correspond with each other and to be cognate, descended from some common ancestor word. Lining up these correspondences, he noted that where the ancient languages showed a *p* sound, in the corresponding words the Germanic languages showed a fricative *f*.

In 1822 Jacob Grimm, one of the brothers who collected fairy stories, revised his *Deutsche Grammatik* by adding a 595-page account of the phonology of some 15 different languages and stages of languages, a serious way of revising an earlier edition. He built on the work of Rask and gave a detailed exposition of the Germanic consonant shift (*Lautverschiebung*), formulating a historical cycle (*Kreislauf* "rotation") that came to be known as "Grimm's Law." He observed that the ancient languages showed a voiceless stop (*p*, *t*, *k*) where Germanic languages such as Gothic and English showed a corresponding fricative (*f*, *th*, *h*).

	Sanskrit	Greek	Latin	Gothic	English
p		*pod-*	*ped-*	*fotus*	*foot*
t	*trayas*	*treis*	*tres*	*threis*	*three*
k		*kardia*	*kor*	*hairto*	*heart*

Similarly, where the ancient languages showed a voiced stop, Germanic showed a voiceless stop.

		Greek	Latin	Gothic	English
b		*turbe*	*turba*	*thaurp*	*thorp*
d	*daśa*	*deka*	*decem*		*ten*
g		*agros*	*ager*	*akrs*	*acre*

And where the ancient languages showed an aspirate (a stop pronounced with a puff of air and written *b^h*, etc.), Germanic showed an unaspirated voiced stop.

b^h	*b^hārāmi*	*p^hero*	*fero*	*baira*	*bear*
d^h	*d^hā-*	*tit^hēmi*	*facio*		*do*
g^h	*stig^h-*	*steik^ho*		*steiga*	"go" staigat

He took the ancient languages to manifest the consonants of the hypothetical parent language, Proto-Indo-European, more or less directly. The manifestation was not always direct: so the PIE voiced aspirates *d^h* and *g^h* were realized as voiceless *t^h* (written θ, theta) and *k^h* (χ, chi) in Greek, the aspirates *b^h* and *d^h* as a voiceless fricative *f* in Latin. This meant that there were some changes between PIE and the ancient languages. Grimm was interested mostly in the changes between PIE and early Germanic. One can view these changes as a cycle (see figure 2.2).

There were several exceptions, cases in which the correspondences that Grimm hypothesized did not hold, but he showed no interest in them. Others were more interested, however. Two generations of scholars sought to explain away the exceptions, and succeeded with the discovery of Verner's Law.

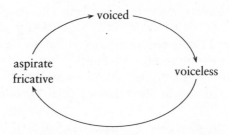

Figure 2.2   Grimm's cycle.

Many people soon noticed that a voiceless stop in the ancient languages corresponded to a voiceless stop in Germanic when it was preceded by a fricative. So, while the third person singular of the verb "to be" was *asti* in Sanskrit, *esti* in Greek, and *est* in Latin, Germanic also showed a *t* in the equivalent position: *ist*. Similarly, Latin has *captus* "taken" and *noctis* "night", while Gothic has *hafts* and *nahts*. In each case, the *t* does not change when it is preceded by a fricative like *f* and *h* in Germanic.

Next, in 1863, the ingenious mathematician/linguist Hermann Grassmann noticed that certain voiced consonants seemed to be preserved in Germanic, not changing to a fricative, as Grimm's cycle would lead one to expect. So, while Sanskrit had *duhītā* "daughter" and *bodhāmi* "offer", Gothic had *dauhtor* and *-biudan*, where the initial *d* and *b* are preserved. Grassmann showed that these are not really counterexamples to Grimm's Law, but just cases where Sanskrit does not manifest the proto-language, PIE, directly. He demonstrated that the *d* of "daughter" and the *b* of "offer" must have been the aspirates d^h and b^h respectively in PIE, corresponding then, as Grimm would expect, to unaspirated, voiced stops *d* and *b* in Germanic. He examined the internal structure of Greek and Sanskrit and showed that they underwent a change: if a word contained two aspirated consonants, the first was de-aspirated. This operation, which came to be honored as "Grassmann's Law," explained some puzzling curiosities. In general, Greek and Sanskrit nouns show different case markings in the suffixes attached to the end of the stem, and the stem is invariant. However, in some rare instances, the initial consonant of the stem may differ, depending on the case form. So the nominative case of "hair" in Greek is t^h*ríks* (written θρίξ), and the genitive is *trik^{h}ós* (τριχός), with an unaspirated *t* initially. Grassmann explained this oddity by assuming that the most primitive form of the root was t^h*rik^h-*, with two aspirates. The nominative ending was *-s*, and the genitive was *-os*. Because aspirates cannot stand immediately before a sibilant *s*, k^h is de-aspirated with the nominative *-s* ending, yielding t^h*ríks*. On the other hand, the most primitive form of the genitive was $t^h rik^h os$, where the k^h is not immediately before a s. Now Grassmann's Law explains why one finds $trik^h ós$: the first of the two aspirates, t^h, must be de-aspirated.

The *coup de grace* came in 1875. Grimm's Law, revised first to accord with the observations regarding fricatives, then by Grassmann, worked quite well for initial consonants, but there were still many apparent exceptions in medial position, which were now explained away by Karl Verner. Certain voiceless stops in the ancient languages did not become voiced stops in Germanic, as Grimm's Law would lead us to expect, but became voiced fricatives. So Sanskrit *pitār*, Greek *patēr*, and Latin *pater* show two voiceless stops, presumably indicating that the consonants for the word for "father" in PIE were *p-t-r*. The first of these stops behaved according to Grimm's Law and became a fricative *f* in Germanic: Gothic *fadar*, English *father*, etc. However, the second stop, the *t*, did not become a voiceless fricative as in English "thin"; unexpectedly, it became a voiced stop *d* in Gothic. On the other hand, the word for "brother" worked as expected: Sanskrit shows a medial *t* (*bʰrātā*), which corresponds to a voiceless fricative in Gothic (*brōþar*). Verner showed that the different histories of the medial *t* in "father" and "brother" were a function of the phonetics of the words: in one case the ancient accent preceded the *t* (*bʰrātā*) and in the other case it followed (*pitá*). This observation, not surprisingly, entered the canon as Verner's Law.

Verner's Law yielded a more or less complete understanding of the evolution of the Germanic consonantal system and led to the triumphant notion that this was the way things always were: sound change was always regular, exceptionless, and phonetically conditioned. Verner had found a phonetic conditioning factor, something in the word itself, which would predict how the medial consonant would behave: namely, the position of the accent. At the end of the century, people like Eduard Sievers (author of *Grundzüge der Lautphysiologie* (1876)) made phonetics into more of an empirical, experimental science, which promised to provide explanations for the changes represented by sound laws. The laws were thought to be reducible to facts about speech articulation, along with some general principles (see below).

The year 1876 brought a lot of productive work and is often referred to as the *annus mirabilis* of the nineteenth century (Hoenigswald 1978). The idea that sound change was regular and systematic was formulated in 1878 in the preface to Osthoff and Brugmann's *Morphologische Untersuchungen*, and the people who held the idea of exceptionless regularity were referred to as the *Junggrammatiker*, the "neo-grammarians." Davies (1998) describes them as "the instigators of a sort of Kuhnian revolution in both technique and methodology," whereas Hockett (1965: 188) saw them as "a group of young Turks, armed with a vitally important idea and with enormous arrogance, winning converts and making enemies as much through charisma as by reasonable persuasion." Davies says that early on "they were covered with opprobrium but they were also revered with the sort of devotion which is more suitable for the followers of a religious sect than for members of a scholarly movement." Eventually they turned into members of the establishment and were accused of stuffiness, dogmatism, and inflexibility. Davies has the details, which will remind her readers of other intellectual power plays.

This nineteenth-century work on the Germanic consonant shift illustrates a more general point. The field of linguistics first identified itself by claiming that language history was *law-governed*, even if the notion of law (Grimm's Law, Grassmann's Law, Verner's Law) was scarcely that of Boyle's Law or the law of gravity, which are timeless. The term referred to specific sound changes, or "correspondences," affecting specific languages at specific times. One could formulate precise correspondences of the form $a \rightarrow b$ *in some phonetically definable context*, where a and b were sounds in corresponding words at two stages of history. The input was the inventory of words in some language (attested or reconstructed), and the output was the inventory of corresponding words at some later stage. Sound a became something else, b, systematically. In any event, languages were supposed to change in systematic ways, and historical linguists, perhaps more than other kinds of linguists, have always been concerned with issues of explanation. The question then arises as to what kind of explanation could be offered for sound changes of this type.

2.3 Historical Explanations

Work on language history at this time reflected the two dominant models of what a science should be: Newtonian mechanics and Darwin's theory of evolution. It also reflected the influence of Hegel, as was explicit in the work of Schleicher on the *Sprachgeist*; Schleicher tried to write stories in Proto-Indo-European, as if it were a real language, and posterity has not treated him kindly. Nonetheless, even though he died early, at 47, he was very influential in his day, as is clear from the introductory comments in Lehmann 1967: 87–9, and the Hegelian approach to history that he expressed was widely shared. *What*

Newton saw all phenomena as describable by deterministic laws of force and motion, such that all future states were, in principle, predictable in a "straight-line," linear fashion from a complete knowledge of the present state. This inspired the notion of sound *laws* to describe the history of changes. The term *Lautgesetz* "sound law" was first coined by Bopp in 1824, and he even offered a mechanical explanation for ablaut alternations (i.e. alternations like English *fell-fall*, *take-took*, *foot-feet*, where the difference in the medial vowel determines the difference in meaning) by invoking a "law of gravity" and postulating that syllables had different "weights." As we have just seen, the concept of the sound law became more rigorous as the century proceeded, until eventually in 1878 sound change was declared to be regular and exceptionless.

Darwin was inspired by work on language history, and he in turn inspired linguists to view languages as natural organisms, on a par with plants and animals. This influence was explicit in the writing of Schleicher, as we have noted, and of Bopp and August Pott. The linguist's language families, languages, dialects, and idiolects were the biologist's genera, species, varieties, and individuals. Languages, like species, compete with each other in a struggle for survival, in the view of Schleicher, and there were inexorable laws of change to be discovered.

Nineteenth-century linguists knew that language reflected psychological properties. Karl Brugmann wrote at the beginning of his career that "the human speech mechanism has a twofold aspect, a mental and a physical" (Lehmann 1967: 198), and went on to talk about the "psychophysical mechanism." At the end of his career, he wrote a monograph the title of which translates as "Varieties of Sentence Formation according to the Basic Psychological Functions in the Indo-European Languages" (1918), and many of the central ideas recur in Brugmann 1925: ch. 6. Heymann Steinthal (1823–99), strongly influenced by Hegel, was a linguist who wrote extensively about psychology and its links with language. He, in turn, influenced Hermann Paul, who strikes us now as an early kindred spirit in the way he thought about psychology. Furthermore, there were psychologists who dealt with language and its acquisition: Wilhelm Wundt (1832–1920) and others. Wundt was known to, and greatly admired by, Leonard Bloomfield when he was young, before he discovered Watson and the behaviorists.

The psychological notions of the time were problematic, in part because they were expressed in ideas of Hegel's. Grimm, for example, adopted a mystical belief in a Hegelian *Sprachgeist*, which had some existence above and beyond individuals (see below). This idea was formulated as *Völkerpsychologie* by Wundt, Steinthal, and Moritz Lazarus, and this group psychology was attacked by Paul (1891: xxxiv f) as being incoherent:

All psychical processes come to their fulfilment in individual minds, and nowhere else. Neither the popular mind (*Volksgeist*), nor elements of it, such as art, religion, etc., have any concrete existence, and therefore nothing can come to pass in them and between them. Away, then, with these abstractions!

Whatever the problems, linguists separated this kind of psychologizing from their day-to-day work. Pedersen's (1931) survey of nineteenth-century work on language scarcely refers to the psychologists at all. William Dwight Whitney, professor of Sanskrit and comparative philology at Yale College, expressed the demarcation rather clearly:

The human capacity to which the production of language is most directly due is, as has been seen, the power of intelligently, and not by blind instinct alone, adapting means to ends. This is by no means a unitary capacity; on the contrary, it is a highly composite and intricate one. But it does not belong to the linguistic student to unravel and explain ... it falls, rather, to the student of the human mind and its powers, to the psychologist. So with all the mental capacities involved in language. (1875: 303)

This was the general view of linguists, through Bloomfield and the structuralists: leave psychology to the psychologists. Winfred Lehmann, in drawing attention to Whitney's views on the proper division of labor, writes to me that, as far as the nineteenth-century linguists were concerned, he has "always assumed that they felt there was plenty to do in getting the data together, and then analyzing them, without explaining them." He adds that it is important to remember that Brugmann pointed out in the preface to his *Grundiss* (see below) that he was providing a systematic account; it is not historical. *Everything* is listed and described, but he was not writing a grammar of a given language.

So linguists generally did not appeal to psychology to explain historical changes. Instead, there were independent laws of history to be found. These historical laws operated on the sounds of languages and were manifested in the relationship between corresponding words in different, historically related languages.

The neo-grammarians were the culmination of this research paradigm, but they confronted two major problems. First, there were regularities of language change which could not be stated in purely phonetic terms, which suggested that it wasn't the language or the sounds that were changing, but rather some kind of abstract system. This matter was dealt with by a terminological move: these linguists were dealing with the law-governed regularities of "sound change," but there could be other kinds of change which worked differently: namely, what were called "analogical changes," which were not law-governed in the same way. Analogy was a different, somewhat more mysterious kind of regularity.

It may make sense to think of words being transmitted from one generation to another, and if they are transmitted in different form, then change has taken place. But in this regard the nineteenth-century linguists were focusing on the products of human behavior, rather than on the internal processes that underlie the behavior. Not all aspects of language can be treated productively in this way, and sometimes one has to deal with the underlying processes and abstract systems. This is true for Grimm's Law, for example, which affected many consonants in a kind of cycle (see figure 2.2); it is also true of more complex changes, such as the famous Great English Vowel Shift, which changed all the long vowels of Middle English in another kind of cycle (raising all vowels by one step and making diphthongs of the highest vowels: so /tiːm/ "time" became /taim/, /sweːt/ "sweet" became /swiːt/, and /huːs/ "house" became /haus/. Grimm's Law and the Great Vowel Shift affect many sounds and represent changes in systems.

Because the neo-grammarians were working with the products of language, rather than with the internal, underlying processes and abstract systems, there were principled reasons why they did not extend their ideas of phonetic change to the domain of syntax.[5] It makes no sense to think of (sets of) sentences, products of behavior, being transmitted from one generation to another, because language acquisition is clearly not just a matter of acquiring sets of sentences, as will become clear in the next chapter. None of this bothered nineteenth-century linguists, because they thought of language as a collection of words, with everything else attributable to either universal "logic" or individually variable "habits." So there wasn't anything to have a history of except words, their pronunciations, and their meanings.

So, as far as one can tell, the first problem, and the matter of abstract systems, assumed very little, if any, importance at the time. By contrast, there was much debate about the second problem, the causes of sound change.

Grimm's, Grassmann's, and Verner's Laws were not general laws like Boyle's Law; therefore they required a deeper explanation. Changes were taken to be *directional*, as in biology, where the replacement of one species by another was taken to result from a mutation which yielded an organism which was more successful in the struggle for survival in a particular environment. Rask (1818) held that languages became simpler. Schleicher (1848) identified a progression from isolating to agglutinating to inflectional types, although this was said to hold for preliterate societies, whereas Rask's drive to simplicity was relevant for postliterate societies. There was widespread agreement that language change followed fixed developmental

laws and that there was a direction to change, but there was active dis-
agreement about *what* the direction was. This was a matter of live dispute.
By the end of the nineteenth century there was an enormous body of work
on sound correspondences between historically related languages and vast
compendia of changes which had taken place in many Indo-European languages. The great monument was Karl Brugmann and Berthold Delbrück's
multi-volume *Grundiss der vergleichenden Grammatik der indogermanischen
Sprache* published between 1886 and 1900. But, such compendia notwithstanding, there were few ideas of why those changes had happened. Eventually the directionality view crumbled.

The notion that languages became simpler/more natural/easier to pronounce was, first of all, circular. "Simpler" etc. was what languages change
to, and there was no independent definition in a framework dealing entirely
with historical change. Since linguists regarded their work as essentially
concerned with language change, they sealed it off from other concerns, and
did not work on language acquisition in an integrated way. Consequently,
they had no independent way of defining their central notions. (Once
we move beyond the nineteenth century, we find less restricted approaches;
linguists like Jespersen broke out of the circle by developing independent notions of simplicity. Even in the late nineteenth century, the beginning
of instrumental phonetics enabled people like Sievers to link changes
to possible assimilation patterns that change sounds in certain phonetic
environments.)

Second, the idea that languages change towards greater simplicity (or
whatever) gives no account of why a given change takes place when it
does – unlike the laws of gravity, etc. which apply to all objects at all
times. To that extent, invoking notions of directionality was no more law-
like than the laws of Grimm, Grassmann, and Verner, which directionality
was intended to explain.

There was much discussion of the causes of sound change in the contemporary literature, and this was where the problems were perceived to
lie. There were occasional attempts to break out of the circle by invoking
psychology, but the psychology was implausible. So Grimm explained his
law of consonant shifts as

> connected with the German's mighty progress and struggle for freedom ...
> the invincible German race was becoming ever more vividly aware of the
> unstoppability of its advance into all parts of Europe ... How could such a
> forceful mobilization of the race have failed to stir up its language at the
> same time, jolting it out of its traditional rut and exalting it? Does there not
> lie a certain courage and pride in the strengthening of voiced stop into
> voiceless stop and voiceless stop into fricative? (1848: 417–37)

Of course, Grimm's contemporaries did not accept such explanations uniformly, but this style of explanation was not unique. If this seems a bit
wild and farfetched, it is not substantially different from a claim made by
Otto Jespersen. As we noted in chapter 1, the verb *like* shifted its meaning
in the fifteenth century and ceased to mean "cause pleasure for" or "please."
One could no longer say things like *The pears like the king,* meaning "The
king likes the pears," as was possible in earlier English. Jespersen claimed
that this shift was due to the "greater interest taken in persons than in
things."[6]

Explanations of this kind may never have had much going for them, but
they were curiously resistant and were never decisively and explicitly refuted.
One has to see them for what they are: psychological elements introduced
into an essentially historicist and a-psychological theory as an attempt
to break out of a narrow circle and reach some level of explanation. The
psychology invoked was never convincing.

By the early twentieth century the data of linguistics seemed to consist in
an inventory of sound changes occurring for no good reason and tending
in no particular direction. The historical approach had not brought a
scientific, Newtonian-style analysis of language, of the kind that had been
hoped for, and there was no predictability to the changes. The psychological move of Paul, Jespersen, and others could not provide the necessary
underpinning. Consequently, the program was not viable. No sustainable
explanations were available for the observed phenomena – i.e. historical
changes – and there was no science of history which met nineteenth-
century demands. The main problem here was that the demands were too
ambitious.

Stephen Anderson (personal communication) emphasizes that we often
have competing, mutually antagonistic principles that make different predictions. For example, "ease of articulation" for the speaker competes
with "clarity of perception" for the hearer, and one or other of those
two notions can account for many phonological changes. That is, when a
change takes place, we can often relate it, after the fact, to one or the other
motivation. Although we might not have been able to predict the change in
advance, we do have some kind of understanding of what happened, some
explanation in a weaker sense. A theory is not empty or nonexplanatory
simply because it fails to predict accurately, and we should not be too
demanding in our goals.[7]

Another way of looking at this is to note that some changes in language
may be brought about by contact with other languages (there are very few
well-established cases in the literature, but let us agree that they may exist)
or by novel expressions taking root in the language as speakers strive for

unusual or striking forms. Also, the use of some constructions may change in frequency of occurrence. In that case, one cannot predict the development of Portuguese, for example, unless one is able to show which foreign influences will succeed and which novel expressions, once adopted, will survive. So linguistic history cannot be determined by structural factors alone. One cannot give a good description of the current state of one's favorite language and expect historians to engage in a kind of Newtonian determinism and provide a computer program that will predict the state of the language in, say, 200 years. For all the talk of directionality, the evidence is that nineteenth-century linguists were not altogether at ease with it; certainly their analyses allowed for particular, contingent factors. After all, under certain circumstances some forms of spoken Latin developed into some form of French, and under other circumstances other forms of Latin developed into Spanish and Sardinian; there was nothing intrinsic to Latin which forced it to develop into French. If a grammarian, *qua* grammarian, regards linguistically unpredictable factors as due to *chance*, one must then ask whether language change is attributable only to chance.

Probably the most thorough discussion of the causes of change in recent times is Lass 1980 and Lass's answer to that question was essentially yes. Lass assumed that scientific explanations are deductive-nomological, involving general laws and deductions from those laws. Since laws are essential, Lass looked for "developmental laws" and "straight-line explanations of language change" – essentially the kind of thing that nineteenth-century linguists had formulated. He found none that met his standards. He gave an accurate critique of efforts to find historical laws but then despaired and decided that he could pursue only a "metaphysical research programme."[8] What was remarkable about his book was its exclusive concern with the nature of linguistic change and its neglect of what it is that changes. It was as if a biologist had tried to account for evolutionary change in an organism without considering the organism's internal structure. Lass's pessimism regarding historical linguistics came from taking too narrow a view; but his view reflects the perspective of the nineteenth century, which was concerned exclusively with matters of language change and sought predictive, deterministic accounts. In his most recent publication, Lass, now older and wiser but still not one to mince words, sees that his earlier book was "partly ill-advised," and even "bigoted, coarsely positivist" (Lass 1997: xv, 332).

The historicist paradigm criticized by Lass – the notion that there are principles of history to be discovered, which would account for a language's development – was largely abandoned in the 1920s. Indeed, there was a virulent anti-historicism in the writing of the structuralists Franz Boas,

Leonard Bloomfield, and Edward Sapir. They worked on language change up until their deaths, showing that the traditional methods of historical and comparative linguistics were as applicable to the unwritten, indigenous languages of North America as they were to Indo-European; Bloomfield worked on the reconstruction of Proto-Algonquian for most of his career. They also perpetuated many of the analytical procedures of the historical linguists in their own synchronic work. However, they abandoned *historicism*, and with it the earlier program of seeking to explain how it was that languages came to be the way they are. The perceived problems related to the circularity of invoking historical principles and to the psychological claims. Sapir (1929) wrote that the psychological interpretation of language change was "desirable and even necessary," but that the existing psychological explanations were unhelpful and "do not immediately tie up with what we actually know about the historical behavior of language." Bloomfield (1933: 17) complained about the circularity of Paul's psychologizing, saying that there was no independent evidence for the mental processes other than the linguistic processes they were supposed to explain. The historicist paradigm was not really refuted or shown to be seriously inadequate by Bloomfield, Boas, Sapir, and the structuralists; rather, it was abandoned as yielding diminishing returns. The paradigm had turned to psychology to avoid an inbuilt circularity and then collapsed because of the inadequacy of the psychology invoked.[9] Work on language change flourished, but structuralists, by and large, did not appeal to historicist explanations.

2.4   Determinist Views of History

The highly deterministic view of history that the linguists sometimes articulated, the idea that there are laws which determine the way that history proceeds, is a hallmark of the nineteenth century. We have seen how it guided the systematic study of language in the nineteenth century, and it played a role in the development of Darwinian ideas and in the domain of political history.

We know that Darwin read the linguists, and vice versa, and that Marx dedicated *Das Kapital* to Darwin. Darwin was too much of a Victorian not to appeal to the notion of progress, but he was critical of the notion and modest in his appeals to it. Marx too had an interesting theory of change, whereby ideas are socially embedded and are amended through conflict, through the clash of theses and antitheses. One changes by negating some previous idea, and then one negates that negation without going back to the first idea, having already moved on somewhere else. Marx's view of social change and revolution, in which small insults to the system build up until the system itself breaks, is a very sensible approach and quite compatible with what I shall sketch in later chapters for language change. However, Marx was very much a nineteenth-century thinker, in that he was caught up in notions of predestiny and determinism, particularly in theories of history. He developed historical laws prescribing that a feudal society must necessarily develop into a mercantilist society, a mercantilist into a capitalist society, capitalism into socialism, and socialism into communism (Cohen 1978). For Marx, the real task of economics was to explain how society evolved over time. At his funeral, Engels eulogized him in a way that he would have liked: "Just as Darwin discovered the law of evolution in organic nature, so Marx discovered the law of evolution in human history."

Marx's approach to political history grew out of the idea that there is a political *science*, a science of the relationships of human beings to each other and to their environment, meeting usual scientific standards and consisting of deductive-nomological laws which permit one to formulate verifiable hypotheses, to discover new facts, and to make predictions about future behavior. This was an idea of Hobbes and Spinoza and their followers, and it became more and more powerful in the eighteenth and nineteenth centuries, as the natural sciences flourished and as the view emerged that anything not reducible to a natural science could not properly be called knowledge at all.

> The more ambitious and extreme scientific determinists, such as Holbach, Helvétius, and La Mettrie, used to think that, given enough knowledge of universal human nature and of the laws of social behavior, and enough knowledge of the state of given human beings at a given time, one could scientifically calculate how these human beings, or at any rate large groups of them – entire societies or classes – would behave under some other given set of circumstances. (Berlin 1996: 41)

The scientifically minded philosophers of the eighteenth century believed passionately in such laws, and in a science of society. The great politicians, even if they did not know it, must have acted on principles which could be extracted and reduced to an accurate science, just as the principles of mechanics or of biology were once established. This tradition, still maintained by optimistic and ambitious sociologists, has proved to be quite resilient. It turned out to explain only small parts of actual human behavior and failed to explain, for example, events surrounding the Jacobin Terror or the rise and violence of nationalism or the unpredictable play of irrational factors. Nonetheless, the early social scientists remained confident that new principles would be more successful.

> Messianic preachers – prophets – such as Saint-Simon, Fourier, Comte, dogmatic thinkers such as Hegel, Marx, Spengler, historically-minded theological thinkers from Bossuet to Toynbee, the popularizers of Darwin, the adaptors of this or that dominant school of sociology or psychology – all have attempted to step into the breach caused by the failure of the eighteenth-century philosophers to construct a proper, successful science of society. Each of these nineteenth-century apostles laid some claim to exclusive possession of the truth. What they all have in common is the belief that there is one great universal pattern, and one unique method of apprehending it, knowledge of which would have saved statesmen many an error, and humanity many a hideous tragedy. (Ibid. p. 42)

It has been argued that not only is there a single, coherent, evolutionary process to history, but that it has an end point. Hegel and Marx believed that there was an end point: the evolution of human societies would end when mankind achieved a form of society that satisfied its deepest, most fundamental longings. For Hegel, this was the liberal state; for Marx the end point was communism. Francis Fukuyama (1992) has argued that the natural end point is a liberal democracy, and that this end point has now been reached, at least as an *ideal*. The idea that there is a coherent, directional history to human society, a Universal History, is the historicism criticized by Popper, who believed that it was responsible for "the unsatisfactory state of the theoretical social sciences (other than economic theory)" (1957: 3).

The "inexorable laws of history" never rose above the level of truisms ("most revolutions are followed by reaction"), and they helped the tyrants of the twentieth century – Lenin, Stalin, and Hitler – not as a system of knowledge, but as a way of justifying ruthless acts and suppressing opposing doubts and reservations. As a system of knowledge, the fundamental problem is that the laws are too principled and exclude contingency – accidental, unpredictable factors which may have large consequences. That is where proponents of a determinist science of history are quite wrong.

This problem is aggravated by another problem: adopting gross categories like classes and types of society (mercantile, capitalist, etc.). By contrast, Jon Elster has emphasized the need to approach political psychology through what he calls "methodological individualism": one must "study the individual human action as the basic building block of aggregate social phenomena" (1993: 8). Elster's is a self-consciously reductionist account, seeking to explain the complex by the simple – "the principle that has brought about scientific progress in the face of all kinds of holistic obscurantism" (ibid. 7). When we get down to talking about linguistic change, we shall face a precisely analogous problem in deciding the scale of our categories, as discussed in chapter 4. We shall echo Elster's view and argue that we understand language change best as an aggregate of changes in individual grammars.

At the other extreme, many scientists do not consider history a part of science, because it deals with particulars and contingency. But this too is not right and reflects a false taxonomy. History may resist straightforward analysis because it is so contingent, but this does not necessarily make it not part of science, rather just a different type of science, as emphasized recently in much of the writing of Stephen Jay Gould.

My goal in this book is to broaden our perspective on language change. Rather than looking for "straight-line," deterministic explanations of language change, I shall take a more indirect approach, leaving plenty of room for contingent factors. In this way we will get an account of language change which is better than that of the nineteenth-century linguists, and one that is different in kind. Those linguists reflected and contributed to the determinism of the nineteenth-century approach to history, at least when they were in their ideological phases. Similarly, we shall reflect and contribute to an alternative, more contingent view of history developed by biologists and historians.

Richard Lewontin has emphasized that

> a complete understanding of organisms cannot be separated from their histories. So the problem of how the brain functions in perception and memory is precisely the problem of how the neural connections come to be formed in the first place under the influence of sights, sounds, caresses, and blows. (1995: 119)

The biology of the nineteenth century was consumed with the problem of bringing the individual and collective histories of organisms into one grand mechanical synthesis, and the two great monuments of biology in that century were the evolutionary system of Darwin and the development of experimental embryology by the German *Entwicklungsmechanik*.

We may distinguish three levels of history in the domain of biological matters. First, one has the evolution of collective properties in a species. Second, there is the development of one set of properties from one generation to another, reflecting the plasticity and variability permitted by the evolved properties of the species. So Lewontin reports a classic experiment in plant genetics, in which seven individuals of the plant *Achillea* were collected in California and each plant was cut into three pieces. One piece from each plant was grown close to sea level, one at 1,400 meters, and one in the High Sierras, over 3,000 meters above sea level. The sets of three pieces were genetically identical, each from the same original plant, but each one grew very differently at each elevation.[10] Similarly, humans have the capacity not only to become speakers of Japanese, if they are raised in an appropriate environment, or Swedish, but also speakers of modern or Middle English. As the third level of history, we have the emergence of mature capacities in an individual. We all began life as a single fertilized egg cell, which grew and transformed itself to produce, in our cases, a reader of books on language change written in English.

Each of these three kinds of history is *contingent*. The environment matters, and it influences history at all three levels. Lewontin notes that "Darwin's radical difference from Lamarckism was his clear demarcation of inside and outside, of organism and environment, and his alienation of the forces within organisms from the forces governing their outside world" (ibid. 129). Mechanisms internal to the organism cause them to vary in their heritable characteristics. These variations – mutations of the genes – are not induced by the environment but happen at random with respect to the demands of the outside world. Quite independently, there is an outside world constructed by forces beyond the influence of the organism itself that set the conditions for the survival and reproduction of the species. The inside and outside interact with each other only through the selection induced by differential survival and reproduction of those forms which best match the independent, external world. This is a matter of *chance*. Those that match, survive to reproductive age and thrive; the others perish. This means that there will be no "straight-line" explanations of history which will reliably predict sequences of events, and there is no reason to believe that there are laws of history.

History is often chaotic in a more or less technical sense. In equations involving x and y, any value for x gives one a value for y. One can think of history as an iterated algorithm: each time one works out a value for y, one uses it as the next value for x. This is a feedback process, in which the solution is fed back into the equation and it is then solved again. At any point, there may be a chance factor which will affect the equation. A slight perturbation may be followed by more perturbations, and the system may be sensitive to slight variations in initial conditions. This is why Edward Lorenz's butterfly flapping its wings in Beijing may be a factor leading to a storm in upstate New York a month later; but this chain of events, the so-called Butterfly Effect, could never be predicted in advance. The fact

that deterministic rules are at work does not mean that there is predictability; such rules do not govern sequences of events. The deterministic
laws governing weather formation are unstable, and miniscule changes at
one location may percolate through the system to cause major effects elsewhere – sensitive dependence on initial conditions, again. There is no hope
of making long-term weather forecasts taking such elements into account.
Widely separated observations of a chaotic system may appear random,
but more closely spaced observations often reveal regularities. So there is
order underlying chaos, at least some chaos; deterministic rules are at work,
and the techniques of chaos theory may reveal simple causes for complex
and unpredictable effects.

If language or social history works like this, through what we may
think of as scientific chaos, we shall never predict the future development
of German grammars or the US political system, but we may be able to
understand local effects, why some change took place in the way and at
the time it did, if we can identify the source of the perturbation. This
means that if one wants to know what will happen with the weather, the
stock market, US political history, or the development of German, the best
one can do is turn the system on and just watch it unfold. All this differs,
of course, from true randomness, chaos in the lay sense, which has no
fixed, deterministic rules.[11]

Many of the intellectual developments of the nineteenth century had to do
with the nature of historical change. At that time, thinkers in various
domains had a highly deterministic view of history and sought principles
that would yield long-term predictions. Obviously we owe a great deal to
nineteenth-century work in linguistics and other areas of study. However,
the work of the twentieth century has led us to see shortcomings in earlier
work, primarily in the deterministic approach to history and in the characterization of what actually changes when we observe different linguistic
phenomena at different periods. It is a testimony to the persuasiveness of
the nineteenth-century thinkers that these shortcomings are still not fully
understood or corrected; we shall see in chapter 8 that some historical linguists have reverted to nineteenth-century historicism, in effect, despite the
arguments of Bloomfield, Boas, and Sapir.

Here we shall cast off this sort of determinism and see what kinds of
accounts of language history we can give by following a more contingent
approach to the subject. First, we need to ask, when we speak of language
history, what changes. We shall shift away from a study of the products of
behavior: the inventory of words in, say, Gothic, which correspond to a
greater or lesser degree to the words of modern German. Words are the

products of some internal, mental system, and they are transmitted more or less directly from one generation of speakers to the next, in a way that mental systems are not transmitted. We shall shift to a study of the states and properties of the mind/brain that give rise to those products. In doing so, we shall shift from something like a natural history to at least a potential natural science. In the next chapter I shall argue that what changes is a biological grammar, which is represented in the mind/brain of an individual. If we apply what we have learned about grammars and acquisition, we can sometimes understand how languages change in big, systematic ways.

Notes

1   I am no historian, and my goal here is to view nineteenth-century work not in its own terms, but rather in terms of questions arising in late-twentieth-century research. I have been helped greatly in this by some true historians: Giorgio Graffi, Winfred Lehmann, and Richard Price.

2   Some argue that Japanese is distinct from Ryukyuan, and that Ryukyuan is a cover term for a number of languages which are not mutually intelligible: Okinawan, Miyako, Hateruma, and Yonaguni. Similarly, a person from Tokyo will not understand a person from Toohoku in the northeast. So "Japanese" is best seen as a cover term for a set of languages. Likewise, "Korean" is used to cover Chechudo, a dialect spoken on the island of Ceycwuto, and the northeast Hamkyeng dialect, neither of which is comprehensible to a speaker from Seoul. The same point holds for all the "large" languages: there are many different forms of English, Spanish, and Chinese.

3   Gould (1985) offers a fascinating, accessible account of how recent work on DNA hybridization has made it easier for biologists to distinguish homologies from analogies, by examining the molecular structure of organisms.

4   Robins (1967) gives an excellent account of work on language before the nineteenth century, and Pedersen (1931) describes the efflorescence in the nineteenth century, adorning his story with photographs of the major players and detailed accounts of individual contributions. Sampson (1980) has a good chapter on the nineteenth century and stresses the influence which philologists and biologists had on each other. Now Anna Morpurgo Davies (1998) has written a rich history of the century, which supersedes all earlier work on nineteenth-century linguistics; she was kind enough to send this to me in typescript.

5   Children acquire some sort of finite, abstract *system*, which characterizes their syntactic capacity and enables them to use an infinite number of sentences. This finite system may change from generation to generation. The neo-grammarians had no appropriate notion of such an abstract system, and therefore no plausible account of what changed in the domain of syntax over the course of time. I discussed this matter more extensively in Lightfoot 1979.

6 I discuss these changes in chapter 6. Jespersen's explanation has been repeated in recent times by McCawley (1976) and Tripp (1978).

7 Anderson (1979) discussed this point in connection with competing principles which predict rule orderings: paradigm uniformity, feeding/bleeding order, transparency, morphology before phonology, etc. He distinguished explanation from prediction and pointed out that the neo-grammarian notions of sound change and analogy sometimes make contradictory predictions, but may still be illuminating and explanatory.

8 Lass attacks explanations of language change based on "naturalness" and teleological "functions." If a certain property p is "natural" or statistically common, one can explain a change whereby p emerges; one cannot explain a change where p does not emerge or is the case less than before the change occurred. Functional notions like ease of pronunciation are simply nonpredictive: they can explain some changes but not those where pronunciation is not made easier. So, Lass concluded, developmental laws based on these notions are inadequate.

9 A similar kind of internal collapse took place later with the structuralists. This is probably no accident, because the structuralists essentially adopted the analytical approach of the neo-grammarians. They applied it to synchronic analysis, avoiding all but the most superficial abstractions and working with implausible psychological theories. But that's another story.

10 While each of the three segments grew differently at different elevations, taken as a whole, there is no predictability from one environment to another: the tallest plant at one elevation may have the poorest growth at another, and vice versa for another plant.

11 Casti 1994: ch. 3 offers a lucid account of chaos theory.

3

Grammars and Language Acquisition

In this chapter we consider what it means to know a language. Individuals grow grammars, which are biological entities represented in people's brains and which characterize their linguistic knowledge. We shall move away now from talk of languages and focus instead on these biological grammars. Cutting some corners, we can say that grammars grow in accordance with genetic or developmental principles, and we can discover what those principles are.

Grammars vary from one person to another, and they may change in groups of people from one generation to the next. This happens if the initial conditions change somewhat, if people are exposed to different childhood experiences. We'll go on to argue in the next chapter that if we observe a language undergoing some significant shift over the course of time, what really is occurring is that grammars are changing in certain individuals and that grammatical change then spreads through a population of speakers. In this way, we adopt Jon Elster's "methodological individualism," mentioned in the last chapter, and study individual behavior as the basic building block of aggregate social phenomena, explaining the complex by the simple. For now we shall deal with the prior matter and argue that a person's mind/brain contains a grammar, which characterizes his or her linguistic capacity and interacts with other mental components.

3.1 We Know More than we Learn

A striking property of language acquisition is that children attain infinitely more than they experience – literally so, we shall see. They attain a productive system, a grammar, on the basis of very little experience. So there is more – much more – to language acquisition than mimicking what we hear in childhood; and there is more to it than the simple transmission of a set of words and sentences from one generation of speakers to the next.

To understand some fundamental aspects of language acquisition, let us go straight to a few simple but specific phenomena. I want to convince you that you know far more than you are consciously aware of, that you're smarter than you think you are.

Consider some subtleties that people are not consciously aware of. The verb *is* may be used in its full form or its reduced form: people say *Kim is happy* or *Kim's happy*. However, certain instances of *is* never reduce: for example, the underlined items in *Kim is happier than Tim is* or *I wonder where the concert is on Wednesday*. Most people are not aware of this, but we all know subconsciously not to use the reduced form here. How did we come to know this? As children, we were not instructed to avoid the reduced form in certain places. Yet, all children typically attain the ability to use the forms in the adult fashion, and the ability is quite independent of intelligence level or educational background. Children attain this ability early in their linguistic development. More significantly, children do not try out the nonoccurring forms as if testing a hypothesis, in the way that they "experiment" by using forms like *goed* and *taked*. The ability emerges perfectly, as if by magic.

Another example: pronouns like *she, her, he, him, his* sometimes refer back to a noun previously mentioned in a sentence (1a–c). However, one can understand (1d) only as referring to two men, Jay and somebody else; here the pronoun may not refer to Jay, unlike in (1a–c).

1 (a) Jay hurt his nose.
   (b) Jay's brother hurt him.
   (c) Jay said he hurt Ray.
   (d) Jay hurt him.

As adults we generalize that a pronoun may refer to a preceding noun *except* under very precise conditions (1d). But then, how did we all acquire the right generalization, particularly knowledge of the exception?

Recall the nature of our childhood experience: we were exposed to a haphazard set of linguistic expressions. We heard various sentences containing pronouns; sometimes the pronoun referred to another noun in the same sentence, sometimes to a person not mentioned there. Problem: because we were not informed about what cannot occur, our childhood experience provided no evidence for the "except" clause, that pronouns sometimes do not co-refer. That is, we had evidence for generalizations like "*is* may be pronounced *z*" and "pronouns may refer to a preceding noun," but no evidence for where these generalizations break down.

As children, we came to know the generalizations and their exceptions, and we came to this knowledge quickly and uniformly. Yet our linguistic experience was not rich enough to determine the limits to the generalizations. We call this the problem of the "poverty of the stimulus." Children have no data which show them that *is* may not be reduced in some contexts, and they have no data showing that *him* may not refer to Jay in (1d). These two small illustrations are examples of the form that the poverty-of-stimulus problem takes in language. It may look as if children are behaving magically, but there is no magician, and magic is no answer.

There are two "easy" solutions to the poverty-of-stimulus problem, but neither is adequate. One is to say that children do not overgeneralize, because they are reliable imitators. That is, children do not produce the reduced *is* in the wrong place or use a pronoun in (1d) wrongly to refer to Jay, because they never hear language being used in this way. In other words, children acquire their native language simply by imitating the speech of their elders. We know that this approach is not tenable, because everybody constantly says things they have never heard. We express thoughts with no conscious or subconscious consideration of whether we are imitating somebody else's use of language. This is true of the most trivial speech: in saying *I wanna catch the 3:25 p.m. bus, which leaves from outside Border's bookstore*, I am using a sentence that I have almost certainly not heard.

A variant on this approach is that children learn not to say the deviant forms because they are corrected by their elders. This view offers no better insight for several reasons. First, it would take an acute observer to detect and correct the error. Second, where linguistic correction is offered, young children are highly resistant and just don't get the correction. Third, in the examples discussed, children do not overgeneralize, and therefore parents have nothing to correct; this will become clearer towards the end of this chapter, when we discuss experimental work on young children.

So the first "easy" solution to the poverty-of-stimulus problem is to deny that it exists, and to hold that the environment is rich enough to provide evidence for where the generalizations break down. The problem is real, but the "solution" does not address the problem.

The second "easy" answer also denies that there is a problem, but it denies that there is anything to be learned and holds that a person's language is fully determined by genetic properties. Yet this answer also cannot be right, because people speak differently, and many of the differences are environmentally induced. There is nothing about my genetic inheritance that makes me a speaker of English; if I had been raised in a Dutch home, I would have become a speaker of Dutch.

The two "easy" answers attribute everything either to the environment or to the genetic inheritance. Neither position is tenable. Instead, language emerges through an interaction between our genetic inheritance and the linguistic environment to which we happen to be exposed. English-speaking children learn from their environment that the verb *is* may be pronounced *iz* or *z*, and native principles prevent the reduced form from being used in the wrong places. Likewise, children learn from their environment that *he*, *his*, etc. are pronouns, and native principles dictate where pronouns may not refer to a preceding noun. The interaction of the environmental information and the native principles accounts for how the relevant properties emerge in an English-speaking child.

We'll sketch the relevant principles in a moment. It is worth pointing out two things. First, we are doing a kind of Mendelian genetics here. Working in the mid-nineteenth century, Mendel postulated genetic "factors" to explain the variable characteristics of his pea plants, without the slightest idea of how these factors might be instantiated biologically. Similarly, linguists seek to identify information which must be available independently of experience, in order for a grammar to emerge in a child. We have no idea whether this information is encoded directly in the genome or whether it results from epigenetic, developmental properties of the organism; it is, in any case, native. As a shorthand device for these native properties, I shall write of the "linguistic genotype," that part of our genetic endowment which is relevant to our linguistic development. Each individual's genotype determines the potential range of functional adaptations to the environment (Dobzhansky 1970: 36), and I assume that the linguistic genotype – what linguists call "Universal Grammar," or "UG" – is uniform across the species (short of pathological cases). That is, linguistically we all have the same potential for functional adaptations, and any of us may grow up to be a speaker of Catalan or Hungarian, depending entirely on our circumstances and not at all on variation in our genetic makeup.

Second, our ideas about how this a priori information is represented are very tentative. There are different models of UG, and those models all change frequently as researchers learn more about language variation, acquisition, and change. I shall invoke the technicalities of particular models as little as possible. Where I do need theoretical ideas, I pick them from what are known as Government-Binding or Minimalist models, but I am not concerned here with outlining a coherent model of UG and shall simply pick ideas which help us understand the phenomena under discussion. I shall be eclectic and opportunistic in this regard, and not much concerned about consistency. There may be equally useful ideas in other models. I am interested in arguments to the effect that property p needs to be postulated at the level of UG, and am less concerned about the form that property *p* might take or how property *p* is biologically encoded.

Since children are capable of acquiring any language to which they happen to be exposed between infancy and puberty, the same set of genetic principles which accounts for the emergence of English (using "genetic" now in the extended sense I have indicated) must also account for the emergence of Dutch, Vietnamese, Hopi, or any other of the thousands of languages spoken by human beings. This plasticity imposes a strong empirical demand on hypotheses about the linguistic genotype; the principles postulated must be open enough to account for the variation among the world's languages. The fact that people develop different linguistic capacities, depending on whether they are brought up in Togo, Tokyo, or Toronto, provides a delicate tool with which to refine claims about the nature of the native component.

So there is a biological entity, a finite mental organ, which develops in children along one of a number of paths. The paths are determined in advance of any childhood experience. The language organ that emerges, the grammar, is represented in the brain and plays a central role in the person's use of language, whether for speaking, listening, writing poems, or solving crossword puzzles. We have gained some insight into the nature of people's language organs by considering a wide range of phenomena: the developmental stages that young children go through, the way language breaks down in the event of brain damage, the manner in which people analyze incoming speech signals, and more. At the center is the biological notion of a language organ, a grammar.

3.2   The Nature of Grammars

So children acquire a productive system, a grammar, in accordance with the requirements of the genotype. If asked to say quite generally what is now known about the linguistic genotype, I would say that it permits finite grammars, because they are represented in the finite space of the brain, but that they range over infinity. Finite grammars consist of a limited, precise set of operations which allow for infinite variation in the expressions that are generated. The genotype is plastic, consistent with speaking Japanese or Quechua. It is modular and uniquely computational.

By "modular" I mean that the genotype consists of separate subcomponents each of which has its own distinctive properties, which interact to yield the properties of the whole. These modules are, in many cases, specific to language. Research has undermined the notion that the mind possesses only general principles of "intelligence" which hold of all kinds of mental activity. One module of innate linguistic capacity contains abstract structures which are compositional (consisting of units made up of smaller units) and which fit a narrow range of possibilities. Another module encompasses the ability to relate one position to another within these structures by movement, and those movement relationships are narrowly defined.

To see the kind of compositionality involved, consider how words combine. Words are members of categories like noun (N), verb (V), preposition (P), adjective/adverb (A), etc. If two words combine, then the grammatical properties of the resulting phrase are determined by one of the two words, which we call the "head." So, if we combine the verb *visit* with the noun *Chicago*, the resulting phrase *visit Chicago* has verbal, not nominal, properties. It occurs where verbs occur and not where nouns occur: *I want to visit Chicago*, but not **the visit Chicago*, or **We discussed visit Chicago*. So the expression *visit Chicago* is a verb phrase (VP), where the verb *visit* is the head projecting to VP. This can be represented as a labeled bracketing (2a) or as a tree diagram (2b). The verb is the head of the VP, and the noun is the "complement." (Here I adapt the novel, bottom-up approach to phrase structure of Chomsky 1995: 244ff.)

2   (a) $_{VP}$[$_V$[visit] $_N$[Chicago]]

    (b)

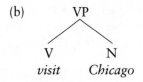

In general, two categories *merge* to form a new category. So an "inflectional" element like *will* might merge with the VP *visit Chicago*, to yield the more complex expression *will visit Chicago*, with a structure $_{IP}$[$_I$[will] $_{VP}$[visit Chicago]]. The inflectional *will* heads the new phrase and projects to a phrasal category IP. This means that *visit Chicago* is a unit (VP), which acts as the complement of *will*, but *will visit* is not a unit; that is, there is no single node which dominates *will visit* and nothing else in this example. This is how grammars assign structures to phrases.

A full sentence like *The student from Denver will visit Chicago* is formed by successive merger, yielding the structure of (3). *The student from Denver* is a unit which acts as the subject of the clause. It is formed by successive merger. *From* merges with *Denver* to yield a preposition phrase (PP), which merges with *student* to form a NP, which merges with *The* to form a constituent called, in recent work, a "determiner phrase" (DP). This DP, in turn, is the *specifier* of the inflectional head *will*, acting as the subject of the clause.[1]

3

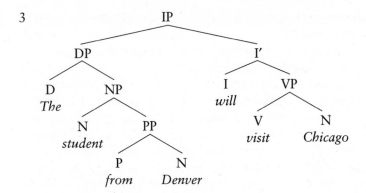

This means that there are two kinds of phrase, one consisting of a head and its complement, *visit Chicago*, in (3), and the other, a more complex phrase consisting also of a specifier, like the IP in (3).

The units defined by these trees are the items which the computational operations manipulate; they are the items which move and can be deleted and which receive indices. Non-units are not subject to these operations.

One of the computational operations involved is that of overt movement to account for the displacement of elements. So an expression like *What city will the student visit?* (where *What city* is understood as the complement of *visit*) has a structure along the lines of (4). Here we need more structure to enable *will* to merge with the IP, and then to enable *What city* to merge with the rest of the clause. *Will* is a head (labeled C for "complementizer"), which merges with the IP, and the determiner phrase (DP) *What city* is a specifier of that head. I indicate the positions from which these elements have moved.

4

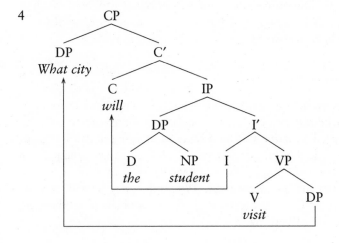

Let us return now to the problem of the reduced *is*, which we discussed earlier. A computational operation attaches the reduced *is* not to the preceding word but to the *following* word, contrary to what the apostrophe *'s* spelling convention suggests. That makes it one of very many instances where orthography does not reflect grammatical reality. Orthography reflects the direction of *phonetic* assimilation: the reduced *'s* takes on phonetic characteristics of the preceding word (compare *Pat's here*, where *'s* is voiceless, and *The dog's here*, where *'s* is voiced, pronounced like *z*). However, rightward attachment at the syntactic level explains why, if there is no following word, the reduced form does not occur, because there is nothing to the right for it to attach to: *Kim is happier than Tim is*. The same holds for *'ve*, *'re*, and the reduced forms of *am*, *will*, *would*, *shall*, and *should*. Poets make linguistic jokes from these principles: the Gershwins were famous for contraction jokes, and in *Girl Crazy* (1930) a chorus begins "I'm bidin' my time / 'Cause that's the kind of guy I'm."

An intervening understood element also blocks attachment to the right, so that there is no reduction: *I wonder where$_x$ the concert is x on Wednesday*. Here *where* has moved from the position indicated and is understood in the position *x*. This shows that the reduced *is* has to be in a certain kind of structural relationship with the following word: it has to *govern* it. *Is* does not govern *on Wednesday* in this example. The distinction is illustrated in (5). In (5a) *is* governs the following word, *happy*, and therefore may be reduced: *happy* is the complement of *is*. Similarly with the first *is* of (5b). However, the underlined form in (5b) does not govern the following word, *Tim*, and therefore may not reduce; in this case, the subject *Tim* and the copula verb *is* have permuted. Intuitively, a head like *is* governs a following word which is its complement (in due course, we shall need to extend this definition slightly). So now we have an answer to the problem sketched at the beginning of this chapter: a reduced *is* is attached to a word to its immediate right which it governs.

5 (a) Kim's happy.
   (b) Kim's happier than is Tim.

Consider another reduction process, whereby *want to* is often pronounced *wanna*: *I want to be happy* or *I wanna be happy*. Here, the *to* may be attached to the preceding *want* and then reduced to give the *wanna* form. But an intervening understood element blocks the reduction process. For example, *Who do you want to see?* has the logical structure of (6a) (corresponding to the statement *You want to see Jill*), and it may be pronounced with the *wanna* form. *Who* is understood as the direct object (complement) of the verb *see*, indicated here by *x*.

6   (a) Who_x do you want $_{IP}[_I$to see $x]$

      (b) Who_x do you want $[x$ to go]$

However, when an understood element intervenes between *want* and *to*, *wanna* does not occur in the speech of most people. So an expression *Who do you want to go?* has the logical structure of (6b) where *who* is understood in the position *x* as the subject of the verb *go* (corresponding to the statement *I want Jill to go*). Logical structures like (6b) do not have a corresponding phonological structure where *want to* is reduced to *wanna*.

The government restriction also holds for the reduced *wanna* form, even though *to* attaches to its left: the reduced form occurs only if *want* governs *to*. *Want* governs *to* in (6a) and therefore may be reduced. However, *want* does not govern the following *to* in the sentences of (7), and it may not be reduced.[2] I give some partial structure in (7a′, b′), enough to show the lack of government between *want* and the immediately following *to*. In (7a′) *want* does not govern the IP *to win games*, because the IP is not its complement; it acts as the subject of the next IP, which, in turn, is the complement of the verb *want*. Similarly, *to vote for the incumbent* is not the complement of *want* in (7b′) and therefore is not governed by it.

7   (a)   They don't want to win games to be their only goal.

      (a′)   . . . want $_{IP}[_{IP}[_I$to win games] $_I$to be their only goal]

      (b)   They expect people who continue to want to vote for the incumbent.

      (b′)   They expect $_{IP}[_{NP}[$people who continue to want] $_I$to vote for the incumbent]

The restrictions on reduced forms, as we have them now, are general: reduced items must be in a government relation with a lexical element. One productive approach is to treat reduced *to* and reduced *is*, etc. as *clitics*. Clitics are little words which occur in many, perhaps all, languages and have the property of not being able to stand alone. There are rightward clitics, which attach to a word to the right, like reduced *is*, and leftward clitics, which attach leftwards, like reduced *to*. Part of what a child developing a grammar needs to do is to determine the clitics in his or her linguistic environment, knowing in advance of any experience that these are small, unstressed items left- or right-attached to an adjacent element under a structural relationship of government, with no other (phonetic or "understood") element intervening. This predetermined knowledge is contributed by the linguistic genotype and is what the child brings to language acquisition. So hearing a reduced form like *'s cold in here* and knowing that it is equivalent in some way to *It is cold in here* suffices to show the child that *'s* is a rightward clitic.

On this approach, the child is faced with a chaotic environment and scans it, looking for rightward and leftward clitics – among many other things, of course. This is my solution to the problem with which I opened this chapter, and it is an answer of the right shape. It makes a general claim at the genetic level (clitics and their behavior are predefined) and postulates that the child arrives at a plausible analysis on exposure to a few simple expressions like *'s cold in here*. The analysis that the child arrives at predicts no reduction for the underlined *is* in *Kim is happier than Tim is*, *I wonder where the concert is on Wednesday*, and countless other cases, and the child needs no correction to arrive at this system. The very fact that *'s* is a clitic, defined in advance of any experience, dictates that it may not occur in certain contexts. It is for this reason that the generalization that *is* may be pronounced as *'s* breaks down at certain points and does not hold across the board.

The mature grammar treats *'s* as a rightward clitic and *-na* as a leftward clitic. This is a feature of an English speaker's phenotype, the mature expression of the potentiality defined by the genotype. By pointing to a plausible triggering experience, linguists show how the English speaker arrives at the relevant analysis, given specific claims at the genotypical level. Linguists spend a lot of time analyzing a wide range of languages, sensitive always to the poverty-of-stimulus problems which each grammar throws up and seeking a single body of information, the invariant linguistic genotype, which solves the poverty-of-stimulus problems in all grammars.

Consider now the second problem: the reference of pronouns. They taught us in school that pronouns refer to a preceding noun, but the data of (1) show that this just isn't right. As we saw, in (1d) *him* may not refer to Jay; in (1b) *him* may refer to Jay but not to Jay's brother. The best account of this complex phenomenon seems to be to invoke a native principle which says that pronouns may *not* refer back to a local nominal element, where "local" means contained in the same clause or in the same DP. This is known as Principle B of the Binding Theory, which deals with the indexical properties of NP/DPs and whose effects have been studied in many languages.[3]

In (8) I give the relevant structure for the corresponding sentences of (1). In (8b) the DP *Jay's brother* is local to *him*, so *him* may not refer back to that DP – we express this by indexing them differently. On the other hand, *Jay* is contained within the DP and therefore is not available to *him* for indexing purposes, so those two nouns do not need to be indexed differently – they may refer to the same person, and they may be co-indexed. Again we see the constituent structure illustrated in (2), (3), and (4) playing a central role in the way in which the computations of the Binding Theory are carried out. In (8d) *Jay* is local to *him*, and so the two elements may not be co-indexed; they do not refer to the same person. In (8c) *Jay* is not local to *he*, because the two items are not contained in the same clause, and Principle B does not block co-indexing: *Jay* and *he* may refer to the same person. In (8a) *his* is contained within a DP and may not be co-indexed with anything else within that DP; what happens outside the DP is irrelevant to Principle B; so *his* and *Jay* may co-refer and do not need to be indexed differently.

8   (a) $_{IP}$[Jay$_i$ hurt $_{DP}$[his$_{i/j}$ nose]]
      (b) $_{IP}$[$_{DP}$[Jay$_i$'s brother]$_k$ hurt him$_{i/j}$]
      (c) $_{IP}$[Jay$_i$ said $_{IP}$[he$_{i/j}$ hurt Ray]]
      (d) $_{IP}$[Jay$_i$ hurt him$_j$]

We could have illustrated this principle equally well with data from French or Dutch, because the principle applies quite generally, to pronouns in all languages. If we assume Principle B as a native principle, available to the child independently of any actual experience, language acquisition is greatly simplified. Now the child does not need to "learn" why the pronoun may refer to Jay in (8a) or (8b, c) but not in (8d). Rather, the child raised in an English-speaking setting has only to learn that *he, his, him* are pronouns – that is, elements subject to Principle B. This can be learned by exposure to a simple sentence like (1d) (8d), uttered in a context where *him* refers to somebody other than Jay.[4]

One way of thinking about the contribution of the linguistic genotype is to view it as providing invariant principles and option points, or "parameters." There are invariant principles to the effect that clitics attach to elements in a government relation and that pronouns are not locally co-indexed. Meanwhile, there are options such that direct objects may precede the verb in some grammars and follow it in others, that some clitics attach to the right and some to the left. These are parameters of variation, and the child sets these parameters one way or another in light of her particular linguistic experience. As a result, a grammar emerges in the child, part of the linguistic phenotype. The child has learned that *'s* is a clitic and that *her* is a pronoun; the genotype ensures that *'s* is attached to a lexical category in a government relation and that *her* is never used in a context where it refers to a local nominal.

Here we have looked at a couple of specific acquisition problems and considered what ingredients are needed for their solution. Now let us stand back and think about these matters more abstractly.

3.3   The Acquisition Problem: The Poverty of the Stimulus

The child acquires a finite, generative system – a grammar – which generates structures which correspond more or less to utterances of various kinds. Children acquire these grammars despite a poverty of stimulus on three levels.

First, the child hears speech from adults, peers, and older children. This stimulus does not consist uniformly of complete, well-formed utterances; it also includes sentence fragments, slips of the tongue, incomplete thoughts, ill-formed utterances from people who do not know the child's language well, and even sentences artificially simplified, supposedly for the benefit of children. Even if only 5 percent of the expressions the child hears are of this latter type, there will be a significant problem in generalizing to the set of grammatical sentences of the language, because the pseudo-sentences do not come labeled as defective.

Second, a child encounters only a finite range of expressions, but she comes to be able to produce and understand an infinite range of novel sentences, going far beyond the sentences heard in childhood. We know this at the intuitive level when we recognize that we constantly encounter novel sentences that we have not heard or used before. Consider the sentences on this page; it is unlikely that the reader has encountered any of them before in the precise form in which they occur here.

More formally, to understand that there is an infinite number of English sentences, one has only to realize that, in principle, any given sentence may be of indefinite length. Three iterative devices permit this and they may occur in various combinations:

Relativization: This is the dog that chased the cat that killed the rat that caught the mouse that nibbled the cheese that . . .
Complementation: I think that Jim asked me to tell Kim that Tim thought that I said that . . .
Co-ordination: Jay went to the movies and to the concert, and Ray and Kay went out for dinner, and Fay stayed at home, and . . .

If a sentence may be of indefinite length, then it follows that people have a capacity to use and express an indefinite number of sentences. Since a person's experience is finite and the mature capacity ranges over infinity, the stimulus alone cannot fully determine the mature capacity.

Third, people come to know things subconsciously about their language, things for which no direct evidence is available in the data to which they are exposed as children learning to speak. People eventually understand

and utter complex, ambiguous sentences, identify paraphrases, and distinguish sentences that may occur in their language from ones that may not. We have just spent a few pages illustrating this kind of thing, and the subconscious, mature capacity that ordinary people have involves language properties made explicit by linguists. However, the crucial properties lie outside the primary linguistic data available to young children. Children are not systematically informed that hypothetical sentences do not in fact occur (e.g. *Who do you wanna go?, *Kim's happier than Tim's), that a given sentence is ambiguous, or that certain sets of sentences are paraphrases of each other. Also, many legitimate, acceptable sentence types may never occur in a child's linguistic experience. Such data are not available to preschool children and are not part of their verbal experience. The distinction between the range of data known to the linguist and the much more limited data available to the beginning speaker is of vital importance for the biological view of language development.

This third deficiency is quite crucial. The first two, the imperfection and finiteness of the stimuli, are not decisive kinds of data deficiencies. They do not deny that relevant experience for language learning is available; they simply assert that the experience is "degenerate," hard to sort out. The fundamental deficiency is the third, which says not that relevant experience is degenerate but that in certain areas it does not exist at all. This deficiency shapes hypotheses about the linguistic genotype.

Some structural principle prevents forms like *Who do you wanna go? from occurring in the speech of English speakers, as we have seen. Children are not exposed to pseudo-sentences like this and informed systematically that they are not said. Speakers come to know subconsciously that they cannot be said, and this knowledge emerges somehow, even though it is not part of the input to the child's development. Furthermore, it is hard to imagine how the inventory of sentences and sentence fragments that constitute the child's linguistic environment could provide even indirect evidence that such sentences do not occur. It is not enough to say that people do not utter such forms because they never hear them. This argument is insufficient, because people say many things that they have not heard, as we have noted. Language is not learned simply by imitating or repeating what has been heard.

This third deficiency of the stimulus is of particular importance in defining our approach to language acquisition. A good deal of evidence exists that the contrast between the child's experience and the range of data available to the linguist is quite substantial. Over the last 40 years, much of the linguistic literature has focused on areas where the best description cannot be derived directly from the data to which the child has access, or is underdetermined by those data, as in the examples with the clitics *to* and *'s* and the pronouns. If the child's linguistic experience does not provide the basis for establishing a particular aspect of linguistic knowledge, another source must exist for that knowledge. That aspect must be known a priori, in advance, in the sense that it is available independently of linguistic experience. We tentatively assume that it is available through genetic prescriptions, while not ignoring other possibilities – for example, that it arises as a consequence of other, nonlinguistic experience.

All this is not to say that imitation plays no role: just that it does not provide a sufficient explanation, given the third data deficiency. This is worth emphasizing, because antagonists sometimes caricature this approach to language acquisition as "denying the existence of learning," when in fact its adherents merely deny that learning is the whole story – a very different matter. The quotation is from a remarkable article in *Science* magazine, in which the authors assert that "Noam Chomsky, the founder of generative linguistics, has argued for 40 years that language is unlearnable," and that they, on the other hand, have "rediscovered" learning (Bates and Elman 1996)!

Caricatures of this type show up in the writing of people who claim that *all* information is derived from the environment, and that there is no domain-specific genetic component to language acquisition. These people deny the poverty-of-stimulus problems, claiming that children derive all relevant information from their linguistic environment. Bates and Elman provide a recent, particularly clear and striking instance of this line, claiming that artificial neural networks can learn linguistic regularities from imperfect but "huge computerized corpora of written and spoken language."[5]

Others have appealed to a structured input which allows children to circumvent the poverty-of-stimulus problems (Snow 1977). Parents and other people often adopt a simple, sometimes artificial style of speech when addressing children; but it is scarcely plausible that this "Motherese" provides sufficient structure for language acquisition to take place on a purely inductive basis. Children do not simply generalize patterns without the aid of genetically determined principles.

There are at least four reasons why this kind of pattern generalization is not the answer to how children acquire speech. First, although children no doubt register only part of their linguistic environment, there is no way of knowing exactly what any individual child registers. Therefore, there is no factual basis for the claim that children register only what is filtered for them through parents' deliberately simplified speech. Children have access to more than this, including defective utterances, sentence fragments, and all the imperfections that the world throws at us. Second, even supposing that they register only perfectly formed expressions (and hence that the first data deficiency does not hold), this isn't enough to show that the child has a sufficient inductive base for language acquisition. The third data deficiency still holds, and the child would need to know that *wanna* fails to occur in certain contexts. If children learn by induction, we must ask why quite ordinary inductive generalizations like this – that *want to* may be pronounced *wanna* – break down. The artificial, simplified speech of the Motherese style does not show where inductive generalizations must stop. Third, if the child registered only the simplified, well-formed sentences of Motherese, the problem of language learning would be *more* difficult, because the child's information would be more limited. Fourth, careful studies of parents' speech to children (like Newport et al. 1977) show that an unusually high proportion consists of questions and imperatives, and that simple declarative sentences are much rarer than in ordinary speech. This suggests that there is very little correlation between the way the child's language emerges and what parents do in their speech directed to children. The existence of Motherese in no way eliminates the need for a genetic basis to language acquisition. The child is primarily responsible for the acquisition process, not parents or playmates.

Nobody denies that the child must extract information from her environment; it is no revelation that there is "learning" in that technical sense. My point is that there is more to language acquisition than this.

Children react to evidence in accordance with specific principles. It is not at all clear what role induction plays. Induction does not enable a child to determine what a well-formed sentence is; nor does it explain how children "learn" the meanings of even the simplest words. Children do not have sufficient evidence to induce the meaning of *house*, *book*, or *city*, or of more complex expressions, even if we grant everything to advocates of Motherese or those who argue that it's all data processing of huge corpora (see n. 5). The biggest problem with ordinary sentences like *Kim is too clever to catch* or *Everybody saw him* is not that they exist, but to characterize their meaning and the meanings of the individual words. There is another problem with the Motherese hypothesis, which is more trivial than this but nonetheless real: children typically acquire the language not of their parents, but of their older siblings and peers.

The problem demanding explanation is compounded by other factors. Despite variation in background and intelligence, people's mature linguistic capacity emerges in fairly uniform fashion, in just a few years, without much apparent effort, conscious thought, or difficulty; and it develops with only a narrow range of the logically possible "errors." Children do not test random hypotheses, gradually discarding those leading to "incorrect" results and provoking parental correction. In each language community the non-adult sentences formed by very young children seem to be few in number and quite uniform from one child to another, which falls well short of random hypotheses. Normal children attain a fairly rich system of linguistic knowledge by five or six years of age, and a mature system by puberty. This is impressive when compared with the laborious efforts of squads of adult linguists who have made it through graduate school and try with only moderate success to characterize explicitly what people know when they know Estonian, Hopi, or Bengali. In this regard, language is no different from, say, vision, except that vision is taken for granted, and ordinary people give more conscious thought to language.

These, then, are the salient facts about language acquisition or, more properly, language growth. The child masters a rich system of knowledge without significant instruction and despite a triple deficiency of experiential data. The process involves only a narrow range of "errors" or false hypotheses and takes place rapidly, even explosively, between two and three years of age. The main question is how children acquire so much more than they experience.

Given these facts, especially the third data deficiency, certain properties must be available to the organism independently of linguistic experience. These properties permit language growth to circumvent environmental deficiencies and thus to take place quickly and not solely by trial and error. The environmental stimulus is impoverished, unstructured, and fairly random; the child hears a haphazard selection of sentences and pseudo-sentences and receives no significant instruction. So the environmental stimulus is just a trigger. Much of the ability eventually attained is determined by genotypical principles, which are activated by environmental stimuli.

The further fact that children can master *any* human language to which they happen to be exposed in infancy imposes strong limitations on the principles which the scientist can attribute to the genotype. An answer to the problem of acquisition does not lie merely in the properties of the specific language a particular child acquires. This would amount to a claim that the specific properties of, say, Hindi are innately prescribed, which permits no explanation of how a language with a significantly different structure – Polish, say – is acquired. The native principles must therefore be somewhat abstract and not language-specific. The principles must meet strict empirical demands: for each child, the principles must provide a basis for attaining the eventual mature grammar given exposure only to the haphazard and unstructured experience available in the child's community. To require the native principles to give an account of how a child may master *any* natural grammar under the conditions noted is to ask a lot.

The tight empirical demands make language particularly useful as a probe into the intrinsic properties of the human mind/brain.

A grammar represents what a speaker comes to know, subconsciously for the most part, about his or her native language. It represents the fully developed linguistic capacity, and is therefore part of an individual's phenotype. It is one expression of the potential defined by the genotype. Speakers know that certain sentences (in fact, an infinite number) may occur in their speech and that others may not; they know what the occurring sentences mean and the various ways in which they can be pronounced and rephrased. Most of this largely subconscious knowledge is represented in a person's grammar. The grammar may be used for various purposes, from everyday functions like expressing ideas, communicating, or listening to other people, to more contrived functions like writing elegant prose or lyric poetry, or compiling and solving crossword puzzles, or writing a book about language acquisition and change.

Universal Grammar (UG) represents the genetic equipment that makes language growth possible under the conditions assumed here (therefore part of the genotype) and delimits the linguistic knowledge that may eventually be attained – that is, the form and functioning of the grammar. The genotypical principles and parameters can be viewed as a theory of grammar. On this view, the theory of grammar is, in Chomsky's words,

> a common human attribute, genetically determined, one component of the human mind. Through interaction with the environment, this faculty of mind becomes articulated and refined, emerging in the mature person as a system of knowledge of language. To discover the character of this mental faculty, we will try to isolate those properties of attained linguistic competence that hold by necessity rather than as a result of accidental experience, where by "necessity" I of course mean biological rather than logical necessity. . . . The commitment to formulate a restrictive theory of UG is nothing other than a commitment to discover the biological endowment that makes language acquisition possible and to determine its particular manifestations. . . . we can explain some property of attained linguistic competence by showing that this property necessarily results from the interplay of the genetically-determined language faculty, specified by UG, and the person's (accidental) experience. (Chomsky 1977: 164)

It need hardly be pointed out that there is nothing necessary or God-given about this research goal; nor do I want to give the impression that all linguists adopt it. Crucially for our purposes, the vast majority of people who have worked on language change have not adopted this research goal. In fact, people have studied language with quite different goals in mind, ranging from the highly specific (to describe Dutch in such a way that it can be learned easily by speakers of Indonesian), to the more general, such as showing how a language may differ from one historical stage to another (comparing, for example, Chaucerian and present-day English). However, this is the goal I adopt, and this is the sense in which I shall construe a grammar, seeing it as a biological object; and it is important to keep this idea straight and not conflate it with other, more traditional notions of what a grammar is.

3.4   The Analytical Triplet

A grammar, for us, is a psychological entity, part of the psychological state of somebody who knows a language. For any aspect of linguistic knowledge, three intimately related items are included in the account. First, there is a formal, explicit characterization of what a mature speaker knows; this is the *grammar*, which is part of that speaker's phenotype. It is an internal system, what Chomsky 1986 called the I-language, as distinct from the external linguistic production, the E-language. Since the grammar is represented in the mind/brain, it must be a finite system, which can relate sound and meaning for an infinite number of sentences.

Second, also specified are the relevant principles and parameters common to the species and part of the initial state of the organism; these principles and parameters make up part of the *theory of grammar*, or *Universal Grammar*, and belong to the genotype.

The third item is the *trigger* experience, which varies from person to person and consists of an unorganized, fairly haphazard set of utterances, of the kind that any child hears (the notion of a trigger stems from ethologists' work on the emergence of behavioral patterns in young animals). The universal theory of grammar and the variable trigger together form the basis for attaining a grammar; grammars are attained on the basis of a certain trigger and the genotype.

In (9) I give the explanatory schema, using general biological terminology in (9a) and the corresponding linguistic terms in (9b). The triggering experience causes the genotype to develop into a phenotype; exposure to a range of utterances in, say, English allows the UG capacity to develop into a particular mature grammar. One may think of the theory of grammar as making available a set of choices; the choices are taken in the light of the trigger experience, or the primary linguistic data (PLD), and a grammar emerges when the relevant options are selected. A child develops a grammar by setting the parameters of UG in the light of her particular experience.

9   (a)   linguistic triggering experience (genotype → phenotype)
    (b)   primary linguistic data (Universal Grammar → grammar)

Each of the items in the triplet – trigger, UG, and grammar – must meet various demands. The trigger, or PLD, must consist only of the kinds of things that children routinely experience and includes only simple structures.[6] The theory of grammar, or UG, is the one constant and must hold universally, so that any person's grammar can be attained on the basis of naturally available trigger experiences. The mature grammar must define an infinite number of expressions as well-formed, and for each of these it must specify at least the sound and the meaning. A description always involves these three items, which are closely related; changing a claim about one of the items usually involves changing claims about the other two. This tight, ambitious system of description must meet many empirical demands. It is hard to imagine that we might have to choose between two or more descriptions which meet all empirical demands, hard to imagine problems of indeterminacy of the kind that plague the natural historian or the taxonomist who does not take a psychological view of grammars.

The grammar is one sub-component of the mind, which interacts with other cognitive capacities or modules. Like the grammar, each of the other modules is likely to develop in time and to have distinct initial and mature states. So the visual system recognizes triangles, circles, and squares through the structure of the circuits that filter and recompose the retinal image (Hubel and Wiesel 1962). Certain nerve cells respond only to a straight line sloping downward from left to right, other nerve cells to lines sloped in different directions. The range of angles that an individual neuron can register is set by the genetic program, but experience is needed to fix the precise orientation. In the mid-sixties David Hubel, Torsten Wiesel, and their colleagues devised an ingenious technique to identify how individual neurons in an animal's visual system react to specific patterns in the visual field (including horizontal and vertical lines, moving spots, and sharp angles). They found that particular nerve cells were set within a few hours of birth to react only to certain visual stimuli, and, furthermore, that if a nerve cell is not stimulated within a few hours, it becomes totally inert in later life. In several experiments on kittens, it was shown that if a kitten spent its first few days in a deprived visual environment (a tall cylinder painted only with vertical stripes), only the neurons stimulated by that environment remained active; all other optical neurons became inactive, because the relevant synapses degenerated, and the kitten never learned to see horizontal lines or moving spots in the normal way. Thus learning is a selective process: parameters are provided by the genetic equipment, and relevant experience fixes those parameters. A certain mature cognitive structure emerges at the expense of other possible structures, which are lost irretrievably as the inactive synapses degenerate. The view that there is a narrowing down of possible connections from an overabundance of initially possible ones is now receiving more attention in the light of Hubel and Wiesel's Nobel Prize-winning success. At the moment, this seems to be a more likely means of fine tuning the nervous system as "learning" takes place, by contrast with the earlier view that there is an *increase* in the connections among nerve cells.

So human cognitive capacity is made up of identifiable properties that are genetically prescribed, each developing along one of various pre-established routes, depending on the particular experience encountered. These genetic prescriptions may be extremely specialized, as Hubel and Wiesel showed for the visual system. They assign some order to our experience. Experience elicits or triggers certain kinds of specific response, but it does not determine the basic form of the response.

This kind of modularity is very different from the view that the cognitive faculties are homogeneous and undifferentiated, and that the faculties develop through general problem-solving techniques. In the physical domain, nobody would suggest that the visual system and the system governing the circulation of the blood are determined by the same genetic regulatory mechanisms. Of course, the possibility should not be ruled out that the linguistic principles postulated here may eventually turn out to be special instances of principles holding over domains other than language; but before that can be established, more, much more, must be known about what kinds of principles are needed for language acquisition to take place under normal conditions, and similarly for other aspects of cognitive development. Only then can meaningful analogies be detected. Meanwhile,

> we are led to expect that each region of the central nervous system has its own special problems that require different solutions. In vision we are concerned with contours and directions and depth. With the auditory system, on the other hand, we can anticipate a galaxy of problems relating to temporal interactions of sounds of different frequencies, and it is difficult to imagine that the same neural apparatus deals with all of these phenomena . . . for the major aspects of the brain's operation no master solution is likely. (Hubel 1978: 28)

3.5   Real-Time Acquisition of Grammars

In the domain of language, some ingenious colleagues at the University of Maryland have shown that the sophisticated distinctions discussed at the beginning of this chapter do not result from learning, and that the hypothesized genetic constraints seem to be at work from the outset. The experimenters constructed situations in which the overriding temptation for children would be to violate the relevant constraints. The fact that children conformed to the hypothesized constraints, resisting the preferences they showed in other contexts, is taken to be evidence that they have the constraints under investigation, and have them at the earliest stage that they might be manifested (Crain 1991).

Stephen Crain and Rosalind Thornton developed an elicitation task that encouraged children to ask questions like *Who do you wanna go? (cf. 6b), if these were compatible with their grammars. They hypothesized that children would generally show a preference for the reduced *wanna* form whenever this was consistent with their grammars. This preference would be revealed in a frequency count of legitimate forms, like *Who do you wanna see?* (cf. 6a). Comparing the frequency of the reduced forms in these contexts with non-adult reduced forms would indicate whether or not children's grammars contained the hypothetical genetic constraint. If the genetic constraint is at work, there should be a significant difference in frequency; otherwise, not.

In the simplest case, an experimenter asked for a child's help in obtaining information about rats. Help was sought because the rat (a puppet) was too timid to talk to grown-ups. The experimenter said, "The rat looks hungry. I bet he wants to eat something. Ask Ratty what he wants." And the children, who ranged in age from 2 years, 10 months, to 5 years, 5 months, typically would ask "What do you wanna/want to eat?" In this example, the wh- word is understood as the object of *eat*, and the reduced form could occur freely, as in (6a). In fact, the reduced form occurred 59 percent of the time in these examples, and the unreduced form occurred 18 percent of the time. So children do show a preference for the reduced form, and that is the extent of it.

Something very different happened when the wh- word had to be understood in the subject position, as in (6b), *Who do you want to go?* The protocol for this experiment was that the experimenter would ask: "There are three guys in this story: Cookie Monster, a dog, and this baby. One of them gets to take a walk, one gets to take a nap, and one gets to eat a cookie. And the rat gets to choose who does each thing. So, *one* gets to take a walk, right? Ask Ratty who he wants." And the child would typically reply: "Who do you want to take a walk?" Here *who* is understood as the subject of *take*, i.e. between *want* and *to*: who$_x$ you want [x to take a walk]? In these contexts the frequency of the reduced form was quite different: the reduced forms occurred 4 percent of the time, the unreduced forms 67 percent. In fact, one child accounted for all three actual occurrences of the reduced form, which suggests that this particular child had some other analysis of *wanna* forms. So children prefer to use the reduced form in asking questions like (6a), but correctly resist this preference when they should. They use the reduced form in asking questions like (6a), but not in questions like (6b), so they manifest the hypothetical genetic constraint at a stage when their spontaneous production manifests very few instances of long-distance wh- movement. The ingenuity of the experiment shows that even at this stage the relevant principle is operating (Crain 1991).

Wanna contraction is an example of leftward cliticization, but the same story holds for rightward cliticization, in the use of reduced *is*, *will*, and so on. Thornton and Crain conducted a similar experiment to elicit another kind of long-distance question. The target productions were evoked by the following protocols for rightward cliticization:

(10)   *Experimenter*:   Ask Ratty if he knows what that is doing up there.
        Child: Do you know what that's doing up there?
        Rat: It seems to be sleeping.

(11)   *Experimenter*:   Ask Ratty if he knows what that is up there.
        Child: Do you know what that is up there?
        Rat: A monkey.

In (10) the child is invited to produce a sentence where *what* is understood as the object of *doing*: *Do you know what$_x$ that is doing x up there?* Therefore, *is* may be cliticized to the immediately right-adjacent element, *doing*. However, in (11) the child produces a sentence where *what* is understood as the complement of *is*, i.e. between *is* and the following item: *Do you know what$_x$ that is x up there?* (cf. *That is a bottle up there*). The intervening x marker prevents the *is* from cliticizing on to *up* in adult speech; no adult would say **Do you know what that's up there*, with the reduced form (cf. *That's a bottle up there*). Thornton and Crain found that young children behaved just like adults, manifesting the hypothetical genetic constraint. The children tested ranged in age from 2 years, 11 months, to 4 years, 5 months, with an average age of 3 years, 8 months. In the questions elicited there was not a single instance of the reduced form where it is impossible in adult speech. Children produced elaborate forms like those of (12), but never with the reduced *is*.

12 (a) Do you know what that black thing on the flower is? (4 years, 3 months)
   (b) Squeaky, what do think that is? (3 years, 11 months)
   (c) Do you know what that is on the flower? (4 years, 5 months)
   (d) Do you know what that is, Squeaky? (3 years, 2 months)

The experiments just described deal with elicited production, but comprehension studies also show that hypothetical genetic constraints are in effect in very young children, at the earliest stage at which they can be tested. Thornton (1994) reported children's comprehension of yes/no questions containing negation, such as (13). The difference between the two forms lies in the structural position of the negative: in (13a) the negative is inside the IP (partial structure given in (13a')), whereas in (13b) it has cliticized to *did* and moved out of the IP to C (13b').

13 (a) Did any of the turtles not buy an apple?
   (a') $_{CP}$[did $_{IP}$[any of the turtles **not** buy an apple]]
   (b) Didn't any of the turtles buy an apple?
   (b') $_{CP}$[did**n't** $_{IP}$[any of the turtles buy an apple]]

The position of the negative corresponds to two distinct interpretations. That correspondence between meaning and structural position follows from principles of UG, which we need not go into here; essentially, a negative "scopes over" any element within its complement. The phenomenon is clear. Suppose that turtles A and B bought an apple but turtle C did not. Then if somebody asked question (13a), an appropriate answer would be that turtle C did not. If somebody asked (13b), then the appropriate answer would be very different: turtles A and B did. So children's responses to questions like (13a) and (13b) reveal how they interpret negatives. In particular, responses to (13b) show whether children interpret the negative in the higher structural position. This is worth testing, because Thornton found that all her children *produced* non-adult negative questions. Most doubled the auxiliary verb (*What do you don't like?*), and one failed to move the auxiliary to the position of C (see structure (4)): *What you don't like?*

In testing comprehension, Thornton found that the children had no difficulty interpreting negative questions in adult fashion; significantly, all children were able to access interpretations like (13b), where the negative needs to be interpreted in the position of C. She tested children between the ages of three-and-a-half and four-and-a-half. The comprehension test used a modified form of the Truth Value Judgment Task (Crain 1991). A

story was acted out by one experimenter and was watched by the child
and a second experimenter, who played the role of a puppet, in this case
"Snail." At the end of each story, the experimenter asked Snail a targeted
question. Snail had difficulty with the question ("That's a hard one . . ."),
and requested help from the child. If the child was cooperative, she answered
the question for Snail.[7] The scenarios used to test children's comprehension of questions like (13a) and (13b) were designed so that either (13a) or
(13b) could be asked appropriately; children's answers, however, indicated
their analysis of the structural position of the negative. Thornton found that,
while these children made *production* errors with expressions like adult
What don't you like?, their *comprehension* was adult-like and manifested
the UG principles which determine the scope of negatives.

So there is a clear production/comprehension asymmetry, which, of course,
is no surprise on the modular view of mind that I have articulated. Whatever it is that causes the delay in producing the adult forms, the fact that
children interpret the negative questions in adult fashion shows that they
have access to whatever principles of UG assign scope relations. The difficulty evidently lies in the behavior of the clitic *n't*: children produce non-
adult questions which retain the *n't* in the inflection phrase IP until they
figure out that *n't* may cliticize to *did* and move with it outside the IP to
the higher complementizer position C.

This last experiment illustrates the obvious fact that young children are
not entirely like adults in their syntactic behavior, even if they seem to
manifest at the earliest stage possible the hypothesized genetic constraints
that we have been discussing. In another study, Thornton analyzed an
intriguing type of non-adult speech. She observed wh- questions like (14)
in some three- and four-year-old children, where a copy of the wh- word
shows up at the front of the clause where it is understood; such sentences
do not occur in adult English, but analogues to them occur in dialects of
German and in other languages (Thornton 1995).

14 (a) What do you think what pigs eat?
    (b) Who do you think who eats trash?

Furthermore, even after children stop using medial wh- words in object
extraction questions like (14a), they persist in using them in subject extractions like (14b). That developmental sequence illustrates principles of UG:
the extra wh- word in subject extraction questions is an overt manifestation of the "agreement" properties needed to license an empty subject. That
won't make much sense until we get to chapter 9 (section 9.3) and consider subject extraction in the context of the evolution of UG in the species,

but my point here is more primitive: some children systematically produce things like (14), even though they never hear such sentences uttered by adult speakers of English. Children do not simply imitate models; they develop a system, a grammar, which at certain stages of development yields things which no child hears from English-speaking adults. When we study the development of these grammars, we can often understand the properties they have, even when they do not reflect what children have heard.

There is, of course, much more to be said about grammars and their acquisition, and there is an enormous technical literature. Here I have tried to sketch the essence of the biological view of grammars, because it is central to my account of language change. Now we shall proceed to investigate language change as change in individual grammars, and we'll see where that gets us.

Meanwhile, we have an approach to the riot of differences that we find in the languages of the world and even within individual languages: there's a universal language, and it is this UG which makes us accessible to one another. As children, our linguistic experience varies tremendously; no two children experience the same set of sentences, let alone the same pronunciations. Nonetheless, the approach I have sketched enables us to understand the universality of our development, why we categorize the linguistic world so similarly and can talk to each other, despite the enormous variation in our childhood experience.

For centuries people have held that organisms grow according to the prescriptions of an internal regulatory program. As a result of twentieth-century work in molecular biology, we now understand much about how that regulatory mechanism works, how it is transmitted, how it can be amended, and so on. But the idea that there must exist an internal regulatory program long antedates recent work in molecular biology. For centuries scientists theorized that the sperm contained a perfect miniature creature, a "Russian doll," or "homunculus," which simply grew bigger as time went on. This was preformationism, which was quite a reasonable theory to hold in the eighteenth century. Earlier, Plato held that the basic ideas and elements of thought were innate, and that at birth we drank of the River Lethe, the river of forgetfulness, which rendered this equipment subconscious. We no longer hold such ideas, but they do suggest that the question of how to account for the way in which living things develop has been a basis for theorizing. People have long thought that the development is internally directed in some way. The reason for this belief has always been that environmental factors alone cannot determine certain features of the mature makeup of an organism.

Recently, theoretical developments have brought an explosive growth in what we know about human languages. Linguists can now formulate interesting hypotheses, account for broad ranges of facts in many languages, with elegant abstract principles. Work on human grammars has paralleled work on the visual system and has reached similar conclusions, particularly with regard to the existence of highly specific computational mechanisms. In fact, language and vision are the areas of cognition that we know most about; we know much more in these domains than we know about memory, the emotions, or, for heaven's sake, consciousness. Much remains to be done, but we can show how children attain certain elements of their language organs by exposure to only an unorganized, haphazard set of simple utterances; for these elements we have a theory which meets basic requirements. Eventually, the growth of language in a child will be viewed as similar to the growth of hair: just as hair emerges with a certain level of light, air, and protein, so, too, a biologically regulated language organ emerges under exposure to a random speech community.

Our focus here is grammars, not the properties of a particular language, or even general properties of many or all languages. A language on the view sketched here is an epiphenomenon, a derivative concept, the output of certain people's grammars (perhaps modified by other mental processes). Relegating the notion of a language in this way avoids various problems of classification: we no longer need to decide whether dialects of Swedish and Norwegian belong to one of two distinct languages, or whether two dialects of Chinese would be better classified as different languages. A grammar has a clearer status: it is the finite system that characterizes an individual's linguistic capacity and that is represented in the individual's mind/brain. No doubt the grammars of two individuals whom we regard as speakers of the same language will have much in common, but there is no reason to worry about defining "much in common," or about specifying when the outputs of two grammars constitute one language. Just as it is unimportant for most work in molecular biology whether two creatures are members of the same species (as emphasized, for example, by Monod (1972: ch. 2) and Dawkins (1976)), so too the notion of a language is not likely to have much importance if our biological perspective is taken.

So when we think about change over the course of time, diachronic change, we shall now think not in terms of sound change or language change, but in terms of changes in these grammars, which are represented in the mind/brains of individuals and emerge and grow in the way that we have discussed in this chapter. Under certain conditions, if the linguistic environment is a little different, a child's brain may grow a grammar somewhat different from that of her mother. We'll investigate what those conditions are, and how that growth takes place.

Notes

1 Other examples of specifiers are *American* in *American attempts to dispose of Saddam Hussein*, *have* in *They have read the article*, *straight* in *Go straight to Chicago*.

   We see that *will visit Chicago* is represented as a constituent, but it is labeled a I′ in 3. The I′ is an intermediate inflection projection; it designates an inflectional projection which is larger than ₁[will] but which itself projects to a still larger inflectional structure, the IP. The category IP does not project to a larger type of inflectional expression and is, in this sense, maximal. Similarly, *Students from Denver* would be a NP, hence maximal, when part of a sentence *I met students from Denver*. However, these nodes are recursive, so one also finds expressions like *Students from Denver with green trumpets*. When embedded in this way *Students from Denver* is not maximal and is a N′, part of a larger NP. We reserve the XP notation for a node which is maximal. An element might be both a N and a NP, as *Denver* and *Chicago* in (3).

2 Government was an important notion in work conducted within the Government-Binding (GB) model of the 1980s, but it is not a primitive in more recent work conducted under the Minimalist Program (Chomsky 1995; Radford 1997; Uriagereka 1998). Nonetheless, the distinctions captured by the idea of government also need to be made in all models of grammar. Reformulating government in ways congenial to minimalist goals involves technical issues that I don't want to get into here, so I maintain the anachronism, although I define it in a more strictly local fashion than was used in much GB work.

3 Binding Theory, in fact, divides nouns into three types: anaphors (*herself*, *each other*, etc.), pronouns, and names. Each noun type has different indexical properties, defined by a principle of the Binding Theory. So Principle A applies to anaphors and says that they must be locally co-indexed; Principle B applies to pronouns, as we have seen; and Principle C applies to names. On this view, the child classifies each noun she encounters as belonging to one of the three classes; that is the learning involved. The indexing conventions apply only to the largest NP/DP available; that restriction is characterized in the technical literature as a function of "c-command" relations.

   Until 1976 grammarians made the traditional assumption that structural conditions determined when pronouns might be co-indexed with other phrases. Then in a seminal paper, Howard Lasnik (1976) turned things around and argued that more elegant analyses would postulate structural conditions under which pronouns might *not* be co-indexed with other phrases.

4 In Old English, pronouns like *her*, *me*, etc. did double duty and behaved sometimes as pronouns subject to Principle B and sometimes as anaphors (subject to Principle A of the Binding Theory – see n. 3). So we find expressions like *Ic behyde me*, "I hid myself," which we discussed in chapter 1. Here *me* acts as an anaphor and needs to be glossed "myself" in modern English.

5 For good discussion of the viability of these neural networks as a basis for explaining language acquisition, see Lachter and Bever 1988 and Pinker and

Prince 1988. Jerry Fodor also has an excellent, accessible article on this topic in *The Times Literary Supplement* (1997). Where these connectionist models are worked out, contrary to their advertisements, they make strong, language-specific innateness assumptions throughout (Marcus 1997).

"Learning" is a slippery term. Languages are *learned* in the sense that children derive information from their linguistic environment and then converge on some grammar in accordance with specific principles. That, however, is a specialized sense of "learning," and not the way the term is used in informal discourse. If we understand learning in a nontechnical sense, then it is not clear that learning plays any role in the acquisition of language. In that case, we may be better off not to talk about children "learning" a language, but to talk instead in terms of the growth of language. This was Chomsky's point in the passage that Bates and Elman misrepresent.

6 One idea about limiting the trigger to simple structures is the "degree-0 learnability" of Lightfoot 1989, 1991, 1994, which posits that triggers are limited to elements from unembedded binding domains.

7 The child was not asked the question directly, in order to alleviate any feeling she might have of being tested; in this setup, Snail is being quizzed, not the child. Here I am giving only the briefest description of the experiments, but the experimental techniques used for this kind of work require great ingenuity and are of enormous interest in themselves. For excellent discussion, see Crain and Thornton 1998.

4

Gradualism and Catastrophes

Grammars, then, are real, biological entities represented in individual mind/ brains. They characterize a person's mature linguistic capacity, or a significant part of it. On the other hand, a language, like Odysseus, turns out to be a mythical, imaginary creature. It may be a convenient and useful fiction, like Odysseus and like the setting of the sun, but in reality it is derivative, the aggregate output of some set of grammars. We shall see that a language is not a coherent, definable entity.

So, when traditional historical linguists speak of a language changing, somebody with a biological view of grammars takes a reductionist stance and thinks of individual grammars changing and the changes spreading through a population. When others ask why a language should have changed in some way, we ask why grammars should have changed, aiming to explain the complex by the simple. This shift in perspective makes a big difference.

4.1 Grammars and Change

Let us consider how the biological view of grammars affects how we think about diachronic change, and let us distinguish it from other views of a grammar commonly invoked in discussions of language change. A grammar grows in the mind/brain of an individual upon exposure to relevant childhood experience. The grammar interacts with other aspects of a person's mental makeup, in a modular conception of mind. Different experiences may give rise to different grammars in different individuals, but it is a plausible initial assumption that grammars are subject to the same principles, parameters, and learning constraints, which are common to the species.

Looked at from this biological perspective, there is no single grammar of English – rather, various grammars which exist in the minds of English speakers. Grammars may vary somewhat, even among people whom we call speakers of English. Speakers of English are not uniform, and grammars exist for people, not for languages. Let us distinguish terminology from reality here: proponents of the biological view of grammars occasionally speak of "the grammar of French" to refer to the grammars of French speakers in a generalized way, a kind of shorthand which abstracts away from individual variation. This usage may be misleading, but, as I have noted elsewhere, it is comparable to references to the French liver, the American brain, or the Irish wit; nobody believes that there is such an entity, but sometimes it is a convenient abstraction. Similarly, biologists standardly refer to "the fruit fly" or "the nematode," even in technical work, also abstracting away from variation which is irrelevant to the purpose at hand.

Grammars, then, are individual entities which exist in people and do not define languages as such. They exist in the minds of individual speakers, just as livers and brains exist in individual bodies. There is no such thing as "the grammar of English"; rather, there are thousands of speakers, all of whom have internalized grammars, some differing from others. That *set* of grammars generates much of the recorded body of what we call English, and much more that goes unrecorded.

Hermann Paul articulated this general view of language change clearly and fiercely in the nineteenth century. He emphasized the individual/ biological view of grammars, noting in an early work that "dass die reelle Sprache nur im Individuum existiert" (actual language exists only in an individual) (1877: 325). His notion that "each individual has his or her own language" (1891: 23) is essentially the idea that there is no such thing as "the grammar of English." In attacking the group psychology of Lazarus and Steinthal (see chapter 2), he wrote in the original, 1880 German version of his famous *Principles* (1891): "Wir müssen eigentlich so viele Sprachen unterscheiden als es Individuen gibt" (we must in fact distinguish as many languages as there are individuals) (p. 31). His emphasis on the individual was a minority perspective and played no important role for a long period.

We can learn about the general principles, parameters, and learning constraints common to the species by studying how different grammars (in this biological sense) arise in children when the relevant experiences change minimally, from one generation to another. No two children have exactly the same primary linguistic data; they hear different things. Nonetheless, despite variation in experience, children often attain the same mature structural system. Initial experiences may vary indefinitely, but grammars show structural stability and vary only in limited ways. This structural stability is what enables us to communicate with each other. For Paul, variation and individuality were no mystery: "the problem which challenges solution is this: how comes it that while the language of each individual has its own special history, this degree of agreement . . . maintains itself within this miscellaneously constituted group of individuals?" (1891: 23).

Sometimes, however, minor changes in the relevant childhood experience cross a threshold and have consequences for the grammars which emerge. In that case, we have a different grammar, and this may entail far-reaching surface effects in terms of the class of sentences generated by the new grammar. The conditions under which grammars change can illuminate the general principles, parameters, and learning constraints, as we shall explore in the next few chapters. We investigate the change in grammars and ask how the change might have come about – that is, how childhood experience must have been different and what principles, parameters, and learning constraints were involved.

4.2 Social Grammars

Other linguists use the term *grammar* to refer to other, very different objects: pedagogical tools, inventories of morphological properties of languages, and, in a common usage, descriptions of socially defined entities. On this latter, social view of grammars, people speak of "the grammar of French" or of some dialect of French to allude to an algorithm which supposedly characterizes some socially defined idea of French encompassing the language of Michel Platini, François Truffaut, Jacques Chirac, and many others. This view of grammars remains common among certain historical linguists. Grammars are taken to be devices which generate a corpus of sentences belonging to some socially or politically defined entity, not the knowledge of an individual person. Such algorithms, if they exist, would define the conventional idea of a language.[1]

Biological and social views of grammars are very different from each other. The distinction between an individual's grammar and the group notion of a language is analogous to the biologist's distinction between individual organisms and species, and to the distinction made by historians and social scientists between individuals and societies or social classes. Species and societies are group notions. There is nothing right or wrong about working with one or other notion, but there is a difference – a vast difference. Certain questions need to be dealt with at the level of an individual organism, and for certain purposes we can abstract away from individual variation and operate at a macroscopic level of aggregate species, societies, and languages.

Questions arise which only make sense in one or other view of grammars. On the biological view, countless questions arise about the internal properties of these grammars: how they are represented in brains, how they emerge in young children, and so on. None of these questions is relevant if one thinks of a grammar as a social entity. And some questions get construed very differently.

Take the question: Do adults change grammars? For proponents of a social definition of grammars, the answer is yes, and that is a simple certainty. Since a grammar characterizes the corpus of English expressions, adult innovations will change that grammar insofar as they change the corpus. However, on the biological view of grammar that I have adopted, it is a logical possibility but by no means self-evident. It is undisputed that individual speech often changes through the course of a lifetime – we can track this nowadays through letters and tape recordings. In particular, idioms and slang expressions are known to change very rapidly. But the fact that an individual's speech changes does not entail that the individual's *grammar* changes. There is more, much more, to an adult's use of language than his or her grammar. Certain forms may be produced more or less frequently over the course of an individual's lifetime, sometimes deliberately, sometimes subconsciously. Some forms may be incorporated into a person's usage without being incorporated into the productive system characterized by the grammar; they may be specifically learned as forms to be used in particular contexts. It is quite possible that adults change their grammars in the sense in which I am using the term, but I know of no argument to that effect.

Adult innovations constitute grammatical changes for social grammarians, but that does not mean that they also reflect grammatical change for biological grammarians, because the latter are working with a different conception of grammar. Since grammars have structural stability, they may or may not be changed in adulthood. Although adult innovations may not affect grammars, they are nonetheless significant for the biological grammarian: they reflect changes to the primary linguistic data (PLD), the input experience for the next generation of language learners. Adult innovations, then, constitute one reason why an individual might be exposed to PLD which differ from what his mother was exposed to. There are other reasons, of course, relating to population movement, language contact, and the constant, ever-demanding need for strikingly expressive forms.

If one believes that there is a single grammar which generates the corpus of sentences found in English or some variety of English, then questions about how that entity changes will have little to do with language acquisition by children. Changes will be explained not by considerations of individual psychology but by historical principles which are independent of individual minds; in chapter 8 we shall discuss some actual explanations of this type.[2]

Different views of what a grammar is give rise to different questions, but a stronger point needs to be made: it is not clear that there can actually be such a thing as a social grammar. The sentences of, say, Old English do not constitute a recursively enumerable set. That is, there is no single, finite algorithm which can be acquired by a child and which generates the sentences of Old English and no nonsentences (we shall see this when we discuss optionality in grammars, later in this chapter). There is no reason to believe that such an algorithm exists in any real sense: it cannot be a psychological entity represented in an individual brain. Nor is it clear whose sentence patterns or pronunciation it would characterize – not any particular individual's, evidently. There is no comprehensive, central archive of English or French available to be consulted by William Safire or the Académie Française in order to determine whether something is a sentence of English or of French; nor is there any "social matrix" in which grammars might be located, except in postmodernist fantasies. It is hard to imagine what other kind of existence it might have, beyond being an intellectual construct in a researcher's notebook. In that case, the *social* grammar of Old English, whatever it is, would not be a generative algorithm. Although some historical linguists assume some sort of informal social grammar, the assumption is usually tacit, and the grammar is not explicated.

I know of only one context in which social grammars have been explicitly argued for, and that is in the studies inspired by William Labov's work (1994) on "variable rules." However, Labov works with a psychological grammar which has a different domain of application; it is not a social grammar in the sense outlined above. His claim is that speakers' grammars are psychological/biological entities existing in the minds of individual speakers in pretty much the same sense that I have argued here, but that these grammars incorporate rules which contain variables.

Labov's variables are socially induced in the sense that if a speaker uses and/or recognizes two past tense forms, say *dived* and *dove*, *sneaked* and *snuck*, both forms are incorporated into the speaker's grammar, along with an indication of the probability of each particular form occurring. All this information, including information about different dialects, is learned on exposure to the alternating forms. And likewise for syntactic operations such as movement from one structural position to another. So the individual's grammar incorporates knowledge of varying forms and their probability of occurrence. What is at issue here is not whether the grammar is biological or social; Labov's grammars are clearly biological. The difference between his grammars and the ones I have described is that his incorporate much more information. Labov builds into his model of a person's linguistic knowledge information about social variability. Later in this chapter we shall discuss an alternative and, I think, superior approach to variability in terms of coexisting grammars.

Even if it is productive to work with a nonbiological, social notion of grammars, believing that grammars hold of social groups of one kind or another, that view leads to very different questions about historical change and very different answers. For the moment, I shall treat social grammars as fictions; but, in any case, they would entail a very different research program.

Adopting a biological notion of grammars enables us to approach an old debate from a new angle. The debate concerns the question of whether linguistic change is gradual or catastrophic. This debate is very similar to an analogous debate among evolutionary biologists. Some biologists believe that species evolve gradually, others that they evolve abruptly. Biologists, of course, are dealing with genotypical change, whereas we are dealing with change in phenotypes, change in grammars. We shall follow the first woman writer to be elected to the Académie Française. In her novel *Memoirs of Hadrian*, Marguerite Yourcenar wrote:

> When . . . two ideas are in contradiction, be ready to reconcile them rather than cancel one by the other; regard them as two different facets, or two successive stages, of the same reality, a reality convincingly human just because it is complex.

We shall see that "language" change is indeed gradual in certain respects, but that grammars undergo sudden, abrupt change from time to time. The debate about the gradualness of change turns on the categories used, languages or grammars.

4.3   Gradualism, Imagined and Real

Everyday common sense rests to some degree on the notion of continuity and gradual change. The basic idea is that if there is a little distortion, the patterns, processes, and structures of life don't change very much. Similarly with language. The overwhelmingly most common view among historians is that language change is gradual. Languages change in piecemeal fashion, and there are thought to be no major discontinuities, except, of course, where the textual record has significant gaps. Recently, some writers have been aggressive in denying that abrupt, catastrophic change *ever* happens, with many phenomena changing simultaneously (see Carden and Stewart 1988; Harris, forthcoming; Harris and Campbell 1995 (48ff, 77ff, etc.), Hopper and Traugott 1993).

Gradualism has pretty much had complete hegemony. However, I'll argue here that whether or not change is generally gradual depends on what units of analysis are employed and which lens is used. It is languages which change gradually; grammars are a different matter. If we use biological grammars as our unit of analysis, then abrupt change happens. In fact, it must happen. Some changes may be small-scale and therefore may appear to be gradual, but appearances can be deceptive.

If we think macroscopically, in terms of changes in sets of more or less unanalyzed phenomena, using a wide-angle lens, then change always seems to be gradual. My favorite illustration is a study reported by Fries (1940). English used to have object–verb order, and one said things like "John said that Susan apples ate" (with the direct object preceding the verb in the embedded clause); present-day speakers would say *John said that Susan ate apples.* Fries offered statistical data showing that Old English alternated between object–verb and verb–object order freely, and that "the order of ... words ... has no bearing whatever upon the grammatical relationships involved" (p. 199). He found that object–verb order occurred 53 percent of the time around the year 1000, and that it was "gradually" replaced by verb–object order, reducing to 2 percent by the year 1500. He provided one set of statistics for each century but offered no analysis.

Fries's counts ignored the distinction between embedded and simple, unembedded clauses, and he had no analysis of the fact that the finite verb often appeared in second position in simple clauses. If we make such distinctions, we see that Old English grammars had object–verb order underlyingly and an operation moving finite verbs to yield verb-second order in main, unembedded clauses (van Kemenade 1987). Consequently, we find object–verb order uniformly in embedded clauses, but not often in simple clauses. Kroch and Taylor (1997) show that there was a dialect difference involving movement of finite verbs: in Middle English northern dialects moved verbs more than southern dialects.

In fact, two changes took place at the grammatical level: underlying object–verb order was replaced by verb–object order, and the verb-movement operation was lost. The *grammatical* change consisted in a change in the head-order parameter and the loss of northern "verb-second" grammars, each of which were abrupt. We'll see the details in chapter 6, but my point here is that if our units of analysis are as gross as Fries's, change will look gradual.

At the other end of the scale is the microscopic approach, using a long, telescopic lens. The speech of no two people is entirely identical. It follows naturally that if we take manuscripts from two periods, even two periods in the lifetime of one individual, we shall be able to identify differences and so point to language "change." In this sense everything is in flux, and languages are constantly changing in piecemeal, gradual, chaotic, and relatively minor fashion – an example of the world of Heraclitus. Again we see gradual change. But the fact that a person's speech changes does not mean that his or her grammar changes.

Where historical records are rich, it is difficult to distinguish marked discontinuities merely by looking at the texts. In fact, nobody would have argued that linguistic change is abrupt and bumpy just by looking at textual records. Where the records seemed to suggest some bumpiness, it was assumed that fuller records would fill in the gaps and provide gradual curves. Sometimes those intermediate stages were reconstructed, as if there were an independent way of knowing what happened when the records were silent.

In this respect, the gradual/catastrophic debate among historical linguists differs from the analogous debate among evolutionary biologists. There gradualism has also been the dominant view, but the fossil record generally does not show gradualness. Rather, discontinuities are the norm, and punctuated equilibrium is overwhelmingly reflected in the fossil record. Consequently, proponents of abrupt change, punctuated equilibrium, derive very direct support from the relevant records (Eldredge and Gould 1972). Evolutionists committed to gradualism need to argue that the gaps in the fossil record are accidental. In language, the textual record, where rich and viewed with no analytical spectacles, has often suggested that speech changes gradually.

Not only do the texts suggest that change is gradual in the linguistic domain, but some changes really do progress gradually. Initial experiences are never entirely the same for any two speakers, and they may differ from each other in minor and insignificant ways. So in that sense, if one looks at them diachronically, they may change gradually. These changes may even be cumulative to some extent, while grammars remain structurally stable and invariant. Some construction type might become more frequent, perhaps as a result of taking on some expressive function. This would reflect a change in the way in which grammars are used, but not in the grammar itself. Such changes in frequency do not reflect a change in grammars, but they do constitute a change in the PLD for the next generation of speakers.

Not only may primary linguistic data change gradually, but the very nature of language acquisition ensures a certain kind of gradualness under usual circumstances. Normally the output of a person's grammar is a significant part of the linguistic environment that triggers the emergence of the grammar of that person's child. This works against major discontinuities in the class of expressions and their associated meanings and guarantees some stability from one generation to the next; generally one does not find a grammar yielding fairly uniform object–verb order being replaced abruptly by a grammar yielding uniform verb–object order. However, we shall see in chapter 6 that sometimes population shifts entail that parents' speech may be very different from that of their children, and one may find big discontinuities.

As historical linguists recorded and tried to understand the flux in the textual record, they overcommitted themselves to the proposition that change is necessarily gradual. This overcommitment takes the form of claiming that *grammars* themselves change only gradually. The internal properties of grammars, it is said, may differ only slightly from one generation to the next. A pair of rules may come to be reordered (Klima 1964; Harris 1980), or features may change in one generation (Allan 1988; Lieber 1982), or conditions on rules may be reformulated (Hausmann 1974). In a very early work (1969), Traugott formulated "diachronic processes," which mapped one grammar into another, and discussed the formal properties of those "processes," as if there was a formal mapping from one internal system to another. The idea here was that grammars, in general, may differ to a certain extent, but that grammars of adjacent generations of speakers may differ from each other in only minor ways. There were supposed to be formal constraints on the ways in which adjacent grammars may differ, and those formal constraints were to constitute a theory of change, quite independent of a theory of grammar.

This kind of gradualism has never amounted to much, in my view, but it is widely advocated. It is sometimes characterized through a theory of language types and sometimes through lexicalist models of grammar. In an approach which dominated work on syntactic change in the 1970s, the self-styled "typologists" distinguished "consistent" from "transitional" language types. Consistent languages exhibited harmonic properties, and those properties were mixed in various ways in transitional languages. They held that languages progressed from one "consistent" type to another, losing and acquiring harmonic word-order properties in a prescribed, long-term order. A consistent subject–object–verb language might gradually acquire all the harmonic properties of a consistent subject–verb–object language in the appropriate order. The new verb–object order would emerge before the new noun–determiner or noun–adjective order, etc. The hierarchies were elaborate, sometimes involving 15 or 20 word-order properties; but no single language's history ever manifested more than one or two changes in these relationships. People postulated many unattested stages to account for instances where a fairly complete typological change was thought to have taken place, as between Latin and the modern Romance languages. Not unexpectedly, these linguists conducted the most detailed work on reconstructed histories, where problems of attestation did not arise. The commitment to gradualness in this model was more an article of faith than an empirical result based on investigation.

Alternatively, gradual changes have sometimes been modeled in "lexicalist" theories of grammar, in which particular grammars differ from each other not in terms of harmonic properties or of settings of abstract parameters, but only in terms of features of individual lexical items. The parameters of variation among grammars are defined by the available features. As a particular verb is recorded in a new syntactic environment, a feature in its lexical specification is changed accordingly (Allan 1988; Lieber 1982). The models invoked have allowed unrestricted systems of features, including features determining whether the lexical item undergoes a particular syntactic operation. Their virtue is that they permit accurate codifications of what occurs in historical texts at any period. Their drawback is that they are powerful enough to be compatible with just about any set of data. This approach to change implies that language acquisition is highly data-driven, that children match their input, which may vary pretty much without limit. However, these models, being too powerful, underestimate the bumpiness of variation and cannot represent a person's mature linguistic capacity, because they are demonstrably not attainable by children.

One way of seeing this is to consider cases of obsolescence, where a verb ceases to occur in a certain construction, and this is codified by a new lexical feature of that verb. The problem is that this new feature is sensitive to the *absence* of some form, and in general children do not acquire their grammars and set grammatical parameters on the basis of negative data (information that certain forms do not occur), as we saw in the last chapter. We'll see in a few pages that changes involving obsolescence of forms are particularly enlightening about the nature of parametric variation among available grammars.

Unconstrained lexicalist models have been popular with historians, because they are powerful enough to state even the narrowest of generalizations; but they cannot be models of a person's mature capacity, attained through normal childhood experience. They are powerful enough to be observationally accurate, systematizing what is recorded in the texts at some point by ever-changing lexical features; but the models characteristically offer no explanations for the changes being recorded. They reflect too narrow a concern for accuracy. Accuracy is not enough and may, in fact, be misleading. These models miss the fundamental property that grammars must be learnable. They also ignore the fact that texts from some period – say, the year 1354 – offer only a miniscule record of what could be generated by grammars of that period; consequently, there is no special merit in a system which generates exactly the set of sentences in that corpus.

The problem lies not with the features as such, or with the lexicalist models as such, but with their expressive power. A constrained lexicalist model would allow only a narrow range of features functioning in a narrow range of ways. For example, current work within the Minimalist Program (Chomsky 1995) allows functional heads to have certain features, which force the movement of categories. If they define only a narrow range of options, then they will not be compatible with just any data set, and they will allow us to capture the bumpiness of variation.

4.4 Catastrophes

As we have seen, the textual record, looked at casually, has suggested to many people that linguistic change progresses gradually. However, the Victorian economist Alfred Marshall once warned that "the most reckless and treacherous of all theorists is he who professes to let the facts and figures speak for themselves."

Considerations of language acquisition in children forced us in the last chapter to adopt an approach to grammars which predicts a bumpiness in variation and change. Natural languages are replete with partial generalizations which do not hold all the time and therefore cannot be learned inductively; one example is that *is* may be pronounced *z*. Consequently, linguists have postulated a rich linguistic genotype, UG, which provides the basic structures of grammars independently of any particular linguistic experience. Linguistic experience then refines the details and leads to the emergence of a mature grammar. That refining process consists in assigning words to a small number of categories, and that is one way in which grammars differ from each other, albeit within narrow limits. It also includes adopting abstract, structural properties. English grammars have a VP which includes a verb and then a noun phrase, $_{VP}$[V NP]; we say *ate an apple*.

Japanese grammars have the reverse order, noun phrase, then verb, $_{VP}$[NP V]; people say "an apple ate," pronounced *ringo tabeta*. Grammars like English are verb–object, and grammars like those of Japanese are object–verb.[3] Some grammars have an operation which raises verbs overtly to an independent inflectional position; others do not (section 6.3). Structural parameters like these introduce a kind of bumpiness into linguistic variation. Grammars which differ by a single parameter setting may generate very different classes of sentences, so speakers with these two grammars may be quite different from each other in terms of the class of sentences they use.

If grammars may vary in bumpy ways, then we would expect that they change in bumpy ways. That is, there must be points in history when grammars differed in terms of some structural parameter setting. In that case, changes are abrupt and catastrophic, with many surface effects. This follows simply from viewing language as manifesting a biological capacity represented in individual mind/brains, and then viewing change in the light of attempts to understand language acquisition as the emergence of these grammars in children under natural conditions.

Other changes in grammars may be small-scale (chapter 7). Lexical items may come to be categorized differently, and the recategorization may affect certain words before others, progressing in piecemeal fashion. In English, words like *must*, *can*, *may*, etc. were once more or less ordinary verbs, but they came to be categorized as instances of an inflectional element as a result of morphological changes which simplified the verb classes of Old English. Linguists have discussed this change intensively. The literary records suggest that the morphological changes affected some verbs before others. Likewise, the recategorization was piecemeal, with certain verbs being recategorized before others.[4] Each of the grammatical innovations, morphological and categorial, even if they are small-scale, must take place in direct or indirect response to changes in the PLD; there can be no other explanation.

Whether the changes are small-scale or large-scale, they constitute differences between grammars of different speakers. Those differences (which are what we mean by "change") do not have temporal properties, and therefore cannot be "gradual." Mark Hale put the issue well when he wrote to me that "the gradualness is a mirage created by our failure to distinguish between independent change events." He offers a good analogy. If we define *death* as the point at which some well-defined electrochemical activity in the brain ceases, it would make no sense to argue that death is gradual, either because it is followed by many further changes (e.g. changes in property ownership) which seem to be part of the same phenomenon, or because death moves from organ to organ gradually, or because it gives rise to "variation" in the population (dividing it into those who show the effects of death and those who do not). None of this would add anything to our understanding of death as a biological phenomenon.

The view I am advocating assumes that grammars hold not of languages, but of individuals. If there is no grammar of, say, Old English, then there can be no gradual shift in that grammar. In the same way, there can be no gradual shift in an aggregate French liver if alcohol ceases to be available, because that aggregate liver does not exist in any real sense. Grammars of individuals may differ from each other, just as individual livers may differ, perhaps as a result of differing alcohol consumption. If there are abstract, structural properties, then two grammars may differ in terms of one property, and that may entail many superficial differences; the set of sentences generated by those two grammars may differ quite significantly, although the grammars differ only in one property. This is true also for the grammars of two adjacent generations, where there has been grammatical change. In chapters 5–7, we shall see what sort of story this view of grammars allows for language acquisition and change.

I have found it helpful to think of change in grammars in the context of work on catastrophe theory. Catastrophe theory, developed originally by the French mathematician René Thom, is an attempt to provide a mathematical framework for modeling various kinds of discontinuous processes. For example, one can lower the temperature of a body of water, and a catastrophic change takes place at $0°$ Celsius, when it turns to ice. The water does not gradually become more ice-like: the phase transition is sudden. In chapter 2, I recommended John Casti's account of chaos theory; he also offers a good, balanced discussion of work on catastrophes (Casti 1994: ch. 2). He debunks the intuition that small, gradual changes in causes give rise to small, gradual changes in effects. The term *catastrophe* may be a little overblown to describe water changing to ice or the output of object–verb grammars changing to the output of verb–object systems; but Casti points out that the French *catastróphe* is not quite as catastrophic as the English *catástrophe* (p. 53). For us, "catastrophes" are the bumpy discrepancies that we find from time to time between the input that a child is exposed to and the output that the child's mature grammar generates. We shall see in chapter 6 that these discrepancies occur in a number of contexts, not just through the changes chronicled by historians of English, French, etc.

Casti illustrates elementary catastrophe theory (the only part that is in good shape mathematically), which deals with systems whose attractors are fixed points. One example is the gross national product (GNP), a measure of the performance of the economy, which is determined by many factors – interest rates, money supply, consumer habits, industrial production, and so on. The level of GNP is a fixed-point attractor of the economic process.

> For every level of the inputs, the economy moves to a particular level of GNP, which can be envisioned as a point in the space of states of the economy. And since every setting of the inputs produces such a point, there is a whole surface of GNP points that the economy may produce – at least one for every level of interest rates, money supply, production facilities and all the rest. Catastrophe theory is designed to study the geometrical structure of this surface. (Casti 1994: 46)

Usually, if we change the inputs slightly, the corresponding level of GNP shifts only a little. However, sometimes we find combinations of input values such that a minor change entails a discontinuous shift to an entirely new region of the GNP surface. Such a value of the inputs is what is called a "catastrophe point."

> As it turns out, these catastrophe points arise at just those input levels where there is more than one possible fixed point to which the system can be attracted. And the jump discontinuity is a reflection of the system's "deciding" to move from the region of one attractor to that of another. Catastrophe theory shows us that there are only a small number of inequivalent ways in which these jumps can take place, and it provides a standard picture for each of the different geometries that the surface of attractors can display. (Ibid.)

Biophysicist Stuart Kauffman offers another example, which he takes to illustrate his notion of "the edge of chaos," a close cousin of the "self-organized criticality" findings of physicists Per Bak, Chao Tang, and Kurt Wiesenfeld.

> The central image here is of a sandpile on a table onto which sand is added at a constant slow rate. Eventually, the sand piles up and avalanches begin. What one finds are lots of small avalanches and few large ones. If the size of the avalanche is plotted on the familiar x-axis of a Cartesian coordinate system, and the number of avalanches at that size are plotted on the y-axis, a curve is obtained. The result is a relationship called a power law. The particular shape of this curve . . . has the stunning implication that the same-sized grain of sand can unleash small or large avalanches. Although we can

say that in general there will be more tiny avalanches and only a few big landslides ... there is no way to tell whether a particular one will be insignificant or catastrophic. (Kauffman 1995: 29)

Catastrophe theory deals with input values where the fixed point reflecting the system's behavior shifts from being a stable attractor to being an unstable one. This change in stability forces the system to move abruptly to a new stable fixed point. A small change in an input value leads to a discontinuous shift in the fixed-point attractor. This is not a predictive theory, and Casti shows that much of the bad press that catastrophe theory has received results from people interpreting it as a predictive system. It is explanatory, in much the way that evolutionary theory is explanatory, helping us to understand what has happened, rather than predicting what is to come.

The natural way for linguists to think of this is that different childhood experiences, different sets of primary linguistic data (PLD), sometimes cross thresholds, which entails that the system shifts, and that a new grammatical property results. So the inventory of variable properties constitutes the set of fixed-point attractors. This provides a productive way of understanding what happens in grammatical change and supports the viability of thinking of a small number of parameter settings as defining the structurally stable systems which we call grammars. We shall see in a moment that linguistic variation is typically not a matter of free variance, but rather oscillation between two fixed points of divergence.

The models of catastrophe theory strike me as particularly germane to work on grammatical change, and they may help us reach new levels of understanding. Conversely, work on abrupt change in grammars may help the mathematicians.

Why do mathematical theorems, obviously invented by human minds, apply so accurately to the outside world? This is the question posed by Eugene Wigner in his often cited paper "The unreasonable effectiveness of mathematics in the natural sciences." The answer lies in Paul Dirac's assertion that God is a mathematician. The cosmos has an astonishingly deep mathematical structure, which pervades many areas of nature. The same mathematics shows up all over the place. Juan Uriagereka (1998), working in the tradition of D'Arcy Thompson (1961), has been impressed by the prevalence of Fibonacci sequences in nature and thinks he has found them at work in grammars. He may be right, or he may be wrong; but it is exhilarating to find common principles at work in the structure of a flower's petals and in phonological inventories. These commonalities represent, in a sense, the deepest insights of science.[5]

4.5   Competing Grammars

Proponents of the biological view of grammars often write as if individuals have only one grammar. However, Tony Kroch and his associates (Kroch 1989; Kroch and Taylor 1997; Pintzuk 1991; Santorini 1992, 1993; Taylor 1990) have argued for coexisting grammars. They postulate that speakers may operate with more than one grammar, in a kind of "internalized diglossia." This work enriches grammatical analyses by seeking to describe the variability of individual texts and the spread of a grammatical change through a population.

In postulating two (or more) coexisting grammars in an individual, a researcher needs to show not only that the two grammars together account for a range of expressions used, but also that the two grammars are learnable under plausible assumptions about the child's trigger experience (PLD). In other words, diglossic grammars are subject to exactly the same learnability demands as any other biological grammar. There is no special issue here, and certainly no reason to believe that diglossic analyses are necessarily unlearnable, as is sometimes argued; nor is there any reason to reject the idea of diglossia because it might sometimes lead to postulating three or four coexisting grammars.[6] We cannot know in advance of investigation how many grammars speakers may have access to; that is precisely what we need to find out empirically. Learners have two or more grammars when their triggering experience leads to incompatible analyses. The difficulty here is not for the child but for the analyst: the analyst must decide when coexisting grammars must be invoked. However, we have no reason to believe that the world was designed in such a way as to make its investigation easy. Nor language. Kroch (1994: 184) notes that "when we reach the point where the linguist has as good a theoretical grasp on Universal Grammar as the language learner has an unconscious one, grammar competition will be as easily recognizable to the former as it already is to the latter."

In fact, this kind of diglossia represents an interesting approach to solving significant learnability problems. It offers a way of eliminating optionality in grammatical operations. Chomsky (1995) has argued that grammars do not permit optional operations. In that case, apparent optionality would be a function of coexisting grammars. Rather than allowing one grammar to generate forms *a* and *b* optionally, we would argue that a person has access to two grammars, one of which generates form *a*, the other form *b*; the speaker has the option at any given time of using one or other of the grammars. This move reduces the class of available grammars, eliminating those with optional operations.

Optionality within a grammar and optional access to two or more grammars may sound like the same idea in different clothing, but they are by no means notational variants. There is a big difference. Modern Dutch, German, Swedish, and other languages are verb-second, and necessarily so. I shall give an analysis of this phenomenon in chapter 6 (section 6.2); for the moment it is enough to say that the finite verb appears in second position, and that this is an obligatory requirement, not just one among a number of options. Dutch speakers say things like (1), not (2), where the verb follows two major constituents.

1 (a) $_{PP}$[In Amsterdam] $_V$live many good linguists.
   (b) $_{NP}$[many good linguists] $_V$live in Amsterdam.
   (c) $_{AP}$[Yesterday] $_V$visited we The Hague.

2 (a) *[In Amsterdam] [many good linguists] $_V$live well.
   (b) *[Yesterday] [we] $_V$visited The Hague.

The obligatory nature of the phenomenon must reflect properties of UG, because it is not learnable; that is, it cannot be a function of the triggering experience of the Dutch or German or Swedish child. The reason is that if the child were free to develop an optional operation putting the verb in second position, it would take negative data to show the Dutch child that this was incorrect for Dutch and that the operation is obligatory. That is, the child would need information to the effect that having the finite verb in, say, third position leads to a sentence type which in fact does not occur in Dutch (2). Negative data of this kind are generally not available to children, as discussed in chapter 3; so the obligatory character of the verb-second property has to come for free, a function of the constraints of UG. So far we have a straightforward poverty-of-stimulus argument. The stimulus that children have, the triggering experience, is not rich enough to instruct the child that the verb-second property is obligatory; therefore we invoke UG.

Here comes the problem: Old English texts show verb-second order alternating with other orders. If we say that verb-second represents an optional operation in the grammars of Old English speakers, we lose our UG-based explanation for the obligatory character of the operation in the modern verb-second languages. We can avoid this problem by appealing to coexisting grammars: some Old English speakers had a grammar which generated consistent verb-second order, just like speakers of modern Dutch. Other speakers had a grammar in which there was no verb-second property, and others had access to each of these distinct grammars. Thus there is no optional operation yielding verb-second structures in any grammar, and we therefore retain our explanation for the properties of the modern languages.

Similarly for the alternation between object–verb and verb–object order. In general, individual grammars do not manifest optional alternations of this type; further, they are precluded by UG for reasons similar to those which preclude an alternation between verb-second and verb-third order. Where a language has such an alternation, we say that this manifests diglossia, and that speakers have access to two grammars. Certain speakers have access only to one grammar; others have access only to the other grammar; and others have access to both grammars in an *internalized* diglossia. As long as each grammar is demonstrably learnable, then, far from raising problems of learnability, this kind of diglossia actually solves what would otherwise be a major learnability problem in the acquisition of optional operations. In general, grammars do not manifest optional, free alternations, and where languages have alternations, they are diachronically unstable and represent a transition whereby one of the grammars is driven into disuse.

Recall my earlier point that there may be no generative algorithm for socially/politically defined inventories. The case just discussed shows that in some cases a social grammar, were it to exist, would necessarily be incompatible with learnability demands, and therefore could not model an individual's capacity. If we write an algorithm generating these incompatible alternations, on the grounds that both forms occur as options in some single speech community, then we cannot write a learnable algorithm which captures the exclusiveness of the verb-second property in another community, like modern Dutch. As a result, there can be no single algorithm generating the options that we find in one speech community, if we are also to provide a learnable account of the exclusiveness that we find in another. For the purpose of accounting for acquisition and change, a "language" is not a good analytical tool; neither is a "grammar" which generates a socially/politically defined language.

On the view developed by Kroch and his associates, "change proceeds via competition between grammatically incompatible options which substitute for one another in usage" (Kroch 1994: 180). One reason for believing that this view of change through competing systems is along the right lines is that alternating forms cluster in their distribution, and the clustering follows from how sets of grammars unify the forms. We do not find free variance, but oscillation between two (or more) fixed points. This is reflected in the Constant Rate Effect of Kroch (1989).

Because parameters are abstract and structural, changing one parameter setting may entail a range of new surface phenomena. We shall see several examples of this in the next chapters. The Constant Rate Effect says that in such an instance all surface phenomena reflecting the parameter setting show usage frequencies changing at the same rate, but not necessarily at the same time. This is easy to understand if one grammar is replaced over time by another, and if that change takes place in a winner-take-all competition between the two grammars. Variation of this type does not stabilize and become a point of optionality within a grammar. We do not find complex arrays of linguistic data changing randomly. Instead, they tend to converge toward a relatively small number of patterns or attractors, as discussed in the context of catastrophes – in a kind of "antichaos" in the terms of Kauffman (1995). It is the theory of parameters which defines those attractors.

Kroch links the quantitative methods of sociolinguistics with the algebraic methods of theoretical syntax. His statistics would be quite mysterious if grammars involving abstract, structural parameters were not involved, restricting the variation to a narrow range. The common rate of change reflects the fact that abstract grammars are implicated. Multiple surface reflexes of single grammatical changes increase in frequency of use at the same rate, supporting the idea that the evolution of syntactic usage is controlled by changes in the underlying generative grammar.

For his simplest illustration, Kroch draws on work by Shawn Noble, who studied the replacement of the simple verb *have* by the complex *have got* in British English. Present-day speakers tend to use the complex form (3) where earlier speakers would have used the simple *have* (4).

3 (a) You've got brown eyes.
   (b) I've got a new job.

4 (a) She has what amounts to a high Cambridge degree.
   (b) They haven't the sense to come in out of the rain.

(3a) and (4a) indicate permanent possession, whereas (3b) and (4b) indicate temporarily bounded possession. The grammars, however, unify this distinction: one grammar has *have* meaning both permanent and temporary possession, and the other grammar has *have got* with both meanings. *Have got* replaces *have* across the board, regardless of whether it indicates permanent or temporary possession. The two meanings are distinct, and the temporarily bounded meaning is favored by approximately 0.65 to 0.35 in all three periods investigated by Noble. While the transition takes place,

Table 4.1   Effect of possession type on the choice between *have* and *have got*

Date	type	% *have got*	total	probability
1750–1849	temporary	12	83	.66
	permanent	4	108	.34
1850–1899	temporary	34	99	.64
	permanent	16	122	.36
1900–1935	temporary	89	74	.66
	permanent	70	43	.34

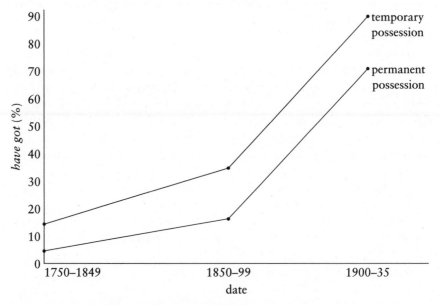

Figure 4.1   Graph for expression of possession type

many speakers use the new *have got* form for temporary possession and the old *have* form for permanent possession. Noble's figures are given in table 4.1.

The figures are shown in graph form in figure 4.1, where one sees that temporary possession occurs with the new *have got* form earlier than permanent possession, but the two types undergo the change at the same rate.

The distance between the two graphs indicates that at all times during the transition some individuals alternate between two grammars, using *have got* for temporary possession and *have* for permanent. This is presumably due to factors independent of the grammars. One such factor might be the processing preferences which lead speakers to prefer one form to another in certain contexts when more than one option is available. An example of this involves the rise of periphrastic *do* in English, which we shall discuss in chapter 6 (section 6.3). Dieter Stein (1986) argued that during the period of their rise the forms with *do* are favored in contexts where its use eliminates certain complex clusters of consonants.[7] Mark Arnold (1995) has argued that *do* is favored where its use enables a transitive verb to stay adjacent to its complement; this would account for the use of *do* with transitive verbs – *Did Kim read the book?* – while intransitive verbs occurred without *do* – *Left Kim early this morning?* These preferences are not well understood, and, whatever they are, they have no effect on the overall progress of the change. They certainly do not entail that grammatically unified phenomena change independently of each other.

The fact that the two graphs proceed in parallel indicates that one abstract system in which temporary and permanent possession are treated alike replaces another; one grammar replaces another over a period of time. So the innovative forms are found at different frequencies, but they enter the language at the same rate. This is the Constant Rate Effect, and it shows up in several studies. It indicates that what changes over the course of time is the propensity of speakers to use one grammar as opposed to another in their language production. The unity of the change is a function of the abstract grammar.

If there is no optionality in individual grammars, then we may ask why and how one grammar replaces another in competition, rather than stabilizing into one system with an optional operation. The answer may lie in the Blocking Effect. Mark Aronoff (1976) argued that there is an economy restriction on lexical items such that morphological doublets do not generally exist; he called this the "Blocking Effect." From the point of view of acquisition, once a child knows that *went* is the past tense of the verb *go*, then it automatically follows from this economy restriction that *goed*, which most children experiment with to a greater or lesser degree, must not be a coexisting form, and it drops out of the child's usage. We do not generally add the productive suffix *-ness* to the adjectives *clear* and *bad* to yield **clearness* and **badness*, because there are preexisting forms *clarity* and *evil*, and the Blocking Effect precludes doublets of this type.[8] We need the economy restriction, and we need to say that it reflects a deep, UG principle, in order to explain the course of acquisition and the fact that doublets generally do not exist in the languages of the world.

However, while doublets generally do not exist, there are exceptions. We might take these exceptions too seriously and weaken the economy principle to some kind of "tendency." However, this would be a mistake: if the no-doublets prohibition is not a principle, but only a tendency, it then loses its explanatory value. If it is just a tendency, then it needs to be explained and cannot itself be invoked as an explanatory notion. In the face of this, we might modify the principle so that it applies only where it holds absolutely. Or we might seek another principle which interacts with the Blocking Effect to yield the observed pattern. These moves are not promising, and Kroch (1994) has argued that the best approach is to retain the principle in its strongest form and to account for doublets, where they exist, sociolinguistically: doublets arise through language contact and compete until one form eventually wins out.

> Due to their sociolinguistic origins, the two forms often appear in different registers, styles, or social dialects; but they can only coexist stably in the speech community if they differentiate in meaning, thereby ceasing to be doublets. Speakers learn one or the other form in the course of basic language acquisition, but not both. Later in life, on exposure to a wider range of language, they may hear and come to recognize the competing form, which for them has the status of a foreign element. They may borrow this foreign form into their own speech and writing for its sociolinguistic value or even just because it is frequent in their language environment. Over time, however, as dialects and registers level out through prolonged contact, the doublets tend to disappear. (Kroch 1994: 185)

Initially, Kroch was obliged to make this move in order to retain the economy principle as an element of UG. This was needed in order to account for the course of language acquisition and for the relative rarity of doublets in the languages of the world. However, rather than being a last-ditch move to save the theory from embarrassing data, the idea of explaining theoretically inconvenient variation through differences in dialect and register turns out to have a new empirical payoff. Reconciling useful theoretical notions with initially contradictory data is, of course, a hallmark of successful sciences. In general, it is the most surprising reconciliations which are the most persuasive.

Kroch points to work on the history of English past tenses by his student Ann Taylor. There are many doublets of past tense forms, but they do not arise gradually, with equal frequency in all dialects at all times. There are occasional instances of new irregular, strong forms (i.e. where the vowel changes), like *dove* and *snuck* for the earlier *dived* and *sneaked*. However, the vast majority go in the other direction: new weak forms are introduced, exploiting the productive *-ed* ending, *walked* for *welk*, *awaked* for *awoke*, etc. Taylor (1994) showed that the appearance of doublets peaked in the thirteenth to fifteenth centuries and was linked to the large-scale borrowing of northern features into written English, which until then was primarily a southern phenomenon. Northern dialects were affected by the large immigration of Scandinavian speakers into the north and north-east of England, sometimes in areas populated only sparsely by Saxons, during the various Danish and Norse invasions of the later Old English period. As adult Scandinavians learned English as a second language, so they simplified inflections – for example, generalizing -ed past tense forms. Naturally, this kind of second-language learning error would have occurred most often with less common verbs, so innovative weak forms are found mostly among the less frequent verbs.[9] Taylor found that doublets were much more frequent in the language of London (e.g. the writings of Geoffrey Chaucer), where there was a great mixture of dialects, than in the vernacular of the countryside (e.g. the letters of the Paston family, who were Norfolk gentry). All this would be mysterious if variation were not limited narrowly by grammatical theory.

When two communities encounter one another, members of one sometimes acquire the language of the other, learning it imperfectly as adults under less than ideal conditions. If one of the languages becomes dominant, then children may be influenced by changes introduced by the parents' imperfect learning. If that new form of the language is then passed on, a speech community may end up with more than one setting for a parameter. Children growing up in that community hear evidence for both settings and develop a diglossic capacity, using various forms to which they have been exposed, even though the forms may be grammatically incompatible. Over time, one form will win out, because of the economy demands of the Blocking Effect, which works against coexisting forms that are not functionally distinct. One example of this would be children in the Middle English period growing up in bilingual, English-Scandinavian communities.

There were competing past tense forms, and in some cases the innovative weak form has come down to present-day English, and in other cases it is the old strong form which has survived. In no case has a Middle English doublet survived to the present day, except in one context. In general, doublets do not last long. The average life span of doublets, measured by citations in the *Oxford English Dictionary*, is about 300 years, Kroch reports; but that figure is misleadingly high; it reflects citations in any dialect and takes no account of archaisms, where the form is used deliberately or unconsciously to replicate the usage of earlier times.

The one context in which doublets do persist is where the rival forms take on different functions. *Shined* and *fitted* persist in some dialects alongside *shone* and *fit*, because they are causative while *shone* and *fit* are not (*He shined the light in her eyes* versus *The light shone in her eyes*; *She fitted him with a new suit* versus *That collar fit him last year*). Many people operate with two plural forms for *leaf*: we see *leaves* on a tree, but we watch the *Maple Leafs* at the hockey stadium in Toronto. The two forms are functionally distinct and refer to different things, leaves and a hockey team. Similarly, we may refer to our irritating colleagues as *Mickey Mouses*, not *Mickey Mice*, because, irritating as they may be, they are not mice and therefore may have a different plural form. If there are, say, three *Superman* films available, I might ask you how many *Supermans* you have seen, referring to the films and not to men, but I might refer to my department chair and my dean as *Supermen*. And my family are the Lightfoots, not the Lightfeet, because we are not feet. Here we find the limit of the Blocking Effect: it prohibits the coexistence of functionally equivalent items but allows them otherwise. That's why *badness* may exist alongside *evil* (see n. 8), because they mean different things.

The hallmarks of morphological doublets are that they are relatively rare. They tend to differ in register, in that only one of the forms is truly native, the other being a later accretion with a specific connotation. If they survive as a doublet, the two forms acquire distinct meanings, but one form is spontaneously overgeneralized in child language. This suggests that they manifest coexisting grammars in an internalized diglossia.

Kroch extends the approach to morphological doublets to account for language-internal syntactic variation, at least in circumstances where the properties of heads are involved. For example, when we find inflection-medial forms (5a) alternating with inflection-final forms (5b) in early English, then the two are considered functionally equivalent morphological variants, like the English past tense doublets. The idea here is that a finite verb like *visited* moved out of its VP to the inflection position (I), which might be medial or final (*e* is a "trace" and indicates an empty position from which a co-indexed item has moved, the verb *visited* in (5).

5   (a)   ... that Kim $_I$[visited$_i$] $_{VP}$[e$_i$ London]
    (b)   ... that Kim $_{VP}$[e$_i$ London] $_I$[visited$_i$]

Like the past tense doublets, the inflection-medial and inflection-final forms compete with each other until one takes over entirely, yielding uniform word order.

The Blocking Effect is inviolable in language acquisition by young children, but it can be overriden as individuals learn a variety of styles and dialects. Over the course of time, however, the economy restriction on acquisition wins out over socially induced variation, unless the doublets acquire different meanings. This means that one grammar spreads through the population, and diglossia, including internalized diglossia, is eliminated. We now have an explanation for the unusualness and instability of apparent optionality, and the explanation is based crucially on the existence of competing, coexisting grammars.

4.6   The Spread of New Grammars

Assuming that individual speakers may operate with more than one grammar also permits a new approach to the replacement of one grammar by another across a society – that is, the spread of change through a speech community. Weinreich, Labov, and Herzog (1968) distinguish between innovation by the individual (which is typically abrupt) and spread across a community (which is typically gradual and manifested by systematic variation). Only the latter constitutes "change" in their view. Reserving "change" for spread of a phenomenon across a community makes little sense for the perspective focusing on biological grammars. However, we agree that individual change is abrupt. The spread of a change across a community raises very different questions for this perspective and is approached through the methods of population biology.

An account of language acquisition at the individual level leads naturally to an account of language change at the group (or population) level. An individual may be exposed to PLD which differ from the parents' PLD, because of population movement, language contact, adult innovations, or perhaps because the PLD happen to be truncated in some way – so do not include certain expressions or do not include them with the frequency of a generation earlier. Recall that the PLD are finite, consisting of certain robust, structurally simple expressions presented to a child, who sets relevant parameters. One individual may set some parameter differently from older people in her community; then it is likely that, because of the grammatical change, she will produce different utterances from other people in her community. These new expressions, in turn, affect the linguistic environment, and she will now be an agent of further change, by virtue of the fact that her younger siblings will have different PLD as a result of what she produces with her new grammar. As the younger siblings also set the relevant parameter in the manner of the older sister, so other people's PLD will differ. Thus a chain reaction is created. It is in this sense that grammatical change can spread analogously to what has been observed in population genetics, replicating aspects of evolutionary change.

Partha Niyogi and Bob Berwick (1995, 1997) have now produced a computer model which analyzes change in this way and *derives* the trajectory of changes. They postulate a learning theory with three sub-components: a theory of grammar, a learning algorithm by which a child generates grammars on the basis of exposure to data, and PLD. They postulate a population of child learners, a small number of whom fail to converge on preexisting grammars. After exposure to a finite amount of data, some children converge on the preexisting grammar, but others do not; they attain a different grammar.

> The next generation will therefore no longer be linguistically homogeneous.
> The third generation of children will hear sentences produced by the second
> – a different distribution – and they, in turn, will attain a different set of
> grammars. Over successive generations, the linguistic composition evolves as
> a dynamical system. (Niyogi and Berwick 1997: 2)

Language change, in this simulation, is a logical consequence of specific assumptions about the theory of grammar, the learning algorithm, and the PLD. Niyogi and Berwick produce a plausible model of population changes for the loss of null subjects in French. Interestingly, their model yields different trajectories for different changes. A common trajectory is the S-curve so familiar to historical linguists studying the spread of changes (e.g. Weinreich, et al. 1968, Kroch 1989). A change may begin quite gradually, then pick up momentum and proceed more rapidly, tailing off slowly before reaching completion.

The fact that changes progressing through populations can be graphically represented by a S-curve is not surprising to those who think in terms of chaotic systems and catastrophic reanalyses. The success of Niyogi and Berwick lies in showing that it is not impossibly difficult to compute (or simulate) grammatical dynamical systems. They show explicitly how to transform parameterized theories and memory-less learning algorithms into dynamical systems, producing results along the way. As a result, they *derive* the S-curve, rather than build it into their model as a specific assumption. Further, not all changes progress in S-curves; we find other trajectories – indeed, their model generates other trajectories for different changes. The model entails that changing specific elements of the theory of grammar or of the learning algorithm produces different trajectories for any given change. This means that their model may be amended in light of the way in which it matches the actual trajectory for specific changes in specific languages. This offers a new empirical demand for theories to meet, in addition to demands of learnability, coverage of data, etc.: theories should provide the

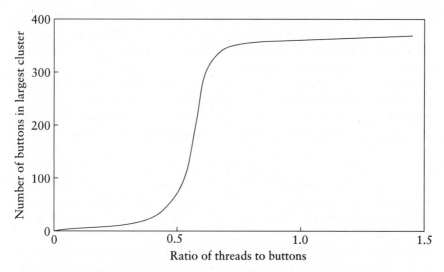

Figure 4.2 Phase transition. From Stuart Kauffman, *At Home in the Universe,* © 1995 by Stuart Kauffman. Used by permission of Oxford University Press, Inc.

most accurate diachronic trajectories for changes. There is more to be said about this work, and we shall return to it in chapter 8.

This reminds me of a toy experiment recounted by Kauffman in the context of "random graphs." Imagine 400 buttons on a dining room table.

> Randomly choose two buttons and connect them with a thread. Now put this pair down and randomly choose two more buttons, pick them up, and connect them with a thread. As you continue to do this, at first you will almost certainly pick up buttons that you have not picked up before. After a while, however, you are more likely to pick at random a pair of buttons and find that you have already chosen one of the pair. So when you tie a thread between the two newly chosen buttons, you will find three buttons tied together . . .
>
> The important features of random graphs show very regular statistical behavior as one tunes the ratio of threads to buttons. In particular, a *phase transition* occurs when the ratio of threads to buttons passes 0.5. At that point, a "giant cluster" suddenly forms . . . As the ratio of threads to buttons passes the 0.5 mark, all of a sudden most of the clusters have become cross-connected into one giant structure. (Kauffman 1995: 56)

Kauffman shows the phase transition in the graph reproduced as figure 4.2.

Kauffman believes that this is a toy version of the phase transition which leads to separate water molecules freezing into a block of ice. The point of using mathematical idealizations in science is that they help to capture the main issues. Kauffman's magical mathematics reveals the kind of pattern that we find in grammatical change and the kind of thing that Niyogi and Berwick have successfully modeled.

For the moment, we may note that Niyogi and Berwick have provided a model of how changes in individual grammars progress through a population of speakers. The fact that the model derives different trajectories for different changes, and that at least some of these trajectories seem to match the real, historical world reasonably well suggests a degree of plausibility. This is a remarkable result, which clearly could not be replicated under a social definition of grammars, which denies the usefulness of individual, biological grammars. The model should impress proponents of social grammars, who must postulate the S-curve as an unexplained primitive.

In discussing competing grammars, Kroch speaks repeatedly of changes progressing slowly and gradually over long periods. There may be slowness and gradualness at the level of the spread of the change through a population of speakers, but grammatical changes need to be instantaneous at the individual level. This follows from the Blocking Effect, which permits coexisting forms only if they are functionally distinct, as discussed earlier. We also know that some changes progress through a population rather rapidly. Earlier we noted that Kroch himself cites the fact that the average life span of doublets, as attested by the *OED*, is 300 years, but that this figure must be greatly exaggerated, since it ignores archaisms and geographical variation in dialects. This all strongly suggests that structural changes are rapid and abrupt at the individual level, and that, in many cases, they also spread through a population rapidly. The speed of the spread depends on many nongrammatical factors relating to social cohesion, facility of communication among different groups, and the like.

My own early work on grammatical change argued for abstract reanalysis on the basis of the dates of initiation and completion, as witnessed by initial and last attestations. For example, if a variety of phenomena drop out of the language at the same time, it might be plausible to claim that those phenomena all manifested a single grammatical change (Lightfoot 1979). Some of the early conclusions have turned out to be sound, whereas others have called for revision. In the early work, there was little concern with intermediate stages or with the spread of a change through a population. Now the work on competing grammars and on population models allows us to model transitions and enriches our understanding of change very considerably.

4.7   Parametric Change

In *As You Like It* (Act III, scene 2), Rosalind explains how time can amble, trot, gallop, or stand still for people in different circumstances. Historians have always known that languages sometimes undergo a period of rapid change, then settle into relative stasis. I have argued here that changes sometimes take place "catastrophically," and that grammars change abruptly. At certain points, dramatic changes take place, often simultaneously. It is natural to try to interpret a cascade of changes in terms of a new setting for some grammatical parameter, sometimes having a wide variety of effects. If we distinguish changes resulting from reanalyses, then we need to know what to look for in seeking grammatical changes. Catastrophic changes, resulting from a new parameter setting, have distinctive features and are quite different from the piecemeal, gradual, chaotic changes which constantly affect the linguistic environment. In earlier work, I identified six distinctive features of grammatical change (Lightfoot 1991: ch. 7).

First, each new grammatical property is manifested by a cluster of new phenomena. For example, the loss of the V-to-I operation in English (see chapter 6) entailed the predominance of forms like *Kim always reads the Bible* in place of the earlier *Kim reads always the Bible*, and the obsolescence of inverted and negative sentences like *Reads Kim the Bible?* and *Kim reads not the Bible*. These apparently unrelated changes took place in parallel, as demonstrated by the statistical studies of Kroch (1989), which showed the singularity of the change at the grammatical level (and led Kroch to postulate his Constant Rate Effect).

Second, not only is a new grammatical property typically manifested by a cluster of new phenomena; it also sometimes sets off a chain reaction. An example from the history of English is the establishment of verb–complement order. I showed (Lightfoot 1991) that this led indirectly to the introduction of an operation analyzing *speak to*, *spoken to*, etc. as complex verbs. Such chain reactions can be understood through the acquisition process: a child with the new verb–complement setting is induced by the constraints of UG to analyze some expressions differently from the way they were analyzed in earlier generations. As a result, the new grammar comes to differ from the old in more than one way.

Third, changes involving new grammatical properties tend to spread rapidly and manifest the S-curve discussed earlier. The old negative patterns associated with the V-to-I raising operation (*Kim reads not the Bible*) were robust and widely attested in the texts until their demise, which was rapid (see chapter 6). The fast spread of new grammatical properties is not surprising if one thinks of it in the context of language acquisition, as

I have just discussed. Once the linguistic environment has shifted in such a way as to trigger a new property in some children, the very fact that some people have a new grammatical property changes the linguistic environment yet further in the direction of setting the parameter in the new fashion. That is, the first people with the new parameter setting produce different linguistic forms, which in turn are part of the linguistic environment for younger people, thereby contributing to the spread of the new setting.

Fourth, obsolescence manifests new grammatical properties. When structures become obsolete, one cannot attribute their obsolescence to the ebb and flow of nongrammatical changes in the linguistic environment. A novel form may be introduced for expressive reasons, at first without affecting any grammar; but a form can hardly drop out of the language directly for expressive reasons or because of the influence of another language. On the contrary, obsolescence must be due to a structural domino effect, a by-product of something else, which was itself triggered by the kind of positive data generally available to children, as we saw in the context of the Blocking Effect.[10]

Fifth, any significant change in meaning is generally a by-product of a new grammatical property, for much the same reason that the obsolescence of a structure must be the indirect consequence of a more abstract change. In chapter 1 I discussed changes affecting the thematic roles associated with particular NP positions in the case of verbs such as *like, repent, ail* (the direct object of these verbs could once be an experiencer, while in modern English only the subject may be an experiencer; so people said things along the lines of "Apples like me" for the modern *I like apples*). It is hard to see how these changes could have arisen as idiosyncratic, nongrammatical innovations that somehow became fashionable within the speech community. Rather, such changes must be attributed to some aspect of a person's grammar, which was triggered by the usual kind of environmental factors – for these English "psych-verbs," the existence of only structural cases (Lightfoot 1991: ch. 6).

Sixth, new grammatical properties occur in response to shifts in simple data, with cues occurring in unembedded domains only; they are not sensitive to changes or continuities in embedded domains. Embedded domains are as likely as unembedded domains to reflect the usual to-ing and fro-ing of the chaotic linguistic environment, but they have no effect on the development of grammars in children. This follows from degree-0 learnability, the claim that grammars are learnable – that is, parameters are set – on the basis of data from unembedded binding domains (Lightfoot 1991, 1994).

All of this will make more sense when we discuss some actual cases of new parameter settings, in the next chapters.

So is change gradual or abrupt? I have argued here that it depends on the lens that one uses. Experience is generally fluid, and if one is concerned exclusively with describing differences in experience, in terms of what one finds in comparable texts of different generations, then change appears to be fluid, gradual, piecemeal, and chaotic. Similarly, if one thinks in terms of some kind of social grammar, where the "grammar" (mythical, I believe) is some kind of codification of the texts produced by some group of speakers, then again change appears to be gradual. Also, if one thinks in terms of a language changing, taking language to be a group phenomenon, change appears to be gradual, like water flowing. However, such commonsensical notions do not get us very far. For a plausible account of language acquisition, we must think in terms of abstract grammars; change is then a function of different grammars emerging in different people.

If we think in terms of biological grammars represented in individual mind/brains, then grammars differ from each other abruptly, a function of the limited variation allowed by UG. From this perspective, we see a series of snapshots – that is, distinct, individual grammars – and we expect languages to differ from each other in bumpy ways. This view may violate common sense, but physicists who view space in eleven dimensions know that common sense is not always a good guide. It provides a way of studying how grammatical shifts affect populations of speakers, an area where historical work has been bedeviled by confusion. One does not find one set of grammars being replaced by another set overnight; the textual record certainly does not suggest that English speakers had object–verb grammars replaced uniformly by verb–object grammars on some National Head-Change Day in the thirteenth century. Nor would we expect such a scenario if we recognize that speakers may operate with more than one grammar, and that grammar change may spread through a population over the course of time. Nonetheless, one does find that certain changes progress rapidly, and we can understand that phenomenon by postulating abrupt change at the level of individual grammars, and new grammars then spreading through a population of speakers.

The characterization of abrupt grammatical change sketched in this chapter makes sense only if we view a grammar as an individual, mental entity, and not as some kind of social entity codifying the data attested in the texts of some period. Making that distinction gives us a way of thinking about the spread of new grammars through a community using the methods of population genetics.

The success or failure of a research program is best determined by seeing whether it is productive or whether, like the neo-grammarian program of the nineteenth century, it leads to diminishing returns. In this chapter we have looked at the speed of change fairly abstractly, and I have made several references to forthcoming arguments in chapter 5 and beyond. It is time to move on to chapter 5, to enter Polyphemus's cave, and to think more concretely. Let us now examine some specific instances of catastrophic change at the grammatical level and see how they enable us to understand the phenomena of language change.

Notes

1   Traugott and Smith (1993), among many others, conceive of a grammar in this way, thinking of it as a device to generate a corpus of sentences belonging to some socially or politically defined entity (Lightfoot 1995). In early work (1969), Traugott took quite an extreme position in this regard, seeking a "diachronic grammar," a single, formal device characterizing different forms and different historical stages of English. This is a very natural logical possibility – in fact almost inevitable – if one thinks in social terms; after all, why should the social unit be defined as just covering one point in time? For discussion, see Lightfoot 1979: 28–35.

     Graffi (1995) discusses the nineteenth-century notion of social grammars which Paul inveighed against.

2   Several groups of researchers have attributed language change to general historical principles, not to changes in PLD. The "typological" explanations offered in the 1970s and the more recent studies on "grammaticalization" both invoke a general theory of change. Grammaticalization is a semantic process, whereby an item with a full lexical meaning comes to acquire a more abstract, functional, grammatical meaning. Those historicist explanations, of course, are not couched in a biological view of grammars, and analyses are formulated in very different terms.

     However, some modern work which adopts the biological view of grammars also invokes general historical principles. This work builds into grammatical theory devices which incline grammars to change in certain directions. This work raises distinct and interesting issues related to the motivation for change, which I return to in chapter 8. I mention it here to show that there is no logical connection between the biological view of grammars and the contingent approach to change that I am adopting, which views structural change as due entirely to prior changes in the PLD rather than to general principles of change or to nineteenth-century-style laws of history.

3   [NP V] order may be base-generated, or it may result from some adjunction operation if grammars have V NP order uniformly in initial structure, as argued by Kayne (1994). I ignore the form of this parametric variation here.

4   Warner (1993) has argued that some changes relating to the English modals were first instantiated earlier than has been claimed. We shall discuss changes in modals in chapter 7.

5   This assumes a realist approach. The universe is patterned in ways that are described by mathematics; the mathematician discovers truths that are independent of his or her culture, and those truths are qualitatively different from traffic conventions or codes of etiquette. As Martin Gardner puts it,

> if all intelligent minds in the universe disappeared, the universe would still have a mathematical structure and in some sense even the theorems of pure mathematics would continue to be true. . . . For a mathematical realist a tree not only exists when nobody looks at it, but its branches have a "tree" pattern even when no graph theorist looks at them. (1996: 281)

This is very different from the postmodernist view that mathematics is a cultural construct, intelligible only within the context of culture. For the "conceptualists," mathematicians do not discover preexisting, timeless things like pi and dodecahedrons; they construct them. Gardner draws this distinction nicely and takes apart the conceptualist stance.

6   Traugott and Smith (1993: 437–8) have argued that diglossic grammars would be unlearnable, and Harris and Campbell (1995: 86) are alarmed at the prospect of "tri- or tetraglossia." There is no reason in principle why diglossic grammars should be unlearnable, although some particular proposals may raise questions of learnability. This just means that we have to be careful in our analyses. I discussed this point in the context of arguments by Susan Pintzuk (1991) for a diglossic treatment of Old English writers, arguing that her particular diglossic analysis is unlearnable (Lightfoot 1997b).

The notion of coexisting grammars is itself a high-level abstraction, but the work of Kroch and his associates is weakened by not discussing how competing grammars might be used by speakers. If their theory allows speakers to switch from one grammar to another in mid-VP, it is probably too powerful.

7   Stein studied the corpus of Shakespeare and argued that the periphrastic *do* is most common where the inflectional ending on the verb would yield a complex consonantal cluster. So *do* is most common in the second person singular, where the ending is -*st*; so *Thou dost sing* occurs more commonly than *I do sing* because it is an alternative to the complex *Thou sing'st*. The frequency of *do* is a function of the consonantal clusters to be avoided. Stein offers some figures: verb stems ending in a vowel occur with *do* 10 percent of the time; verbs ending in a -*k* 24 percent, and verbs ending in a -*t* or a -*d* 38 percent.

Do was well established by the time of Shakespeare, and it is unclear whether Shakespeare's usage reflects common speech at the time or whether it also reflects, to some extent, the poetic demands of euphony.

8   We do, however, use these forms in specialized senses, which are not equivalent to the preexisting *clarity* and *evil*. So linguists often talk of expressions which may not occur in some language as "bad." Then they can go on to compare the "badness" of *Who did you say that left Rio?* with the "badness" of *Who said you that left Rio?* These expressions may be bad in this sense, but they are not evil or immoral in any way. Also, *clearness* has a specialized meaning among Quakers.

9 This conforms to what we know about the storage of forms in the mental lexicon: irregular forms are stored as independent entries (this idea will be important in section 7.2), whereas regular forms are not stored independently, but rather as some kind of stem which then undergoes a productive operation to yield the occurring form. A nice piece of evidence for this division is given by Pinker (1994). In forming compounds, we access lexical entries. If an irregular plural, for example, has its own lexical entry, then we are not surprised to find compounds like *mice eater*, alongside *rat eater*; the compounding exploits the lexical entries *mice* and *rat*. However, we do not find **rats eater*, because *rats*, being a regular plural, is not a distinct lexical entry; therefore the form is not available to the compounding operation.

10 For a recent application of this methodology, see Warner 1995: 542.

5

The Loss of Case and its Syntactic Effects

Rube Goldberg was trained as an engineer but became famous as a cartoonist. He created Professor Lucifer Gorgonzola Butts, an inventor of contraptions that accomplished simple ends in a roundabout manner. One invention was an automatic stamp-licker activated by a dwarf robot who overturned a can of ants onto a page of postage stamps, gumside up, which were then licked by an anteater who had been starved for three days.

He never designed grammars, as far as I know, but grammars have their Rube Goldberg properties. It is true that grammars are formed in a child in accordance with the prescriptions of the linguistic genotype; consequently, they are economical and beautiful in ways imposed by UG. However, they are also shaped by the demands of haphazard experience, and this makes them historically contingent. There is no contradiction here; after all, Rube Goldberg machines conform to the usual laws of mechanics. But there is a tension. Sometimes nature creates situations which display this tension with great clarity, and we get a seat right in front of Professor Butts's contraption, to watch the interplay of general and particular demands. In those situations, the workings of the mechanism may often be revealed by the way that things move and change. So with grammars.

If the linguistic experience of some children shifts a little, there may be dramatic consequences: the resulting grammar may generate a very different set of sentences. Furthermore, the shift may have a domino effect. We shall examine some examples and come to understand how grammars may develop some of their Rube Goldberg properties, seeing how they are contingent, dependent on accidental circumstances. In particular, we shall see that the loss of case endings may have catastrophic effects, entailing changes – sometimes odd-looking changes – in the syntax. Grammatical theory kicks in and shapes the domino effect. As a result, variation is bumpy, and change is catastrophic, many things changing at the same time.

5.1   Case

It is a striking property of natural languages that a noun often shows a different form depending on its function. Modern English manifests these "case" alternations only in the pronoun system. A pronoun shows one form if it is the subject of a finite verb ("nominative"), another if it is governed by a verb or by a preposition ("accusative"), and another if it acts as the specifier of a DP ("genitive") (1).

1 (a)   *He* saw *him* in $_{DP}$[*his* car].
   (b)   *They* saw *them* at $_{DP}$[*their* house].

Other languages have much richer morphological systems. Finnish has, strictly speaking, fifteen different cases, of which nine are local, expressing location, destination, and source, and these may appear alone or with markers for interior and exterior. Source is indicated by the suffix *-tta*; if the phrase indicates "from inside," the noun may have the *elative* case marker *-sta*, and if the phrase indicates "from outside," the noun may have the *ablative* case suffix *-lta*. Other languages have a *comitative* case indicating accompaniment, an *abessive* or *privative* case to mean "not having" (Finnish *rahta-tta* is [money + abessive] "without money, money-less"); some Australian languages encode the opposite idea in a *proprietive* case indicating "having" (Kalkatungu *putu-yan* [stomach + proprietive], means "pregnant"). Languages may display quite an array of different inflectional endings on nouns. If one adds all combinations of orientation markers and regular case markers, one can identify forty or more markings in some Finno-Ugric and Northeast Caucasian languages. Barry Blake's 1994 book *Case* takes his readers on a wonderful trip through a spectacular range of case systems.

Old English had a morphological case system, with essentially four cases – quite simple when compared to Finnish. Table 5.1 gives four sample paradigms, for different types of nouns. The demonstrative (*sē*, etc.) has somewhat richer inflection than the nouns.

Morphological cases are not just ornamental decorations; they interact with core syntactic operations. Polish, like Russian, shows an accusative marking on nouns governed by a verb (2a), but the marking is genitive if the verb is negated (2b).

2 (a)   Janek przyniósł kwiaty
         John brought flowers [accusative]
   (b)   Janek nie przyniósł kwiatów
         John not brought flowers [genitive]

Table 5.1 Some Old English noun inflections

Case	"that stone"		"that ship"		"that tale"		"that name"	
		singular				singular		
nom.	*sē*	*stān*	*þæt*	*scip*	*sēo*	*talu*	*sē*	*nama*
acc.	*þone*	*stān*	*þæt*	*scip*	*þā*	*tale*	*þone*	*naman*
gen.	*þæs*	*stānes*	*þæs*	*scipes*	*þǣre*	*tale*	*þæs*	*naman*
dat.	*þǣm*	*stāne*	*þǣm*	*scipe*	*þǣre*	*tale*	*þǣm*	*naman*
		plural				plural		
nom.	*þā*	*stānas*	*þā*	*scipu*	*þā*	*tala*	*þā*	*naman*
acc.	*þā*	*stānas*	*þā*	*scipu*	*þā*	*tala*	*þā*	*naman*
gen.	*þāra*	*stāna*	*þāra*	*scipa*	*þāra*	*tala*	*þāra*	*namena*
dat.	*þǣm*	*stānum*	*þǣm*	*scipum*	*þǣm*	*talum*	*þǣm*	*namum*

Indeed, the intertwining of case with core syntactic operations shows up even in languages with no overt, morphological case system. This indicates that there is more to case than meets the eye, and that case must represent a significant abstraction, regardless of overt markings. So English grammars permit NP/DPs to occur, to be pronounced, only in certain positions.

The NP/DP may be "understood" in some position, but if that position is not case-marked, the NP/DP must move to another position in which it is case-marked. That, in fact, is the motivation for movement: NP/DPs move in order to be case-marked, even though case marking is often not overt.

So if a NP/DP originates in a position which is not case-marked, it moves to another NP/DP position (3). In (3) *Kay* is understood as the complement of *arrested* and *picture*, and as the subject of *like*, but it may not be pronounced in those positions and must move to a case-marked position: one does not find anything like *Ray was arrested Kay*, *Ray's picture Kay*, *Ray seems Kay to like Jay*, nor *It seems Kay to like Jay*, because, in each example, *Kay* is in a position which is not case-marked.

3   (a) Kay_i was $_{Prt}$arrested e_i.
    (b) Kay_i's $_N$picture e_i (meaning 'picture of Kay').
    (c) Kay_i seems [e_i to like Ray].

If a NP/DP originates in a case-marked position, on the other hand, then it does not move to another NP/DP position. One finds expressions like *Ray arrested Kay, Ray's picture of Kay, it seems Kay likes Ray*, but not the structures of (4), where *Kay* has moved.

4   (a)   *Kay_i $_V$arrested e_i (intended to mean 'Kay arrested herself').
    (b)   *Kay_i's picture $_p$of e_i.
    (c)   *Kay_i seems [e_i likes Ray].

If we are going to distinguish the positions from which movement takes place in modern English in terms of case – (3) versus (4) – we need an abstract notion of case, defined independently of morphological endings, because overt, morphological case does not exist in the language outside the pronoun system. All grammars have some kind of case system, but only some have morphological case; the rest have abstract Case. Abstract Case is what is at work in the distinctions of (3)–(6). From now on I shall use "Case" to refer to that abstract notion of case, and lower-case "case" (sorry) to refer to overt, morphological markings.

The abstract Case system of modern English is simple. Verbs and pre-positions generally assign (accusative) Case to NP/DPs that they govern, as is overt in the form of pronouns: *Kay $_V$saw him $_p$with them*. The subject of a finite verb is governed by an inflectional element and receives (nominative) Case (*he, they left*), and a NP/DP in the specifier of a larger DP is Case-marked by the clitic *'s* and has Case (genitive): *Kay's, his, their book*. These are the positions which receive Case.

In (3a) the trace e_i is governed not by a verb or a preposition or any other Case assigner, but by the participle *arrested*, and it has no Case. Similarly in (3b), the trace is governed by the noun *picture* and has no Case. And in (3c) the trace is the subject of an infinitive verb and is Caseless. As a result, the traces in (3) are movement sites, positions from which a NP/DP moves to another NP/DP position and then receives Case. In (4a), on the other hand, the trace is governed by a transitive verb, in (4b) by a pre-position, and in (4c) by an inflectional element. So all these traces are Case-marked (governed by I in (4c)); a NP/DP may occur in these posi-tions, and these are not positions from which they must move to other NP/DP positions.

Conversely, wh- movement shows the mirror image: a wh- phrase moves to the specifier of CP, not to another NP/DP position, and it may not move there from Caseless positions (5), but only from Case-marked positions (6). (5) and (6) correspond to (3) and (4), respectively. In (6a) the trace is governed by the verb (as in (4a)), in (6b) the trace is governed by the preposition *of* (as in (4b)), and in (6c) the trace is governed by the finite inflectional element (I) (as in (4c)).

5   (a)   *Who$_i$ was Kay $_{Prt}$arrested e$_i$?
    (b)   *Who$_i$ did you see a $_N$picture e$_i$?
    (c)   *Who$_i$ did it seem [e$_i$ to like Ray]?

6   (a)   Who$_i$ did Kay $_V$arrest e$_i$?
    (b)   Who$_i$ did Kay see a picture $_p$of e$_i$?
    (c)   Who$_i$ did it seem [e$_i$ likes Ray]?

This shows that Case is a fundamental item in grammars, even if it is not morphologically marked. Current work within the Minimalist Program is investigating the intertwinement of Case and syntactic operations, with intriguing results. One way of thinking of the relationship between the morphological and abstract systems is to claim that abstract Case occurs in all grammars and must be *realized* in some fashion; morphological case is then just one means of realizing abstract Case.

One way of probing into the relationship between abstract Case and overt, morphological case is to examine what happens syntactically when a morphological case system is eroded and eventually lost. In the next section I shall show some curious syntactic effects resulting from the disappearance of the morphological case system in English. The loss of morphological case enables us to understand to a significant degree the hitherto mysterious emergence of new "split genitives" in Middle English. What is striking is the tightness of the explanation, the way in which one element of a certain theory of Case explains the details of the development. We shall see that if one part of a child's linguistic experience changes – namely, the transparency of the overt case morphology – then other things must also change in the grammars that emerge.

In the theoretical literature there are two approaches to how nouns assign abstract Case. The approach I shall favor links Case to thematic roles. Thematic roles define the semantic relationship of DPs to a verb. The subject DP is an Agent in (7a), a Theme in (7b), a Location in (7c), an Instrument in (7d). These thematic roles are a function of the meaning of the verb and are "assigned" by the verb.

7   (a) $_{DP}$[The forward] kicked the defender.
    (b) $_{DP}$[The forward] received the award.
    (c) $_{DP}$[The Indian Ocean] surrounds Madagascar.
    (d) $_{DP}$[The wind] blew the door open.

On an earlier view, nouns assign Case quite independently of thematic roles. Developing an idea of Jean-Roger Vergnaud's, Chomsky (1981) postulated a UG condition that phonetic NP/DPs (and some movement traces, such as traces of wh- movement, as in (6)) must have Case. That is, NP/DPs are pronounced only in positions which are Case-marked. One can see this analysis at work in the structures (8a, b), where the DPs indicated are empty, positions to which the DP *the city* might move. In general, a noun like *destruction* may be followed directly by (i.e. govern) a DP (8a) or a PP (8b).

8   (a) $_{DP}[_{Spec}[DP's] _{NP}[_N destruction _{DP}[the city]]]$
    (b) $_{DP}[_{Spec}[DP's] _{NP}[_N destruction _{PP}[of the city]]]$

For Chomsky (1981) N does not assign Case. Therefore, in (8a) *the city* is not in a Case-marked position and must move to the specifier of DP, where it is governed by the clitic *'s* and is Case-marked, yielding *The city's destruction*. In (8b) *the city* is Case-marked by the preposition *of* and consequently may not move to another DP position: **The city's destruction of* (it *can* move to Spec of CP by wh- movement: *What did you plan the destruction of?*). *Of* is a meaningless dummy element; it acts as a Case-marker for *the city*, but *the city* receives its thematic role from the noun *destruction*; it is the complement and Theme of *destruction*.[1] In this approach Case marking and thematic role assignment are quite separate.

A more recent approach retains the earlier theory of structural Case but links Case assignment to thematic role assignment (Chomsky 1986, 1995).[2] What is important for our immediate purposes is that N assigns Case (along with a thematic role) to the right or to the left in accordance with the head-order parameter (below) and does so "inherently."[3]

> We must distinguish Case-assignment, at D-structure, from Case-realization, at S-structure. Both Case-assignment and Case-realization fall under government: at D-structure N governs and θ-marks [assigns a thematic role to – DWL] its complement and assigns Case to it; at S-structure N governs both the complement and the subject, so that Case can be realized in either position. (Chomsky 1986: 193)

The key point here is that it is a property of UG that Ns assign inherent Case to the left or to the right, and the Case is linked with a thematic role. This shapes some Middle English innovations.

5.2   Middle English Split Genitives[4]

What has this got to do with language change? We shall see that an approach linking Case to thematic roles gives us a way of understanding Old English grammars rather straightforwardly, and of understanding changes that those grammars underwent as the morphological system was lost.

If UG stipulates that nouns may assign Case to the left or to the right in accordance with the head-order parameter, then it is not surprising to find Old English nouns assigning Case to the left *and* to the right. There is good reason to believe that the head-order parameter was shifting in late Old English: one finds verbs preceding and following their complement, object–verb order alternating with verb–object. There is independent evidence that Old English nouns assigned genitive Case not only to the left (Ælfric's *Godes lof*, "praise of God"; *Cristes læwa*, "betrayer of Christ") but also to the right: *Lufu godes and manna*, "love of God and of men" (Ælfric, *Catholic Homilies*, II. 602. 12), *Ormæte stream wæteres*, "huge stream of water" (ibid. 196. 5). Elizabeth Traugott (1992: 283) notes that one finds possessive–head order alternating with head–possessive. Old English has a very simple analysis. It is more or less a direct manifestation of this UG theory of Case: nouns assign Case to the left and to the right, and only to NP/DPs with which they are thematically related, as we shall see. Case is assigned in that fashion and then is *realized* on both sides of the noun with the morphological, genitive suffix.[5]

If Old English nouns assign Case to the left and to the right inherently, and if in both positions it is realized as a morphological genitive, then it is not surprising to find that Old English also manifested "split genitives" (the term is Eilert Ekwall's (1943)). They are split in that a single genitive phrase occurs on both sides of the head noun. In (9) we see an example in which the split element occurring to the right of the noun was a conjunct (italicized). Jespersen (1909: 300) notes that with conjuncts, splitting represents the usual word order in Old English.

9 (a)   Inwæres broþur *ond Healfdenes* (*AS Chron*. 878)
         Inwær's brother and Healfden's
         "Inwær's and Healfden's brother"
   (b)   Sodoma lande 7 *gomorra* (*West Saxon Gospels* (MS A), Matt. 10:15)
         "The Sodomites' and the Gomorreans' land"

In addition, appositional elements, where two NP/DPs are in parallel, are usually split: the two elements occur on either side of the head noun (10).

10   (a)   Ælfredes godsune *cyninges* (*AS Chron.* 890 (Laud (Peterborough)
             [E] 1122))
             "King Alfred's godson"
     (b)   Þæs cyninges dagum *herodes* (*West Saxon Gospels* (MS A), Matt.
             2: 1)
             "In the days of Herod the king"
     (c)   Iohannes dagum *fulwihteres.* (*West Saxon Gospels* (MS A), Matt.
             11: 12)
             "From the days of John the Baptist"

(10a) is interesting, because it comes from the Peterborough version of
the *Anglo-Saxon Chronicle*, a copy dating from 1122. The Parker [A] version of the *Chronicle*, copied more than 200 years earlier (ca.900), shows
Ælfredes cyninges godsunu, where there is no splitting of the genitive phrase.
The difference between these two manuscripts, noted by Mitchell (1985:
610), suggests either some dialectal or some diachronic variation.

   These split genitives may be part of a wider phenomenon which permits
split constructions not involving genitives. (11a, b) show a split appositional
construction (italicized), and (11c, d) show a split conjunct.

11   (a)   Com *se cyning* to him *Godrum*. (*AS Chron.* 878)
             "The king Godrum came to him."
     (b)   Wearþ *Sidroc eorl* ofslægen *se aldra* (*AS Chron.* 871)
             "Earl Sidroc the elder was slain."
     (c)   Wearþ *Heahmund bisceop* ofslægen *ond fela godra monna* (*AS
             Chron.* 871)
             "Bishop Heahmund and many good men were slain."
     (d)   Ond he *hine* miclum *ond his geferan* mid feo weorðude (*AS
             Chron.* 878)
             "And he much honored him and his companions with money."

It is important to note, however, that splitting within DPs is restricted to
conjuncts (9) and to appositional elements (10). In particular, Old English
seems not to show split constructions with a preposition phrase, along the
lines of *The book's cover about Rio* (= "The book about Rio's cover"). So
there was no general rule "extraposing" a PP. Nor does one find anything like
Þæs cyninges godsune Frances, "The king's godson of-France" (= "The king
of France's godson"), where *Frances* has no thematic relation to *godsune*.

   Split genitives in Old English have a structure along the lines of (12).
Ælfredes is in the specifier of DP. *Godsune* assigns thematic role and Case
to the left and to the right.

12   $_{DP}$[$_{Spec}$[Ælfredes] D $_{NP}$[$_N$godsune [cyninges]]]

These grammars have an overt genitive case on the right or the left of the head noun; and they have split genitives, where the head noun assigns the same thematic role and Case in both directions. So much for splitting in OE grammars.

Now for the mysterious changes. Middle and Early Modern English also manifest split genitives, but they include forms which are very different from the split genitives of Old English (13).

13 (a) The clerkes tale *of Oxenford* (Chaucer, *Clerk's Tale*, Prologue)
    (b) The Wive's Tale *of Bath* (Chaucer, *Wife of Bath's Tale*, Prologue)
    (c) Kyng Priamus sone *of Troy* (Chaucer, *Troilus & Cressida*, I, 2)
    (d) This kynges sone *of Troie* (Chaucer, *Troilus & Cressida*, III, 1715)
    (e) The Archbishop's Grace *of York* (Shakespeare, *1 Henry IV*, III. ii. 119)

The meanings are "The clerk of Oxford's tale," "King Priam of Troy's son," etc., and the genitive is split in the same sense as in Old English grammars: the rightmost part of the genitive phrase (italicized) occurs to the right of the head noun which the genitive phrase modifies. Mustanoja (1960: 78) notes that "the split genitive is common all through ME" and is more common than the modern "group genitive," *The clerk of Oxford's tale.* Jespersen (1909: 293) calls this splitting "the universal practice up to the end of the fifteenth century." However, these Middle English split forms are different from those of Old English grammars, because the rightmost element is neither a conjunct nor appositional, and it has no thematic relation with the head noun *tale, son*; instead, it is related to the leftmost element of the split genitive. How did these new split forms emerge and become so general?

We can understand the development of the new Middle English split genitives in terms of the loss of the overt, morphological case system and Chomsky's (1986, 1995) theory of Case related to thematic role. We can see this through a thought-experiment.

In Early Modern English, grammars emerged which lacked the morphological case properties of the earlier systems, in particular lacking a morphological genitive. We know this because the texts show nouns occurring with no case endings. Old English had four cases (nominative, accusative, genitive, and dative) and a vestigial instrumental case, but they disappeared in the period between the tenth and thirteenth centuries, the loss spreading through the population from north to south, possibly under the influence of the Scandinavian settlements (see section 1.2).

Put yourself now in the position of a child with this new, caseless grammar; your grammar has developed without morphological case. You are living in the thirteenth century; you would hear forms such as *Ælfredes godsune cyninges*, but the case endings do not register. You are not an infant, and you are old enough to have a partial analysis, which identifies three words. *Ælfredes* was construed as a "possessive" noun in the specifier of DP.

The modern "possessive" is not simply a reflex of the old genitive case. Morphological case generally is a property of nouns. By contrast, "possessive" in modern English is a property of the DP, not of nouns: in *My uncle from Cornwall's cat* the possessor is the DP *My uncle from Cornwall*, not the noun *Cornwall* or the noun *uncle*. Allen (1997) shows that the *'s* is a clitic attached to the preceding element, and that the group genitive, where the clitic is attached to a full DP, is a late Middle English innovation.[6] UG dictates that every phonetic NP/DP has Case. The new caseless children reanalyzed the old morphological genitive suffix *-es* as a clitic, which was recruited as a Case marker. The clitic *'s* Case-marks the element in the specifier of the containing DP. So *Ælfred* has Case, and the Case is realized through the *'s* marker (usually analyzed as the head D). In short, the *Ælfredes* of the parents is reanalyzed as *Ælfred's*, although orthographic forms like *Ælfredes* occur when the mental grammar surely yielded *Ælfred's*. Orthographic *'s* is a recent innovation. So far, so good.

What about *cyninges*? The evidence suggests that the phrase became *Ælfred's godsune king*. One finds phrases of exactly this form in (14), where the post-nominal noun is not overtly Case-marked. Jespersen (1909: 283–4) notes that these forms are common in Middle English (where, again, *kynges* and *Grekes* are equivalent to modern *king's* and *Greek's*).

14 (a) The kynges metynge Pharao (Chaucer, *The Book of the Duchesse*, 282)
         "Pharaoh the king's dream"
    (b) The Grekes hors Synoun (Chaucer, *Squire's Tale*, 209)
         "Sinon the Greek's horse"

These forms are direct reflexes of Old English split genitives like (10), corresponding exactly, except that the split element, *Pharao*, *Synoun*, has no overt Case. Despite the absence (for us new, caseless children) of an overt, morphological genitive case, UG prescribes that the post-nominal NP/DP must carry some abstract Case, and that Case must be realized somehow. After the loss of the morphological case system, it can no longer be realized as a genitive case ending. This means that there must be another way of marking/realizing the abstract Case in (14). Well, *Pharao* receives its Case by co-indexing with the Case-marked *kynges*; the two forms are in apposition, and therefore are co-indexed and share the same thematic role. This is exactly what one would expect if there is a one-to-one relationship between Case and thematic role, the key element of the more recent theory of Case. In that event, no independent Case marker is needed for *Pharao*.

There is another option for realizing Case on the rightmost element. The dummy, meaningless preposition *of* could be used as a Case marker, as it is in (13). This is not possible in *Ælfred's godsune king* or the phrases of (14), because if *of* were to Case-mark the NP/DP, one would expect it also to assign a thematic role (given a one-to-one relation between Case and thematic role), and in that event the NP/DP could not be interpreted as an appositional element. The sentences of (13), on the other hand, are not like those of (14) and have different meanings. In (13b), for example, *Wive* and *Bath* are not appositional or co-indexed, therefore an independent Case marker and thematic role assigner is needed; this is the function of *of*. It has often been observed that *of*, which was rare to nonexistent in Old English in a genitival function,[7] takes over the functions of the earlier genitive, and that there are close parallels between early inflected genitives and later *of* phrases (Nunnally 1985: 157; Traugott 1972: 78). On this view, the emergence in Middle English of N *of NP/DP* forms is an automatic consequence of the loss of the morphological case system: *of* was introduced in order to Case-mark a NP/DP which would not otherwise be Case-marked. In particular, the NP/DP could not be Case-marked like the rightmost item in (14), which carries the same Case as *Ælfred's* because it has the same thematic role. So *of* assigns Case to a NP/DP only if it has an independent thematic role.

With the introduction of the *of* Case marker in these contexts, there is a further change, and the split genitive construction is extended, as we have noted (13). In Old English, the post-nominal genitive always had a thematic relation with the head noun; one does not find expressions such as *Þæs cyninges son Frances*, "The king of France's son," where *Frances* is neither a conjunct nor appositional and is thematically related to "king" (Nunnally 1985: 148; Cynthia Allen and Willem Koopman, personal communication). In such a phrase, *Frances* could not be Case-marked by any adjacent element; in particular, it could not receive Case from *son*, because it has no thematic relation with *son*. In Middle English, one does find post-nominal, split DPs even where there is no thematic relation with the head noun, but rather a thematic relation with the noun in the specifier of DP, and the post-nominal items are Case-marked by *of*. So, in (13a) *Oxenford* is thematically related to *clerkes* and not to *tale*, and it is Case-marked by *of.* It is crucial to note that the Middle English split expressions only involve *of* phrases: one does not find *The book's cover about Rio* for "The book about Rio's cover," mirroring the situation in Old English (see above) and showing that there is no general operation "extraposing" PPs in Middle English, as there was not in Old English. Additionally – and this is crucial – the post-nominal noun in (13) always has a thematic role of Locative/Source. I know of no claim to this effect in the literature, but it has been pointed out to me by Cynthia Allen, Olga Fischer, and Willem Koopman in independent personal communications, and it seems to be right. So one does not find forms like (15), where the post-nominal noun is a Theme (15a) or a Possessor (15b).

15 (a) The portrait's painter of Saskia (= the portrait of Saskia's painter)
    (b) The wife's tale of Jim (= the wife of Jim's tale)

The fact that the *of* phrase is associated with a unique thematic role makes sense if UG prescribes a link between inherent Case and thematic role assignment. Consequently, the extension of these split genitives in Middle English is not surprising on a theory which allows nouns to assign Case and which links Case to thematic role assignment (Chomsky 1986, 1995). Similarly in Old English, in (10a), *Ælfredes godsune cyninges, godsune* assigns the same Case to the right and to the left, realized in both instances as an overt, morphological genitive case, as noted above; it also assigns the same thematic role to the two NP/DPs to which it assigns Case. That is what it means for the two NP/DPs to be appositional (same Case, same thematic role), and all of this is easy to understand if Case and thematic role assignment are linked at the level of UG. Likewise for conjuncts (9).

This much we can understand on the more recent theory of Case. The properties of the new grammar must have emerged in the way that they did, if children (a) heard expressions like *Ælfredes godsune cyninges*, (b) did not have the morphological case system of their parents, and (c) were subject to a Case theory requiring all NP/DPs to have Case (assigned and realized) and linking Case with the assignment of thematic roles. We have a tight explanation for the new properties of Middle English grammars, showing how they emerged as children acquired grammars with no overt, morphological case system to realize the abstract Cases, while still subject to the UG condition that all NP/DPs have an abstract Case which is realized in some fashion. In particular, we explain the distinction between (13) and (14), *of* occurring where there is no thematic relation with the head noun (13), but not where there is such a relation (14). We see that change is bumpy; if one element of a grammar changes, there may be many new phenomena. Also, children do not just match what they hear; they may produce innovative forms, as required by UG.

However, our account so far leaves open the question of why these extended split genitives (13) should have arisen. A possible explanation may be found in the reanalysis of one special type of Old English split genitive, that involving double names (henceforth, "split names"). Ekwall (1943: 15) finds "a really remarkable profusion" of these forms in his examination of the English Patent Rolls for the thirteenth and early fourteenth centuries (p. 16). He notes that the documents originated in indictments drawn up by local lawyers, and that "we may assume that the split genitives represent local usage and everyday speech. Many of the descriptions, especially those which contain a pet form of a personal name, have a very homely and colloquial ring" (p. 17). These forms are comparable to the appositional types of (10): *Thomas* and *Doreward* have the same relationship to *prest* in (16a), analogously to the way that *Ælfredes* and *cyninges* have the same relationship to *godsune* in (10a). These surnames often describe social functions: *Doreward* was "ward of the door," *Ward* was "guard."

16 (a) Thomasprest Doreward (1318 *Patent Rolls* (Elmstead Ess.))
          (= priest of Thomas Doreward)
    (b) Simundeschamberleyn Ward (1318 *Patent Rolls* (Hornington YW)) (= chamberlain of Simon Ward)
    (c) Thomasservantcornyssh (1450 *Patent Rolls* (Great Waltham Ess.))
          (= servant of Thomas Cornish)

Ekwall also finds split names where the second part of the name begins with the French preposition *de* and where the DP indicates the place of origin (17). This is a common form of name in Middle English, and "the preposition begins to be dropped already in the first half of the fourteenth century and is sometimes replaced by *of*" (ibid. 48).

17 (a) Nicholesknave de Moeles (1314 *Patent Rolls* (Compton Pauncefoot So.)) (= servant of Nicholas de Moeles)
    (b) Williamesprest de Reigny (1318 *Patent Rolls* (East Lydford So.))
          (= priest of William de Reigny)
    (c) Alicesbailiff de Watevill (1323 *Patent Rolls* (Panfield Ess.))
          (= bailiff of Alice de Watevill)

Comparable split names where the second part begins with English *of* are shown in (18).

18 (a) Thomasefelagh of Barneby (1311 *Patent Rolls* (Lockington, YE))
         (= fellow of Thomas of Barmby)
    (b) Rogereswarenner of Beauchamp (1316 *Patent Rolls* (Bennington
         Hrt.)) (= warrener of Roger of Beauchamp)
    (c) Julianesservant of Weston (1348 *Patent Rolls* (Tetbury Gl.))
         (= servant of Julian of Weston)

Forms like (18), being colloquial and therefore readily available to child
language learners, might have been a trigger for the new split genitives of
Middle English (13). In these names (18) children heard forms introduced
by *of* in a kind of appositional structure. In (18a) *Thomas* and *of Barneby*
are on a par, just like (16a), where *Thomas* and *Doreward* are similarly
on a par, both names of the same person; and initially *of Barneby* was
presumably treated as a unit with no internal structure, a literal translation
of *de* forms like those in (17); if this is correct, then the structure of (18a)
is parallel to that of (10a):

19 $_{DP}[_{Spec}$[Thomas] D $_{NP}[_{N}$felagh $_{NP}$[of-Barneby]]]

It is likely that, as *of* became established as a dummy preposition in
Middle English, *of Barneby* came to be construed with an internal P NP/
DP structure, a necessary step to explain why *of* later tends to get dropped
from names, which then become Thomas Barneby, Roger Beauchamp,
Julian Weston, etc. According to the recent theory of Case, which links Case
with thematic role assignment, we would expect *of* to drop out as it is
recognized as a Case-marking preposition. On the assumption that Barneby,
Beauchamp, and Weston have the same thematic roles, respectively, as
Thomas, Roger, and Julian, a prepositional *of* would be unwarranted,
inviting the interpretation of the following NP/DP as having a distinctive
thematic role. Then we have an explanation for the loss of *of* in these
names. But my point here is more limited: forms such as (18) might have
been a trigger for the extended split genitives like (13). Given that *of* is a
Case marker, then it must have a distinctive thematic role; Locative/Source
is a good candidate given the structure of names like (18), all of which
indicate the place from which the people Thomas, Roger et al. originate.
    This is an explanation for the rise of the split genitives of (13) in Middle
English. They were around for four centuries and then dropped out of the
language. This was a function of the newly available clitic *'s*, which made
possible group genitives like *The clerk of Oxford's tale*, which had not
been possible until *'s* was construed as a clitic (why exactly that was so

does not relate directly to the point of this section), and that in turn was a function of the loss of morphological cases, including the genitive in *-es*. As *'s* was recruited as a Case marker for NP/DPs, there was no reason for splitting, and the split constructions disappeared.

Children know that phonetic NP/DPs have an abstract Case which must be realized somehow. This is a function of UG, and abstract Cases are often realized as morphological cases. Children scan their linguistic environment for morphological cases, and if they find them, they serve to realize abstract Cases. If children do not find morphological cases, parameters are set differently. In that event, a P or V may Case-mark a NP/DP that it governs. This section has shown what happens when everything else remains constant. There came a point in the history of English when children ceased to find morphological cases, for reasons that we shall discuss later in the chapter. Those children were exposed to pretty much the same kind of linguistic experience as their parents, but the transparency of overt case endings had dropped below a threshold such that they were no longer attained. Given a highly restrictive theory of UG, particularly one linking Case assignment by nouns to thematic role assignment and requiring Cases to be realized on phonetic NP/DPs, other things then had to change; that is how and why change is often bumpy. The grammar which emerged under those conditions was shaped by contingent factors, notably by the form of names.

Some of the details of Middle English grammars were shaped in this way, and we come to understand why things changed as they did and why Middle English grammars had their split genitive, Rube Goldberg properties. Conversely, this historical understanding adds to the plausibility of a theory linking Case to thematic role assignment for nouns.

5.3   Inherent Case and Thematic Roles in Early English

In the last section we distinguished the assignment of abstract Cases and the realization of those Cases. One way in which abstract Cases may be realized is through morphological cases, and when that means of Case realization is lost, through the erosion of case endings, there may be elaborate consequences for the new caseless grammars, as we saw.

We saw that nouns may assign thematic roles and inherent Case to dependent NP/DPs. This Case was realized as a morphological genitive in Old English, whether it was on the left or the right of the head noun. Old English verbs, adjectives, and perhaps prepositions were also able to assign thematic roles and inherent Case to dependent NP/DPs, and the inherent Case might be realized as a morphological genitive or dative (20–2).

20 (a) ... deaðes onfoð. (Ælfric, *Catholic Homilies*, I, 21. 308. 2)
death [genitive] he-receives
"... he suffers death."

(b) Ac ge onfoþ þæm mægene Halges Gastes. (*HomS* 46 (*Blickling Homilies* 11), 49)
"But you receive the power [dative] of the Holy Ghost."

21 (a) Þeh hie þæs wyrþe næron. (*Orosius* 104, 5)
though they that [genitive] worthy not-were
"Though they weren't worthy of that."

(b) Monige sindon me swiðe onlice. (*Cura Pastoralis*, 24, 7)
many are me [dative] very similar
"Many are very similar to me."

22 (a) ... neah þære tide. (Bede, *Historia Ecclesiastica*, IV, ch. 24 (*Story of Cædmon*))
"... Near this hour [dative]."

(b) Micele hundas ... ræsdon wið Petres weard. (Ælfric, *Catholic Homilies*, I, 376. 33)
"Huge dogs rushed towards Peter [genitive]."

So other inherent Cases might be realized as oblique morphological cases (i.e. cases other than nominative or accusative), and Old English children found an overt realization of abstract inherent Cases. Here we shall see some more of what happened when this means of Case realization was lost.

If a dependent NP/DP has inherent Case, realized with morphological oblique case, then one would expect that it does not move to another position in which it would receive a second Case, since a NP/DP has one and only one Case. Movement, after all, takes place only where necessary. This can be seen clearly in Latin, where certain verbs assign inherent Case, realized as morphological dative, to the complement NP/DP to which they assign a thematic role (23a). This NP/DP may not move to a position where it would receive nominative Case, the subject of a finite passive verb (23b), and these verbs have so-called impersonal passives (23c), where the complement NP/DP remains in the dative case and does not become a nominative subject.

23 (a)   Calpurnia Marco credit.
           Calpurnia [nominative] Marcus [dative] believes
           "Calpurnia believes Marcus."
    (b)   *Marcus creditur a Calpurnia.
           Marcus [nominative] is-believed by Calpurnia [ablative]
           "Marcus is believed by Calpurnia."
    (c)   Marco creditur a Calpurnia.
           Marcus [dative] it-is-believed by Calpurnia [ablative]

The same phenomenon is illustrated in German and Russian, where NP/DPs with inherent Case, manifested as some oblique morphological case, do not become nominative subjects of passive verbs. It is also true of Old English, but it is less straightforward to illustrate, because most verbs which may assign inherent Case to their complement may also assign a simple structural accusative.[8] So the verb *folgian* "follow" might assign not only a dative (24a), but also an accusative (24b). Similarly, the verb *onfon* "receive" assigns not only a genitive (20a) and dative (20b), but also an accusative (24c).

24 (a)   Him folgiaþ fuglas. (*Phoen. 591*)
           "The birds [nominative] follow him [dative]."
    (b)   And ða folgade feorhgeniðlan. (*Beowulf* 2933)
           "And then he pursued his deadly foes [accusative]."
    (c)   . . . onfoh minne gast. (Ælfric, *Catholic Homilies*, I, 29. 426. 14)
           ". . . receive my soul [accusative]."

Nonetheless, we can see that a noun with an inherent Case does not move in Old English. The verb *give* assigned inherent (dative) Case to its indirect object (25a), and corresponding personal passives along the lines of (25b) are not found until after the loss of morphological dative case.

25 (a)   VP[giefan þæm cyninge þa boc]
           "give the king [dative] the book [accusative]"
    (b)   The king was given the book.

With the loss of morphological case, this means of realizing inherent Case was lost and evidence shows that verbs ceased to assign inherent Case, assigning only structural accusative Case to NP/DPs that they governed. Adjectives and prepositions also ceased to assign inherent Case. Prepositions and verbs became structural Case markers, assigning accusative, but adjectives never came to assign structural Case. So verbs and prepositions may be followed by a phonetic NP/DP that they govern (*see him*, *about him*), but generally adjectives are not (**proud him*) and so require a prepositional Case marker (*proud of him*).[9] In the last section we focused on some consequences of the loss of a morphological means to realize inherent genitive Case in the complement of nouns; in this section we shall investigate the loss of dative case as a realization of inherent Cases assigned by verbs.

The immediate evidence for the fact that the loss of morphological cases coincided with loss of many abstract inherent Cases consists in the loss of overt morphological case, the loss of transitive adjectives, and the emergence of prepositional and indirect passives. Morphological case disappears first in the tenth-century Northumbrian *Lindisfarne Gospels*. Richard Rolle, writing in Yorkshire in the fourteenth century, shows no morphological case. Unfortunately, there is almost no extant northern prose literature for the intervening 300 years, but we know that the loss spread gradually to the south. Visser (1963: 327) notes the rapid decay of transitive adjectives, which were very frequent in Old English and were replaced in Early Modern English by prepositional forms (*similar to*, *worthy of*), where the preposition serves to Case-mark the following NP/DP. The transition seems to begin in the thirteenth century, when new prepositional forms first emerge. Visser gives (26) as the last attestation of a transitive adjective, although *like*, *near*, and *worth* persist in the old form (see n. 9).

26   Enough is me to paint my unrest (1579 Spenser *Shep*. Cal 79)
     "It is enough for me to paint out my unrest."

Prepositional passives (*John was spoken to*) became productive in the thirteenth century, and indirect passives like *John was given the book* (25b) in the fifteenth.[10] Many ·of the earliest examples are found in the Paston Letters (27).

27   (a)   As þow in they vision was opynly schewede. (ca.1400 *Morte Arthure*, 827)
            "As you were openly shown in your vision."
     (b)   He shuld be alowyd mor. (1422–1509 *Paston Letters* (Gairdner), vol. 1, 252)
            "He should be allowed more."

All of this suggests that abstract inherent Case had been lost everywhere by the fifteenth century (except with nouns, as we saw in the last section).

This was manifested by the emergence of indirect passives and the loss of impersonal passives – so impersonal passives do not occur after this time.[11]

Verbs denoting psychological states of one kind or another – "psych-verbs" – underwent some peculiar changes in Middle English. We can understand aspects of these syntactic changes in terms of the loss of the morphological case system.[12]

In many languages psych-verbs often reflect thematic roles in unusual syntactic configurations. This is true of Italian, where one finds patterns like (28).

28　(a)　Gianni teme questo.
　　　　　"Gianni fears this."
　　(b)　Questo preoccupa Gianni.
　　　　　"This worries Gianni."
　　(c)　A Gianni piace questo.
　　　　　"To Gianni pleases this."
　　(d)　Questo piace a Gianni.
　　　　　"This pleases Gianni."

Belletti and Rizzi (1988) offer an influential analysis for these verbs, which is useful for understanding Old and Middle English. The most striking feature of psych-verbs in Old and Middle English is the wide range of syntactic contexts in which they appear – sometimes impersonally with an invariant third person singular inflection (29a), sometimes with a nominative Theme (29b), sometimes with a nominative Experiencer (29c).

29　(a)　Him ofhreow þæs mannes. (Ælfric, *Catholic Homilies*, I, 8. 192. 16)
　　　　　to-him [dative] there-was-pity because-of-the man [genitive].
　　　　　"He pitied the man."
　　(b)　Þa ofhreow ðam munece þæs hreoflian mægenleast. (Ælfric, *Catholic Homilies*, I, 23. 336. 10)
　　　　　then brought-pity to-the-monk the leper's feebleness
　　　　　"Then the monk pitied the leper's feebleness."
　　(c)　Se mæssepreost þæs mannes ofhreow. (Ælfric, *Lives of Saints* (Oswald) 26. 262)
　　　　　the priest [nominative] because-of-that man [genitive] felt-pity
　　　　　"The priest pitied that man."

However, an analysis along the lines of Belletti and Rizzi (1988) predicts the range of psych-verbs attested in early English with appropriate accuracy.

The verbs would be subcategorized to occur with Experiencer and Theme NP/DPs, and this would yield initial structures like (30), with the Experiencer higher than the Theme.

30   $_{IP}$[NP/DP I $_{VP}$[$_{V'}$[verb Theme] Experiencer]]

Belletti and Rizzi's theory of lexical entries would prevent specifying anything beyond the thematic roles with which a verb might occur, the cases manifesting those thematic roles, and an indication as to which (if any) of these roles might be externalized (becoming a surface subject). A set of principles guides the mapping of lexical representations into syntactic structures. Two principles are relevant: (a) V assigns structural Case only if it has an external argument, which is an interpretation of "Burzio's generalization" (a verb Case-marks its complement only if it assigns a thematic role to its subject), and (b) an Experiencer must be projected to a higher position than a Theme DP. Belletti and Rizzi's arguments are not based on the kind of data available to children, so the analysis must be dictated in large part by the demands of UG. In this case, the relevant principles constrain all grammars, including those of OE speakers.

In (31) I list two lexical entries which typify several Old English psych-verbs.

31   (a)   *Hreowan*: Experiencer-dative; (Theme-genitive)
     (b)   *Lician*: Experiencer-dative; Theme

Hreowan "pity", *þyrstan* "thirst", and several other verbs sometimes occurred just with an Experiencer NP/DP in the dative case (*Me hreoweþ*, "I felt pity"); or they might assign two inherent Cases, yielding surface forms *Him* [dative] *ofhreow þæs mannes* [genitive], "He was sorry for the man" (29a). *Lician* "like/please" usually occurred with an Experiencer in the dative case and a Theme in the nominative: *Gode* [dative] *ne licode na heora geleafleast* [nominative], "Their faithlessness did not please God" (Ælfric, *Homilies*, xx. 71). With a lexical entry like (31b), the Theme would receive no inherent Case in initial structure. Nor could it receive a structural Case, because verbs assign structural Case only if they have an external argument (a nominative subject); this would be impossible, because the Experiencer, having inherent Case (dative), could not acquire a second Case. Therefore the Theme could receive Case only on being externalized, moving to a position governed by a finite inflectional element (i.e. becoming a subject with nominative Case).

Belletti and Rizzi (1988: §4.2) argue that a dative NP/DP in (28c) may move to a subject position, carrying along its inherent Case and therefore not receiving structural Case at S-structure; instead, nominative is assigned to the Theme NP/DP, which is adjoined to the VP. Again the arguments are based on negative data; therefore the analysis would not be learnable by children not having access to negative data, and it would have to be dictated by UG if initial structures like (30) are available. This, in turn, suggests that a dative Experiencer could also move to the subject position in Old English, and this seems to be true: dative Experiencers could show some properties of subjects. They sometimes determined the person of the verb (32a), and they could behave like regular subjects in reduced conjoined structures (32b, c), controlling the empty subject in (32c).

32   (a)   Me think we shall be strong enough. (1534, More, *Works* (1557))
     (b)   But moche now me merueilith, and well may I in sothe. (1405 *Mum and the Sothsegger* (EETS) ii I)
     (c)   Us sholde neither lakken gold ne gere, But *e* ben honoured whil we dwelten there. (ca.1374, Chaucer, *Troilus & Cressida*, IV 1523)

Allen (1986: §4.1) pointed to earlier examples and argued that they manifested an operation of coordinate subject deletion under identity with a preceding subject (33). If the understood subject of *asende* is co-indexed with *gode*, then *gode* must be construed to some degree as a subject despite the dative case ending.

33   Ac gode [dative] ne licode na heora geleafleast [nominative] . . . ac asende him to fyr of heofonum. (Ælfric, *Homilies*, xx. 71)
     "But their faithlessness did not please God, but (he) sent them fire from heaven."

Allen also argued that early ME showed "quirky subjects," where a dative NP/DP agrees with the verb and acts as a "quirky" subject (34).

34   Ne rewe [sg.] him nauht ane his sennes. (*Vices and Virtues*, ed. Holthausen, 121)
     "Let him [dative] not only regret his sins [nominative]."

So these datives must be treated as subjects.

A grammar along these lines generates a good sample of the bewildering range of contexts in which psych-verbs may occur. However, there are other possibilities. Some of these, noted by Anderson (1986), require only minor modifications: with some verbs the Experiencer is optional (*Gelomp þæt an swiþe wis mon*, "It happened that a very wise man"; *Gif him gelimpe þæt he þearfa beo*, "If it befalls him that he is destitute"); other verbs develop the option of a *hit* variant in late Old English and come to have an overt subject (*Hit me ofþincþ*, "It grieves me"; *Sore hit me forþynkeþ of þe dede*, "I repent sorely of the deed"). Others are more systematic. The Experiencer might appear in the nominative in a simple "absolutive" construction with no object: *Ic licige*, "I am pleased"; *Ic hreowe*, "I am sorry"; *Ic sceamige*, "I am ashamed." Alternatively, an object might be present: . . . *þæt þu Gode licie*, ". . . that you [nominative] please God [dative]." Furthermore, the Theme might occur in the nominative. Anderson gathered a beautiful paradigm, three examples from Ælfric, one showing the verb *hreowan* being used impersonally, one with the Theme as nominative, and one with the Experiencer as nominative; I reproduced this triplet in (29).

Anderson suggested plausibly that *hreowan*, in showing all three possibilities, represents the typical situation, and that many verbs which manifest only one or two of these possibilities in fact reveal accidental gaps in the texts. Adopting this view, one would not seek to complicate grammars in order to make them generate precisely what is attested in the writings of any given individual. The writings of, say, Bede might show only the patterns of (29a, b) for *hreowan*, not (29c), but that does not entail that Bede's grammar could not generate (29c).

Some historical linguists, many of whom have trained as philologists, have been preoccupied with describing precisely what one finds in the texts, and this preoccupation has led to analyses which simply cannot be right, because they contain grammar-specific elements which are demonstrably unattainable under normal childhood conditions. These linguists have sought textual accuracy at the expense of learnability. I discuss some approaches of this type to the case alternations with psych-verbs in Lightfoot 1991: ch. 6. Nonetheless, if one adopts Anderson's inclusive view, one still needs to account for the variation found with *hreowan* and other verbs.

A straightforward explanation of the variation and of the syntactic changes affecting these psych-verbs lies in the loss of morphological case. If the oblique cases realized abstract inherent Cases assigned by verbs and other heads, their loss meant that the inherent Cases could no longer be realized – or at least, could no longer be realized through these cases. The evidence suggests that as their overt, morphological realization was lost, so inherent Cases were lost at the abstract level. NP/DPs which used to have inherent Case came to have structural Case, and this entailed syntactic changes.

A grammar with oblique cases would generate forms like (29a), given a lexical entry like (31a). Inherent Case would be assigned to the Experiencer and the Theme, realized as dative and genitive suffixes respectively. Similarly, it would generate (35).

35 (a) Him hungreð.
        "He [dative] is hungry."
   (b) Me thynketh I heare.
        me [dative] thinks I hear.
        "I think I hear."
   (c) Him chaunst to meete upon the way A faithlesse Sarazin. (1590, Spenser, *Fairy Queen*, I. ii. 12)
   (d) Mee likes ... go see the hoped heaven. (1557, *Tottel's Misc.* (Arber) 124)

Nouns with an inherent Case could not surface with a structural Case, because nouns have only one Case. If a NP/DP has inherent Case, it has no reason to move to another NP/DP position.

A grammar with no morphological means to realize inherent Case lost those inherent Cases. Consequently, the lexical entries of (31) etc. lost any case specification. Now the NP/DPs had to surface in positions in which they would receive structural Case, governed by I, V, or P. This entailed that one NP/DP would move to the specifier of IP, where it receives Case (governed by I). A verb may assign a structural Case (accusative) only if it has an external argument ("Burzio's generalization"). So the Experiencer NP/DPs in (35), which formerly had inherent Case realized as a dative, came to occur in a nominative position: *He hungers, I think ...*, *He chanced ...*, *I like ...*, etc. With a verb assigning two thematic roles, as one moved to a subject (nominative) position, so the other could be assigned a structural accusative (governed by V), generating forms like *The priest* [nominative] *pitied the man* [accusative].

The account predicts that the new grammar would be manifested by new nominative cases, and that new accusatives would occur only when nominatives have already appeared. There could be no shift to structural accusatives in an impersonal construction. On the version of "Burzio's generalization" adopted, structural Case may be assigned only by a verb with an external (i.e. nominative) subject. Consequently, if a verb assigned inherent (dative) Case to its Experiencer, then the NP/DP could not be externalized to a position in which it would receive a second Case; so the verb could not, in turn, assign structural (accusative) Case. Only when the Experiencer could not have its inherent Case realized with a dative might it be externalized, and only then would the verb be able to assign accusative Case. In (29c) the Experiencer is externalized, but the verb continues to assign genitive Case; later it came to assign a structural accusative.

This account also predicts that a verb assigning inherent Case to its arguments would not occur in the passive agreeing with an externalized nominative; such constructions would occur only after the loss of inherent Case. Before that, inherent Case would be assigned to the NP/DP even if the verb were in the passive form, and the NP/DP would not be able to acquire a second Case. David Denison (1990) shows that although some Old English impersonal verbs occur in what look like passive constructions, they are not in fact so. Instead, one finds "impersonal passives" like (36).

36   Ac him næs þære bene getiðod. (Ælfric, *Catholic Homilies*, II, 35. 302. 115)
     but to-him [dative] not-was that prayer [genitive/dative] granted
     "But he was not granted this request."

Consider now the verb *like*, having the lexical entry (31b). By far the most common pattern for *like*, certainly after the shift to verb–object order, was Experiencer [dative]–verb–Theme [nominative]. *Lician* was a common verb with over 400 citations in the *Concordance to Old English*, and Denison (1990) notes that the type with a dative Experiencer and nominative Theme made up "the overwhelming majority, to the extent that it is doubtful whether the others are grammatical at all." If the Theme has no inherent Case, then the only possibility is for it to move to receive nominative Case.

Now consider a child of the generation without morphological dative case. This child would analyze such forms as Experiencer–verb–Theme, with no inherent Cases. Since the Experiencer often had subject properties, as noted in the context of (32)–(34), was in the usual subject position to the left of the verb, and actually was the subject despite the dative case, the most natural analysis for a new caseless child would be to treat the Experiencer as the externalized subject, hence with nominative Case. The reanalysis of the Experiencer as a subject might be data-driven in this way, or it might simply follow from UG under Belletti and Rizzi's assumption that an Experiencer is projected to a higher position than a Theme (see above). In any case, the reanalysis of an Experiencer as a subject would permit the verb, in turn, to assign accusative Case to the Theme. So externalization of the Experiencer is the most natural option for the new caseless child exposed to Experiencer–verb–Theme sentences, and assignment of nominative Case to the Theme in an adjoined position is automatically eliminated.

This account should be interpreted in terms of grammars spreading through a population of speakers (see section 4.6). There were grammars with morphological case and grammars without. This kind of variation entails that once a grammar without dative case is attested in late Old English or early Middle English, one might find any psych-verb with nominative and accusative NP/DPs. Similarly, as dative cases ceased to be attested anywhere, one would expect to find no more verbs lacking a nominative subject. Beyond these outer limits, the diglossic account does not predict what the texts will manifest at any particular time while the two grammars coexist. Generally, the old conservative grammars with morphological case do not manifest verbs with an accusative Case without a nominative subject; nor would they manifest the indirect passives of (27). Conversely, grammars with no morphological case show psych-verbs with structural accusatives, hence passives with such verbs, indirect passives, and PPs instead of former genitives. These correlations seem to be correct, but the coexistence of two grammars may influence the writing of any individual, and certainly the scribal and editorial transmission, and it is not always possible to distinguish the two systems as cleanly as one would like. It is clear that individuals may operate with more than one grammatical system in an internalized diglossia, although the limits to this capacity are not understood.

A striking property of the loss of the old patterns is its gradualness. The morphological case system was lost over the period from the tenth to the thirteenth century. What this means for us is that the two grammars coexisted for several hundred years. The first nominative-accusative forms are found in late Old English, but impersonal verbs without nominative subjects continue to be attested until the middle of the sixteenth century. The gradualness of the change is to be expected if the loss of inherent Case is a function of the loss of morphological dative case. As the case system was eroded and as caseless grammars spread through the population, one finds many kinds of odd construction in the texts.

Not only does one find verbs assigning different cases (20, 24), but Traugott (1992) even points to an early instance of coordinated NP/DPs with different cases (37).

37   ... [ða ðe þæt tempel and þæra goda gymdon. (Ælfric, *Catholic Homilies*, II, 38. 281. 33)
      those that that temple [accusative] and those gods [genitive] cared for
      "... those who cared for the temple and the gods."

Unless somebody can give a systematic account of why cases are used in this way, it is probably best to treat such forms as aberrations of transitional texts, in fact ungrammatical. Short of this extreme, we know that even in grammars where morphological case remains functional, some thematic roles may not have a case associated with them: e.g. the standard lexical entry for *lician*, where the Theme has no associated case (31b). The paradigm of (29) suggests that while some grammars have a lexical entry for *hreowan* as (31a), yielding (29a), others may have no case associated with the Theme, yielding (29b), and others may have no case associated with the Experiencer, yielding (29c). These are all points of variation within grammars, and people may operate with more than one grammar, including a range of lexical entries. Allen (1995: 169ff) brings a lot of philological skill to this problem and tries to disentangle the actual case system that particular writers must have had (in particular, the scribes of the Peterborough version of the *Anglo-Saxon Chronicle*), picking her way carefully through thickets of distorting textual evidence. Cecily Clark, who edited the *Chronicle* in 1970, believed that the confusion of forms in the section dealing with the years 1122–31 was due to the fact that the scribe was using a system of case marking which he did not actually control. In any case, there is certainly no reason to take the occurrence of some form in some text to indicate that it manifests the grammar of the original author of that text, or anybody else's grammar, for that matter.

As the case system was lost, there is much in the texts that we cannot explain, but some things we can understand. If we view the oblique morphological cases as the realization of abstract inherent Cases, then we can see that the loss of the morphological cases entailed a range of syntactic changes. These include not only the new split genitives discussed in the last section, but also the loss of the so-called impersonal psych-verbs and the rise of nominative-accusative forms. I have offered a minimal account of the changes: the oblique cases were lost and ceased to realize the abstract, inherent Cases. On the theory that I have sketched, this entailed a variety of surface manifestations, and we have an explanation for why certain phenomena clustered in the way they did.

5.4   The Loss and Origin of Case Systems

In the last two sections we have investigated some syntactic consequences of the loss of the morphological case system in English. By postulating an abstract, syntactic Case system, and by treating the oblique cases as a means of realizing the abstract Cases, we have been able to relate some curious-looking syntactic changes to the loss of morphological case, and to provide some tight explanations for the syntactic changes. This presupposes that morphological cases may be lost in the course of history, which is obviously the fact of the matter, and we have seen that this loss takes place despite the fact that it has a wide range of syntactic consequences.

The usual story about the loss of case in English is that it was destroyed by phonological changes. Richard Hogg (1992) tracks the erosion of case endings in comprehensive detail. The case system of Old English is already somewhat degenerate, simplified from what presumably existed at the time of Proto-Old English and the still earlier common Germanic. There were changes in the stress system, so that many word-final vowels became unstressed and were reduced to schwa. This entailed that many final vowels become indistinguishable, so many case distinctions were lost. Also word-final nasal consonants were eliminated. Take those two changes together, and one has an explanation of why all the distinctions of the noun endings in table 5.1 were eliminated except those suffixes ending in -s, the genitive singular of nouns in the general masculine (*stān*) and neuter (*scip*) classes, and the nominative-accusative plural of nouns in the general masculine class. Each of these -s forms was extended to all paradigms, so that by the end of the Middle English period we had the modern system (38).

38	(a)	nom. sg.	*stone,*	*ship,*	*tale,*	*name*
	(b)	gen. sg.	*stones,*	*shippes,*	*tales,*	*names*
	(c)	plural	*stones,*	*shippes,*	*tales,*	*names*

As the case system was lost, the texts show some chaos in the case endings attested, as we have seen. At least we have historical records which tell us something about the way in which a case system might be lost, even if those records need to be interpreted with skill.

We also have some information about the way in which case systems arise, although records are not as rich as we would like. Blake (1994: ch. 6) considers material from a range of languages, which suggests that case endings may be formed by reanalyzing serial verbs as "adpositions" and then as case endings. A serial verb is one which occurs with another verb and carries no tense, mood, or aspect marking of its own. Blake gives some examples from Thai (39).

39 (a) Thân cà bin maa krungthêep.
       he   will fly come Bangkok
       "He will fly to Bangkok."

   (b) Thân cà bin càak krungthêep.
       he   will fly leave Bangkok
       "He will fly from Bangkok."

The second verb has no inflections and no independent subject, and it is functionally equivalent to a preposition. Adpositions have developed in many languages, particularly in West Africa, Southeast Asia, and Oceania. They show some general properties, tending to express notions of locality, instrument, purpose, beneficiary, and accompaniment. There is also some evidence that nouns and adverbial particles may develop into adpositions and then into conventional case endings. Mark Hale tells me that there is plenty of evidence from the history of Baltic that nouns and adverbial particles move precisely along this path and end up expressing things like locality and instrument.

Clearly children may be led to analyze structures differently from their parents, and this is a common mechanism of grammatical change, as we have seen. Case systems may arise and change by this mechanism, and we can see this in the development of some grammars with ergative cases. An ergative-absolutive system assigns one case (ergative) to the subject of a transitive verb and another case (absolutive) to the subject of a transitive verb and the direct object of a transitive verb. So Tongan marks the subject of a transitive verb with a preposition *'e* and the absolutives with *'a*: in (40) the subject of "killed" has an ergative marker, while the other nouns have the absolutive.

40 (a) Na'e tāmate'i 'e   Tēvita 'a   Kōlaiate.
         Past kill   Erg. David Abs. Goliath
         "David killed Goliath."
    (b) Na'e lea   'a   Tolu
         Past speak Abs. Tolu
         "Tolu spoke."

It is sometimes argued that ergative-absolutive languages are fundament-ally different from nominative-accusative languages, but Stephen Anderson (1992: ch. 13) has a nice discussion of the emergence of ergative case systems and shows that this cannot be true. The problem posed by ergative languages is that the morphological categories, absolutive and ergative, do not match the usual syntactic categories, subject and object. In this they dif-fer from nominative-accusative languages, where there is a one-to-one match: nominatives are generally subjects, and objects are generally accusative. He notes two fundamental facts about almost all ergative languages: (a) genu-inely syntactic principles systematically treat the DPs we expect to be sub-jects as constituting a unitary category, regardless of the transitivity of the verb: regardless of their case, they are possible antecedents for reflexives (and cannot be reflexive themselves); they represent positions for an empty, understood subject (technically "controlled PRO"); they may be conjoined with another subject, etc.; (b) so-called ergative languages are almost always "split" systems, showing ergative case systems only under certain circumstances (e.g. with perfect aspect or past tenses), with nominative-accusative elsewhere. In light of this, Anderson treats ergative-absolutive languages as cut from the same cloth as nominative-accusative languages, but with a superficial discrepancy between syntactic and morphological categories.[13]

There are various ways in which this might be implemented. One might take a direct object and the subject of an intransitive verb to move from within the VP to the specifier of the immediately dominating functional category, perhaps an agreement element (41a), while the subject of a transitive verb must move further, to the specifier of the next functional category, perhaps Tense (41b). In a nominative-accusative language, the subject of an intransitive verb moves on to the specifier of TP, but that position is not available to an intransitive subject in an ergative-absolutive language.

41   (a) $_{AgrP}[_{Spec}[DP_i]$ Agr $_{VP}[e_i$ verb]]
     (b) $_{TP}[_{Spec}[DP_j]$ T $_{AgrP}[_{Spec}[DP_i]$ Agr $_{VP}[e_j\ e_i$ verb]]]

Anderson does things differently. He takes agreement to be a syntactic operation which copies features of a NP/DP onto the morphosyntactic representation of the verb, first the object NP/DP, then the subject NP/DP, yielding representations like (42). Then, in an ergative language, a NP/DP which is co-indexed with the *outer layer* of a two (or more)-layer structure (i.e. a transitive subject (42b)) is marked ergative. So he treats ergativity as a morphological, not a syntactic, phenomenon.

42   (a) $_v[V\ dp_i]$
     (b) $_v[[V\ dp_i]\ dp_j]$

The question then is: what would force a child into an ergative analysis? Anderson deals with the closely related question of how such a system might arise historically.

One scenario is that a verb–subject–object language has a rule marking subjects with a -s ending, leaving objects unmarked (43). If such a language undergoes a phonological change whereby final obstruents are lost before a pause, this might affect many final -s markers on intransitive subjects (because they would be sentence-final), but not transitive subjects. So the emergent system would have only transitive subjects marked with -s, which would thus become an ergative marker rather than nominative. Anderson suggests that the emergence of ergativity in Chinook comes close to this scenario.

43   VSO: (a)   V DPs   (b)   V DPs DP

A well-attested source for ergative morphology is the reanalysis of earlier passive constructions. (44) has a notional object with the same case as that of the subject of an intransitive verb, and the notional subject has a special marker *by*; the verb agrees with the notional object – hence all the characteristics of ergative morphology. We don't analyze English passive sentences this way, because they are related to underlying active ones. But if that active–passive relationship were to become unmotivated, sentences like (44) would be indistinguishable from ergatives.

44   They were accosted by him on the way to the subway.

Anderson argues that this is essentially what happened in several unrelated languages: originally passive constructions lost their relation to active forms, and as a result their surface form has been reanalyzed as ergative morphology rather than passive syntax. He cites work by Sandy Chung (1978) showing such a development in Tongan. She took nominative-accusative languages like Maori to reflect properties of Proto-Polynesian: there the passive construction had a much wider distribution than in English; it was much more common, and even obligatory in certain contexts. If passives became still more common in Tongan, effectively obligatory in many structures, the corresponding active sentences would simply have ceased to exist as surface forms. What Chung took to be the syntactically derived status of the "passives" became opaque, and the formal markers were reinterpreted. This represents a new parameter setting, and the evidence suggests that it was triggered by increasingly common passives; that, in turn, was a change in the triggering experience, reflecting not a prior change in available grammars, but rather a change in the ways in which the old grammars were used, a change in the frequency of certain constructions. Anderson goes on to consider instances of "split" ergative systems, ergative case markings being used only with, say, perfect aspect; in each instance he shows that existing structures – e.g. past tenses or possessives – are reanalyzed as a result of shifts, sometimes quite minor, in grammar use.

Grammatical changes of this type are incomprehensible if one views ergative languages as fundamentally different from nominative-accusative languages. On the other hand, if one views ergative systems, or at least a significant class of ergative systems, as involving a parameter setting for case assignment along the lines of what was said in connection with (41) and (42), it is straightforward to understand how such systems might emerge, and why split systems are so common. Specifically, if this is the shape of the parameter, then it is easy to see how trigger experiences might have changed in such a way as to give rise to such grammars. This, in turn, enables us to postulate a plausible trigger experience for (split) ergative systems, and I take it that this is a major goal of our enterprise. So we have learned something about the parameter underlying ergative case systems, and we have seen how some morphological ergative systems might emerge historically as a result of haphazard shifts in a language's PLD.

The split nature of many ergative-absolutive case systems looks like another Rube Goldberg feature of grammars, but we can understand how they might have arisen historically. Their emergence is contingent, dependent on the particulars of earlier grammars. Again we see a chaotic system: we have no basis for predicting the rise of ergative cases, but, when they emerge, we can understand why that development took place, and why they developed where they did.

In this chapter we have looked at some syntactic consequences of the loss of morphological case, and we have asked how case systems might originate in languages. We have seen that as morphological case was lost, so other things happened. The changes are catastrophic, in that they come in clusters. The fact that there were domino effects did not prevent the cases from being lost. Indeed, we have argued that the domino effects had to happen on the theories that we have discussed. This means that we have explanations for the way in which the changes took place, for certain details of those changes, and for the way in which phenomena cluster. If children fail to find morphological cases, then they converge on a quite different grammar; we have been able to show why the new grammar has the form that it does. We have seen what can happen when there is a minimal difference in trigger experiences, when everything remains constant except that morphological case is lost and grammars cease to have that means of realizing abstract inherent Case.

Again, we find children converging on a grammar quite different from earlier ones. All this would be quite mysterious if we viewed language acquisition as a matter of children converging on a grammar which generates the input to which they are exposed. This leads us to adopt a model of acquisition in which children seek pre-specified grammatical cues and do not necessarily match their input. We proceed now to that model.

Notes

1   *Of* phrases occur exactly where PPs generally occur, as the complement or
    adjunct to a noun, verb, or adjective (cf. *book about linguistics, go to Rio,
    angry at him*). For that reason, *of* cannot Case-mark *John* in (i) and thereby
    save the structures; PPs are not permitted in this position.

    (i) (a)   DP seems [John to be smart]   *seems of John to be smart
         (b)   DP was expected [John to win]   *was expected of John to win

    This suggests that *of* is present in the initial structure of (8b), and that the two
    initial structures (8a) and (8b) are equivalent semantically (Lightfoot 1991).
    Chomsky implements things somewhat differently and allows *of* to be inserted
    to save an otherwise un-Case-marked NP/DP, as indicated below in the main
    text. Then a question arises: why may *of* not be inserted to save the structures
    of (i)? Chomsky's answer is that *seems* and *expected* have no thematic relation
    to *John*, and therefore may not assign inherent Case.

2   The relationship is a little complex. Chomsky (1986, 1995: ch. 1) follows a
    suggestion by Joseph Aoun (1985) and takes Case as a condition on visibility
    for thematic role assignment in Logical Form (LF). This involves making
    nouns assign Case inherently. Inherent Case is assigned in initial structure and
    is associated with thematic role assignment (see n. 3).

3   Inherent Case is assigned in initial structure, prior to syntactic movement,
    and is linked to thematic roles, whereas structural Case is assigned after all
    syntactic movement has taken place. If NP/DPs have one, and only one, Case,
    then a NP/DP with inherent Case may not move to another Case-marked
    position (I leave aside the ill-understood matter of "quirky case" in (34) and
    elsewhere).

    This idea of movement being forced by considerations of Case led to a
    wider theory within the Minimalist Program, according to which movement
    takes place only where required by general principles. So an inherently Case-
    marked NP/DP has no reason to move to another Case-marked position, and
    therefore may not do so.

4   The material in this section originated in joint work with Elizabeth Wallace.
    Cynthia Allen, Olga Fischer, and Willem Koopman provided extremely helpful
    comments, which forced me to rethink things fundamentally.

5   Modern English has a wrinkle. It is a little more complex, in that Case is
    realized differently on either side of the N: as possessive *'s* to the left and as *of*
    to the right, *of* being inserted in the course of the derivation. On this approach
    The city's destruction and *Destruction of the city* have the same initial struc-
    ture (8a); (8b), with the preposition *of*, does not exist as an initial structure.
    The city has Case in both positions, but it is realized differently.

6   As the case system was lost, the genitive ending -*s* was reanalyzed as some-
    thing else, a Case-marking clitic. If *'s* comes to be a clitic in Middle English,
    which Case-marks NP/DPs, this might explain why "group genitives" begin to

appear only at that time, as Allen argued. Until then, group genitive DPs would not have been Case-marked in an expression like *My uncle from Cornwall cat. It is not clear why exactly this should be so, but it might be due to some adjacency requirement on Case marking: a head, like cat, needs to be adjacent to a noun that it Case-marks, like uncle. Allen's analysis also predicts Jespersen's observation that splitting was the universal practice (above, main text) until the clitic became available.

It is possible that there was another reanalysis of the genitive ending, yielding the his genitives which were current in the sixteenth and seventeenth centuries: Poines his brother (Shakespeare, 2 Henry IV, II. iv. 308), For Jesus Christ his sake (1662 Book of Common Prayer), meaning "Poines' brother," "For Jesus Christ's sake," etc. The genitive ending in -s was sometimes spelled his, and this form occurs even with females (Mrs. Sands his maid (OED, 1607)) and is juxtaposed with genitive endings: Job's patience, Moses his meekness, and Abraham's faith (OED, 1568).

7 Nunnally (1985: 21) finds no genitival of phrases in his study of the Old English translation of St Matthew's Gospel (of was used frequently to show origin or agency, best translated then by modern from or by).

8 Verbs and prepositions may also assign structural accusative Case, but in addition it is possible that some of the morphological accusatives may realize abstract inherent Cases. I leave aside that possibility here.

9 Exceptions are like, near, and worth. These have the comparative and superlative forms characteristic of adjectives and may be modified by very.

10 There used to be some controversy about the dates of the first indirect passives, but this has been resolved. See Lightfoot 1991: 121–2 for discussion. If prepositional passives came in so much earlier than indirect passives and before transitive adjectives were lost, it might be argued that Old English prepositions did not assign inherent Case (see ibid. 123).

11 All of this is discussed in more detail in ibid., ch. 5.

12 By far the most comprehensive treatment is Allen 1995.

13 There is a vast literature on ergative languages. Bernard Comrie (1978) offers an accessible account of ergative systems and some of the analytical problems that they raise. Dixon (1994) provides a full survey of ergativity splits. He estimates that one quarter of the world's languages have ergative properties, and he discusses changes whereby ergative-absolutive systems emerge from nominative-accusative systems, and vice versa. Alice Harris (1985: chs 14, 15) tracks changes in ergative systems in Georgian and related languages.

6

Cue-Based Acquisition and Change in Grammars

Grammars, in our perspective, are mental entities which arise in the mind/ brain of individuals when they are exposed as children to some triggering and shaping experience. In that case, the central mystery for historical linguists is why they have anything to study: why do languages have histories? Why do changes take place, and why are languages not generally stable? In particular, why do changes sometimes take place abruptly and catastrophically, as we have argued they must? If people produce utterances corresponding fairly closely to the capacity of their grammars, then children exposed to that production would be expected to converge on the same grammar. This is what one would expect if grammars have structural stability, as we have claimed, and children are not "trigger happy," developing different grammars whenever their trigger experiences differ just a little. In that case, diachronic change would be expected only if there were some major disruption due to population movement.

6.1 Models of Learnability

Not only is this what one would expect naively and pre-theoretically; it is also what many learnability models would lead one to expect.[1] For example, Chomsky's *Aspects of the Theory of Syntax* (1965), now a classic, viewed children as endowed with a metric evaluating grammars which can generate the primary data to which they are exposed, along with appropriate structural descriptions for those data. The evaluation metric picks the grammar which conforms to the invariant principles of UG and is most successful in generating those data and those structural descriptions. The child selects a grammar which matches his or her input as closely as possible. Again, if the data and the associated structural descriptions to which the child is exposed correspond fairly closely to the grammatical capacity of some older individual, one would expect the child's evaluation metric to select the same grammar as that older individual's. This expectation is reinforced if the space of available grammars has scattered peaks, as in the *Aspects* view, and if many aspects of the input have no effect on the mature system – for example, the order in which the input is presented to the child.

The same point holds for more recent models. Gibson and Wexler (1994) posit a Triggering Learning Algorithm (TLA), under which the child-learner uses grammars to analyze incoming sentences and eventually converges on the correct grammar. They distinguish global and local triggers, but both are sentence types (p. 409). If the child-learner cannot analyze a given sentence with the current grammar, then he or she follows a certain procedure to change one of the current parameter settings and then tries to reprocess the sentence using the new set of parameter values. If analysis is now possible, then the new parameter value is adopted, at least for a while. So the TLA is error-driven and permits the child to pinpoint which parameter setting is incorrect when the learner's grammar does not give the right results. There is much to be said about the way in which this model works, and Dresher (1998) has some illuminating discussion; but what is crucial here is that the model has the child seeking grammars which permit analysis of incoming data, where the data consist of more or less unanalyzed sentences. Gibson and Wexler's table 3 (1994: 424), here reproduced as table 6.1, correlates three parameter settings (specifier-final/initial, complement-final/initial, +/– verb-second (V2)) and sets of data (listed here in terms of primitives like subject, verb, first object, second object). When exposed to some data set (right-hand column), the child selects the appropriate grammar (left-hand column), although it is not easy for the child to know which data set she is exposed to.

Clark (1992) offers a similar kind of model, but one which differs from that of Gibson and Wexler in that the child cannot pinpoint the source of a grammar's failure and revise particular parameter settings. Clark posits a Darwinian competition between grammars needed to parse sets of sentences. All grammars allowed by UG are available to each child, and some grammars are used more than others in parsing what the child hears. A "genetic algorithm" picks those grammars whose elements are activated most often. A Fitness Measure compares how well each grammar fares, and the fittest grammars go on to reproduce in the next generation, while the least fit die out. Eventually the candidate grammars are narrowed to the most fit, and the child converges on the correct grammar.[2] Clark and Roberts (1993) used this model to give an account of changes affecting the

Table 6.1   Gibson and Wexler's grammar–language pairs

Parameter settings	Data in defined grammar
Spec-final Comp-final −V2 (VOS)	V S, V O S, V O1 O2 S Aux V S, Aux V O S, Aux V O1 O2 S, Adv V S Adv V O S, Adv V O1 O2 S, Adv Aux V S Adv Aux V O S, Adv Aux V O1 O2 S
Spec-final Comp-final +V2 (VOS + V2)	S V, S V O, O V S, S V O1 O2, O1 V O2 S, O2 V O1 S S Aux V, S Aux V O, O Aux V S S Aux V O1 O2, O1 Aux V O2 S, O2 Aux V O1 S Adv V S, Adv V O S, Adv V O1 O2 S Adv Aux V S, Adv Aux V O S, Adv Aux V O1 O2 S
Spec-final Comp-first −V2 (OVS)	V S, O V S, O2 O1 V S V Aux S, O V Aux S, O2 O1 V Aux S, Adv V S Adv O V S, Adv O2 O1 V S, Adv V Aux S Adv O V Aux S, Adv O2 O1 V, Aux S
Spec-final Comp-first +V2 (OVS + V2)	S V, O V S, S V O, S V O2 O1, O1 V O2 S, O2 V O1 S S Aux V, S Aux O V, O Aux V S S Aux O2 O1 V, O1 Aux O2 V S, O2 Aux O1 V S Adv V S, Adv V O S, Adv V O2 O1 S Adv Aux V S, Adv Aux O V S, Adv Aux O2 O1 V S
Spec-first Comp-final −V2 (SVO)	S V, S V O, S V O1 O2 S Aux V, S Aux V O, S Aux V O1 O2, Adv S V Adv S V O, Adv S V O1 O2, Adv S Aux V Adv S Aux V O, Adv S Aux V O1 O2
Spec-first Comp-final +V2 (SVO + V2)	S V, S V O, O V S, S V O1 O2, O1 V S O2, O2 V S O1 S Aux V, S Aux V O, O Aux S V S Aux V O1 O2, O1 Aux S V O2, O2 Aux S V O1, Adv V S Adv V S O, Adv V S O1 O2, Adv Aux S V Adv Aux S V O, Adv Aux S V O1 O2
Spec-first Comp-first −V2 (SOV)	S V, S O V, S O2 O1 V S V Aux, S O V Aux, S O2 O1 V Aux, Adv S V Adv S O V, Adv S O2 O1 V, Adv S V Aux Adv S O V Aux, Adv S O2 O1 V Aux
Spec-first Comp-first +V2 (SOV + V2)	S V, S V O, O V S, S V O2 O1, O1 V S O2, O2 V S O1 S Aux V, S Aux O V, O Aux S V S Aux O2 O1 V, O1 Aux S O2 V, O2 Aux S O1 V Adv V S, Adv V S O, Adv V S O2 O1 Adv Aux S V, Adv Aux S O V, Adv Aux S O2 O1 V

verb-second properties of early French, by allowing an arbitrary degree of misconvergence by children.

What these models have in common is that learners eventually match their input, in the sense that they select grammars which generate the sentences of the input. It is only accurate grammars of this type which are submitted to Chomsky's (1965) evaluation metric, and Gibson and Wexler's error-driven children react to inaccurate grammars by seeking new parameter settings until a sufficient degree of accuracy is achieved. Models of this type can characterize instances of language stability straightforwardly. The child converges on a grammar which analyzes the input successfully, where the input consists of sets of sentences. In that case, the grammar will resemble closely the grammar or grammars which generate that input. Such models can also handle cases of mixed input under conditions of population movement. There again the child is presented with a set of data, in this case data yielded by diverse grammars; he or she converges on a grammar which is most successful in generating that data set, sometimes a grammar quite different from any of those in the previous generation. This would be a case of grammar change, and the new grammar might yield structural descriptions and some sentences which differ from those of the input; but the new grammar would result from the child's effort to match the input sentences as closely as possible.

These are not *pure* input-matching models, of course, of the type advocated by MacWhinney and Bates (1990), in which it is mysterious why children should ever produce non-adult forms in any systematic way. Clark, Gibson, and Wexler's children are not dependent only on the input; they operate in a space defined by UG. Consequently, each intermediate stage for the developing child is represented by some set of UG-defined parameter settings, and that set may generate non-adult forms.

However, it is a fact that sometimes children do not match their input at any stage, including the final stage. One instance would be abrupt, catastrophic change, discussed in the last two chapters. Consequently, it will not be productive to insist that successful language acquisition always has children converging on grammars which generate the sentences that they hear.

It is hard to see how these input-matching models can succeed when children are exposed to unusual amounts of artificial or degenerate data, which in fact are not matched. In particular, it is hard to see how they could account for the early development of creole languages, as described by Bickerton (1984, 1998) and others. In these descriptions, early creole speakers are not matching their input, which typically consists to a large degree of pidgin data. Pidgins are primitive communication systems, cobbled together from fragments of two or more languages. They are not them-selves natural languages, and they tend not to last long, before giving way to a creole with all the hallmarks of a natural grammar. The first speakers of creoles go way beyond their input in some ways, and in other ways fail to reproduce what they heard from their models, arriving at grammars which generate sentences and structural descriptions quite different from those of the input.

Let us call this the "abrupt" view of creolization (following Thomason and Kaufman 1988). There is a dramatic discrepancy between what early creole speakers hear in childhood and what their mature grammars eventu-ally characterize as well-formed, much greater than in noncreole contexts. Bickerton deals with plantation creoles, where new languages appear to be "formed in the space of a single generation" (1998). He argues, surely correctly, that situations in which "the normal transmission of well-formed language data from one generation to the next is most drastically disrupted" tell us something about the innate component and how it determines acquisition. They certainly show that children do not always proceed by converging on a grammar which matches the input.

The abrupt view of creolization is more controversial than it should be. It offends a commitment to the proposition that languages generally change only gradually, which we discussed in chapter 4. This commitment is linked to a highly data-driven view of language acquisition, and it is widely and deeply held, including by creolists. Creolists committed to gradualism – for example, Carden and Stewart (1988) – insist that creoles emerge gradually as a result of changes introduced primarily by adults, as they re-lexify their own languages. However, if this is generally true, if this is most of the story, and if creolization for the most part mirrors adult second language learning and is not abrupt and instantiated by chil-dren, then there is little reason for theoreticians to be interested in the phenomenon. Our data about the early stages of creole languages are gen-erally not very rich, and if one is interested in adult second language learn-ing, one is probably better off refining theories in the light of better data sources.

Here I want to argue the following: that existing models of learnability and existing models of language change commit us to insisting that lan-guages are basically stable. This conforms to the views of some historians that change is inherently piecemeal and gradual. But a better model of learnability enables us to better understand historical change. On this model we shift our focus from language change to change in grammars, and we expect grammar change to be abrupt, sudden, and what in chapter 4 I called "catastrophic." Our learnability model, in turn, will allow us to capture the contingent nature of historical change and to avoid the excessively principled accounts of change offered by some historians.

I shall make some more detailed claims about how grammars are acquired and offer a different model of acquisition. I shall discuss the nature of the experience which triggers the development of grammars, arguing that children scan their environment for designated structures or "cues," and that they are not influenced by the set of sentences generated by their grammars. Indeed, there are no independent "parameters"; rather, some cues are found in all grammars, and some are found only in certain grammars, the latter constituting points of variation.

Ironically, the best-worked-out model of parameter setting comes from phonology and the work of Dresher and Kaye (1990). The notion of binary parameters has not played an extensive role in the phonological literature, but Dresher and Kaye identified parameters for stress systems, a rather well-studied area of phonology. Furthermore, they developed a "cue-based" theory of acquisition, now clarified, elaborated, and generalized by Dresher (1998). On this view, UG specifies not only a set of parameters, but for each parameter a cue. I amend this view slightly and say that cues which are realized only in certain grammars constitute the parameters, the points of variation between grammars. A cue is some kind of structure, an element of grammar, which is derived from the input. The cues are to be found in the mental representations which result from hearing, understanding, and "parsing" utterances. As a child understands an utterance, even partially, he or she has some kind of mental representation of the utterance. These are partial parses, which may differ from the full parses that an adult has. The learner scans those representations, derived from the input, and seeks the designated cues.

The child scans the linguistic environment for cues only in simple syntactic domains; this is the "degree-0 learnability" of some earlier work (Lightfoot 1991, 1994). Learners do not try to match the input; rather, they seek certain abstract structures derived from the input, looking only at structurally simple domains, and they act on this without regard to the final result. That is, a child seeks cues and may or may not find them, regardless of what the emerging grammar can generate; the output of the grammar is entirely a by-product of the cues that the child finds, and the success of the grammar is in no way based on the set of sentences that it generates, unlike in input-matching models. The child's triggering experience, then, is best viewed as a set of abstract structures manifested in the mental representations which result from parsing utterances; some of those representations constitute partial parses, which lack some of the information in mature, adult parses.

Dresher (1998) illustrates the cue-based model of acquisition with some phonological parameters. The essential feature is that a cue-based learner does not try to match target input forms, but uses them as sources of cues. The trigger consists not of sets of sentences, but rather of partially analyzed syntactic structures, elements of the internal grammar, "I-language;" these are the mental representations resulting from parsing utterances. So cues are intensional elements, grammar fragments. A cue-based learner sets a specifier-head parameter (specifier precedes/follows its head) on the basis of exposure to data which must be analyzed with a specifier preceding its head – e.g. $[_{Spec}[\text{John's}]\ _N[\text{hat}]]$. This parameter can only be set, of course, when the child has a partial analysis which treats *John's* and *hat* as separate words, the latter a head noun, etc. In this way, the order in which parameters appear to be set, the "learning path" (Lightfoot 1989), reflects dependencies among cues and follows from their internal architecture. To take another example, exposure to a phrase *student of linguistics* may trigger an analysis which generates complements to the right of their head noun, but this can happen only when the child already knows that *student* is a noun which assigns a thematic role to the phrasal element *linguistics*.

Some version of this cue-based approach is implicitly assumed in some work on acquisition – for example, in the work of Nina Hyams (1986, 1996) and in my own work (Lightfoot 1989, 1991). More recently, Janet Fodor has developed similar ideas, developing the parsing devices needed for a child to identify "structural triggers" – what I have called "cues."

The idea that language acquisition is cue-based and does not proceed directly by input matching results to some extent from work on abrupt language change, where children arrive at grammars which generate data quite different from grammars of an earlier generation. In the next sections I shall suggest that the model gives us a way of understanding two syntactic changes in the history of English. Then I shall turn to the analysis of creoles and signed languages.

The next two sections deal with two well-studied catastrophic changes affecting the history of English, and I shall give a cue-based account of the changes. I will discuss the changes as theory-neutrally as possible, but the change involving V to I raises questions about the relationship between morphological and syntactic properties and needs to be treated in the context of models which postulate a substantive connection between morphology and syntax.

These two changes are partially understood, and they illustrate how the study of a change is intimately connected, on this approach, with work on grammatical theory and with work on cue-based acquisition. They also illustrate what further work is needed for a fuller understanding.

6.2 Cue-Based Acquisition and Loss of Verb-Second

Verb-second languages, like Dutch, characteristically show the finite verb in second position in simple clauses. It doesn't matter how the utterance begins; a finite verb always occurs in second position. The verb is preceded by any phrasal category: a subject NP/DP (1a), a direct object NP/DP (1b), a PP (1c), or an adjective phrase (AP) (1d, e). The verb may not occur in any position other than second (1f).

1 (a) $_{DP}$[Wij] $_V$zagen vele studenten in Amsterdam.
        "We saw many students in Amsterdam."
   (b) $_{DP}$[Vele studenten] $_V$zagen wij in Amsterdam.
   (c) $_{PP}$[In Amsterdam] $_V$zagen wij vele studenten.
   (d) $_{AP}$[Boos over de regering] $_V$zijn de studenten.
        "The students are angry about the government."
   (e) $_{AP}$[Vaak] $_V$zagen wij vele studenten in Amsterdam.
        "Often we saw many students in Amsterdam."
   (f) *$_{PP}$[In Amsterdam] wij $_V$zagen vele studenten.
        *$_{AP}$[Vaak] wij vele studenten in Amsterdam $_V$zagen.

The most familiar verb-second languages are asymmetric and show verb-second order in simple, matrix clauses only, while embedded clauses usually have the verb in some other position. In Dutch, the embedded verb occurs in clause-final position (2), but other verb-second languages like Swedish have the verb in medial position – Dutch grammars have object–verb order, and Swedish have verb–object.

2 (a) . . . dat wij vele studenten in Amsterdam $_V$zagen
        . . . that we many students in Amsterdam saw
   (b) . . . dat de studenten boos over de regering $_V$zijn
        . . . that the students angry about the government are

In chapter 3 (section 3.2) I outlined the basic structure of a clause for grammars of English speakers, but in Dutch and German it would be slightly different, because these languages are I-final and V-final (3).

3

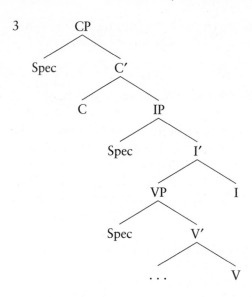

Hans den Besten (1983) assumed this kind of structure when he proposed what became the standard analysis for verb-second languages (4).

4   $_{CP}[$Spec C $_{IP}[$Spec $_{VP}[\ldots$ V $\ldots]$ I$]]$

The finite verb moves to I and then to C, and some phrasal category moves to the specifier of CP; that may be NP, DP, PP, or AP (hence "XP").

But this standard analysis provides (a) no relation between XP-to-Spec movement and V-to-I-to-C movement and (b) no explanation for the obligatory character of the verb-second phenomenon (positing an attractive feature in C merely restates the problem). Linguists know that there is a relationship between the two movements, that an inflected verb *must* move to C if a XP moves to the specifier of CP, and they know this because of negative data, i.e. *un*grammaticality judgments: if some XP moves to the specifier of CP and no finite verb moves to C, the resulting structure is ungrammatical (1f). Therefore, the explanation for the relationship cannot be data-driven; it must come from UG. Similarly for the obligatory character of the verb-second phenomenon, as we saw in chapter 4. The question I want to raise here is: What does the verb-second child learn, and how does he or she learn it?

In Lightfoot 1991 I argued that verb-second children learn that utterances begin with an arbitrary XP with no particular grammatical or thematic role. It is irrelevant whether the XP is a subject or a direct object (1a, b), or whether it is an Agent (1a), a Patient/Theme (1b), a Location (1c), etc. If the specifier of IP is associated with subjecthood, then the arbitrary XP must be in the specifier of some functional category above I, i.e. Spec of CP in the system of (3). Furthermore, as noted, we need a UG condition that lexical material in the specifier of CP needs to be licensed by a lexically filled C; one possibility, due to Uriagereka (1988), is that IP is a barrier to extraction unless it is governed by a lexical C. The only head which can move to C without violating the usual conditions on head movement (Aoun et al. 1987; Rizzi 1990) is a verb, moving through I and therefore picking up finiteness features. This gives rise to the structure (5), and we account for why the finite verb *must* move to C.

5   $_{\text{SpecCP}}[\text{XP}] \; _{\text{C}}[\text{Vf}] \; _{\text{IP}}[\; \dots$

If this analysis is correct, then what the verb-second child learns is that utterances begin with an arbitrary phrasal category. The rest of the information comes from UG. Therefore, the *cue* is (6), an abstract structure and an element of I-language:

6   $_{\text{SpecCP}}[\text{XP}]$

Dutch and German children know that the initial element is in the specifier of CP, because it is invariably followed by a finite verb, unlike, say, topics in English, French, and other non-verb-second languages; the topics in these languages occur in a fronted position but are not followed by a finite verb, and therefore are not in the specifier of CP (7), presumably reflecting some kind of adjoined structure.[3]

7   (a)   Peter, I like (him).
    (b)   Pierre, je l'aime.

Although the initial XP is in principle of arbitrary grammatical function, statistical counts for Dutch, German, Norwegian, and Swedish show that it is a subject about 70 percent of the time in conversational speech (Lightfoot 1993 has the details). Presumably it is those 30 percent nonsubjects which are a crucial trigger for inducing children to postulate that the XP is of arbitrary grammatical and thematic function, hence in the specifier of

CP and not in the specifier of IP (or whatever position is associated with subjecthood). That is to say, the cue (6) must be attested robustly in the primary linguistic data. What we are interested in is the "expression" of the cue (adapting some terminology from Clark 1992), i.e. those utterances which can *only* be analyzed as $_{SpecCP}$[XP]. In this case, this means initial nonsubjects, because a sentence like (1a) might be analyzed with the subject NP/DP in the specifier of IP. Here we can quantify the robustness of the cue: at least 30 percent of matrix clauses express the cue. There is no reason, of course, to believe that there is anything magical about the 30 percent figure, and no reason to believe that there should be a general, cross-cue definition of robustness. We shall return to the matter of the robustness of the cue later in the chapter.

There are many questions glossed over here, but this seems to be a plausible account of how verb-second properties are acquired, which addresses the problems of the standard analysis. Now I shall argue that this cue-based account provides a good basis for understanding how the verb-second phenomenon was lost in the history of English.

Old English/Middle English texts sometimes show verb-second order and sometimes other orders. They *appear* to have optional verb-second, which became more frequent during the Old English/Middle English period. If the appearance were real, this would be highly problematic, because one could now not invoke UG to explain the obligatoriness of the movement in Dutch and German, as we discussed in section 4.5.

Happily, Kroch and Taylor (1997) have provided arguments for the existence of two dialects in Middle English; if they are right, then there is no homogeneous system with optional verb-second. First, there is a northern, Scandinavian-based verb-second grammar (8), which works like Dutch except that it was I-initial and V-initial – in other words a verb-second version of modern English.

8   [Spec C [Spec I [V DP]]

This would yield (modernized) sentences like (9).

9   (a) [We] $_V$saw many students.
      (b) [Many students] $_V$saw we in London.
      (c) [In London] $_V$saw we many students.
      (d) [Angry about the government] $_V$are many students.
      (e) [Often] $_V$saw we many students in London.

Second, there was a southern, indigenous grammar which lacked V + I-to-C and was not verb-second.[4] Early English shows three major alternations (10) (not necessarily three distinct parameters, of course): VPs may show verb–object or object–verb order (10a), I may precede or follow the VP (10b), and there may or may not be an operation moving an inflected verb to C (10c). This leads us to expect the initial structures of (11) with or without V-to-I raising. This is enough to generate what one finds in the texts. Therefore, at least (12) exists alongside (8).[5]

10 (a) VO/OV
    (b) I-medial/I-final
    (c) V + I to C

11 (a) $_{CP}$[Spec C $_{IP}$[Spec I $_{VP}$[V DP]]]
    (b) $_{CP}$[Spec C $_{IP}$[Spec I $_{VP}$[DP V]]]
    (c) $_{CP}$[Spec C $_{IP}$[Spec $_{VP}$[DP V] I]]
    (d) $_{CP}$[Spec C $_{IP}$[Spec $_{VP}$[V DP] I]]

12 . . . $_{IP}$[Spec I $_{VP}$[. . . V . . .]]

(12), assuming verb–object order and V-to-I raising, generates structures like (9a), but not (9b–e) (recall that sentences like (9a) constitute 70 percent of what verb-second children hear). With an adjunction operation, one would get equivalent expressions like (13), which could not occur in a verb-second system like (8).

13 (b) [Many students] we saw in London (equivalent to 9b)
    (c) [In London] we saw many students (equivalent to 9c)

If there were multiple grammars along these lines, then the problem concerning the loss of an optional verb-second system is reconstrued: there were (at least) two coexisting grammars, one obligatory verb-second (8) and one with no V + I-to-C movement, i.e. (12), not verb-second in the usual sense. The first of these ceased to be attained, and was lost. The problem now is to find out why this grammar died out.

On our cue-based model of acquisition and assuming the diglossic analysis of Middle English, we can identify what is likely to have militated against the survival of the verb-second grammar. First, children in Lincolnshire and

Yorkshire, as they mingled with southerners, would have heard sentences whose initial elements were nonsubjects followed by a finite verb less frequently than the required threshold; if we take seriously the statistics from the modern verb-second languages and take the threshold to be about 30 percent of matrix clauses with initial nonsubject in the specifier of CP, then southern XP-Vf forms, where the finite verb (Vf) is not I-final and where the initial element is not a wh- item or negative, are too consistently subject-initial to trigger a verb-second grammar. Southerners overwhelmingly produced only subjects preceding a finite verb, and, as a result, a mixture of southern and northern speech would have less than 30 percent of nonsubject followed by Vf. Ans van Kemenade has provided me with some statistics from *Sawles Warde*, an early-thirteenth-century, southwest Midlands text. She counted 152 matrix clauses, excluding coordinate clauses with missing subjects, dislocated structures (i.e. with resumptive pronouns), and initial *þa*. She found non subject-Vf (where the initial element is not a wh- element, of course) in 26 cases, i.e. 17 percent, well below the required threshold.[6] So the evidence suggests that 17 percent of initial nonsubjects does not suffice to trigger a verb-second grammar, but 30 percent is enough; somewhere between 17 and 30 percent is a phase transition. Of course, we have no idea why there should be a transition at exactly this point, and one might turn for help to the literature on complex systems (e.g. Kauffman 1995).

Second, as those northern children came into contact with southerners, they would have heard verb-third forms like (14), because southerners treated pronouns as clitics, according to most current analyses (e.g. van Kemenade 1987). However, Kroch and Taylor argue that pronouns are not clitics in northern grammars. Therefore, forms with the structure of (14a), i.e. the sentences of (14b, c), would not have been consistent with the verb-second grammars of the earlier generation; they could not be analyzed with initial $_{SpecCP}$[XP]. Prima facie they might have triggered some special adjunction operation, but evidently that didn't happen, because they do not occur in northern grammars.

14 (a) XP – subject pronoun – Vf
    (b) [Æfter his gebede] he $_v$ahof þæt cild up (*Homilies of the Anglo-Saxon Church* (Thorpe) 2.28)
         "After his prayer he lifted the child up."
    (c) [Þis] he $_v$dyde eal for þes biscopes luuen (*AS Chronicle* (Clarke (Peterborough) 1123.73))
         "This he did all for this bishop's love."

Third, the V-to-I operation was being lost from English grammars, as we shall discuss in the next section. If verbs did not raise out of the VP to I, then finite verbs could not raise further to C (*pace* Vikner 1994 and others; see n. 8 below), and there could be no verb-second effect with finite verbs. In particular, if the finite verb could not get to C, nothing could occur in the specifier of CP, given the UG condition requiring anything in the specifier of CP to be licensed by a lexical C. Consequently, sentences corresponding to (9b–e) could not be generated, and it is such sentences which expressed the cue for a verb-second system. This would further reduce the degree to which the cue for a verb-second system was manifested according to the analysis we have offered.

If grammars emerge as children scan for cues, and if $_{\text{SpecCP}}$[nonsubject] is the cue for the grammar yielding a verb-second system, then we can understand why English lost verb-second at the time and in the way it did, and we can understand why the change seems to have taken place rapidly, indeed catastrophically (van Kemenade 1987). On the other hand, if learners simply seek grammars which match the input, there is no reason why verb-second sentences should have been lost, least of all why they were lost rapidly.

I have shown how it is plausible to assume that the trigger experience that northern children had came to differ in critical ways from the trigger experiences that their parents and ancestors had, as there was more contact with the south. This produced a distributional shift in utterances manifesting the cue for the verb-second system. The primary linguistic data (PLD) changed critically, and children converged on new grammars which generated a very different output. We know from acquisition studies that children are sensitive to statistical shifts in input data. For example, Newport, Gleitman and Gleitman (1977) showed that the ability of English-speaking children to use auxiliaries appropriately results from exposure to noncontracted, stressed forms in initial position in yes–no questions: the greater the exposure to these subject–auxiliary inversion forms, the earlier the use of auxiliaries in medial position. Also Richards (1990) demonstrated a good deal of individual variation in the acquisition of English auxiliaries as a result of exposure to slightly different trigger experiences. The question is: When do trigger experiences differ critically? When do they differ in such a way as to trigger a different grammar? That is where work on historical change is so illuminating. Sometimes we can identify points at which there have been clear grammatical shifts, and sometimes we can also identify prior changes in the PLD. What is relevant now is shifts affecting specific elements of I-language, the designated cues. By hypothesis, this shows us changes in PLD having critical effects. In fact, for the immediate future it is work on language change that is likely to be the major source of insight into what triggers particular grammars.

This story about the loss of verb-second systems is based on language contact. Northern children lost verb-second grammars when their PLD changed under the influence of contact with southerners. One may ask why northern children did not simply become bilingual, with two distinct systems internalized, but I have nothing enlightening to say about this beyond the discussion in chapter 4. There we discussed how the Blocking Effect militates against coexisting analyses (section 4.5). We know that children may attain distinct systems, having some kind of English grammar and a French grammar. However, we know little about why distinct systems should emerge under certain circumstances, as opposed to what happened in this case, one grammar being triggered by diverse data generated by more than one prior grammar. The account of the loss of verb-second systems happens to involve language contact, but the expression of the $_{\text{SpecCP}}[\text{XP}]$ cue might drop for other reasons. If early Germanic was verb-second, then southern English must have lost the verb-second system earlier. We have no records of that change, but it may not have been the result of language contact. In the next section we shall discuss the loss of V-to-I movement, showing that the cue changes its distribution, but for reasons which have nothing to do with language contact.

6.3   V-to-I Raising and its Cue

Let us consider now a second case of grammatical change where a cue-based account is illuminating and where language contact plays no role. Operations which associate inflectional features with the appropriate verb appear to be parameterized, and this has been the subject of a vast amount of work covering many languages (see the collection of papers in Lightfoot and Hornstein 1994). We can learn about the shape of the cue(s) by considering how the relevant grammars could be attained, and that in turn is illuminated by how some grammars have changed.

Again, I adopt the familiar clause structure. Since we are now going to discuss English after the change to I-initial and V-initial order, the basic structure is (15), slightly different from the I-final and V-final Dutch system discussed in the last section.[7]

15

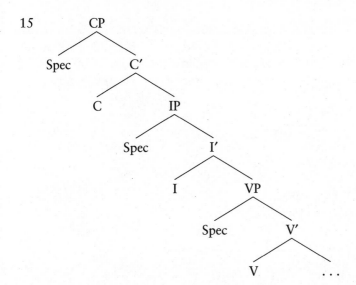

As we noted in the last section, subjects occur in the specifier of IP and wh-elements typically occur in the specifier of CP in the grammars of speakers of English and those of many other languages. Heads raise from one head position to another, so verbs may raise to I and then further to C. In fact, many grammars, like those of French speakers, raise their verbs to the position containing the inflectional elements (16c, d); but English grammars, unusually, do not; instead, they have an operation which lowers I onto an adjacent verb ((16a) but not (16b)). We know this because English finite verbs do not occur in some initial C-like position (17a) and cannot be separated from their complements by intervening material (17b), which strongly suggests that verbs do not move out of their VP in modern English.

16   (a)   Jill $_{VP}$[leave + past]

     (b)   Jill $_I$[leave$_i$ + past] $_{VP}$[e$_i$]

     (c)   Jeanne $_I$[lit$_i$] $_{VP}$[toujours e$_i$ les journaux]
          Jean reads always the newspapers

     (d)   Lit$_i$ $_{IP}$[elle e$_i$ $_{VP}$[toujours e$_i$ les journaux]?
          Reads she always the newspapers?

17   (a)   *Visited$_i$ $_{IP}$[you e$_i$ London last week]?

     (b)   *The women visited$_i$ not/all/frequently $_{VP}$[e$_i$ London last week]

The question I want to raise here is: What is it that forces French children to have the V-to-I operation, and what forces English children to lack the operation?

It is reasonable to construe the English lowering operation as a morphological phenomenon. It doesn't look like a syntactic operation: in general, lowering operations are unusual in the syntax, and a syntactic lowering operation here would leave behind an illicit trace, neither bound nor properly governed (Aoun et al. 1987; Rizzi 1990). Furthermore, one would expect a morphological operation, but not a syntactic operation, to be subject to a condition of adjacency. Therefore, the representation in (16a), reflecting a morphological operation, contains no trace of the lowered I. In any case, the English lowering needs to be taken as the default setting (as argued in Lightfoot 1993; Lasnik 1995; Roberts 1998); there is no nonnegative evidence available to the child which would force him or her to select an I-lowering analysis over a V-raising analysis (16b) for English, if both operations could be syntactic and subject to an adjacency requirement: children would need to know that (17a, b) do not occur (negative data, therefore unavailable as input to children). In that case, let us take the morphological I-lowering analysis as the default setting.

Now one can ask what triggers the availability of a syntactic V-to-I raising operation in grammars where it may apply. Some generalizations have emerged over the last few years. One is that languages with rich inflection may have V-to-I operations in their grammars, and rich inflection could be part of the trigger (Rohrbacher 1994). Indeed, it is striking that the verb *be* is richly inflected in standard English (*am/is/are*) and moves to I and then to C, yielding forms like *Is Bill president?*, while other forms of English (Black English Vernacular, or "Ebonics," and some forms of children's speech) do not inflect *be*, and the uninflected *be* does not move. So alongside (18a) in these types of English, one finds (18b, c), but not (18d).

18 (a)   Bill be angry.
    (b)   Bill don't be angry.
          Do Bill be angry?
          What do Bill be?
    (c)   I don't be angry?
          Do clowns be boys or girls?
          Did it be funny?
    (d)   *Bill ben't angry.
          *Be Bill angry?
          *What be Bill?

However, the presence of V-to-I raising cannot be linked with rich inflection in a simple one-to-one fashion. It may be the case that if a language has rich inflection, then V-to-I raising is available (Lightfoot 1991; Roberts 1998). However, the opposite does not hold: if there is no rich inflection, a grammar may have the raising operation (Danish, Swedish,[8] and, if Otani and Whitman (1991) are correct, Chinese, Japanese, and Korean) or may lack it (English). Indeed, English verb morphology was simplified radically and that simplification was complete by 1400; however, overt V-to-I movement disappeared only in the eighteenth century, so there was a long period when English grammars had very little verbal inflection but did have V-to-I movement. In that case, there needs to be a *syntactic* trigger for V-to-I movement. So, for example, a finite verb occurring in C, i.e. to the left of the subject (as in a verb-second language or in interrogatives), could only get there by raising first to I, and therefore inversion forms like (16d) in French could be syntactic triggers for V to I.

On a cue-based acquisition approach, one would say that the cue for grammars raising V to I is a finite verb in I: i.e. $_I[V]$, an element of I-language. Children seek this cue in the representations resulting from their (partial) parses. One unambiguous instance of $_I[V]$ is an I containing the trace of a verb which has moved on to C, as in the structure of (16d). I would guess that (16d) would be a very important expression of the cue, and I doubt that structures like (16c) or (17b) would be robust enough to trigger V to I in isolation; this can be tested (see below). Again adopting Clark's terminology, one can ask how robustly the cue is "expressed." It is *expressed* robustly if there are many simple utterances which can be analyzed by the child only as $_I[V]$. So, for example, the sentences corresponding to (16c, d) can only be analyzed by the French child (given what the child has already established about the emerging grammar) if the V *lit* raises to I, and therefore they express the cue.[9] A simple sentence like *Jeanne lit les journaux*, "Jeanne reads the newspapers," on the other hand, could be analyzed with *lit* raised to I or with the I lowered into the VP in the English style; therefore it does not express the cue for V-to-I movement.

Early English grammars manifested the V-to-I operation, but later grammars do not; the operation was lost at some point. From the perspective adopted here, the operation ceased to be cued. The cue for V-to-I raising, $_I[V]$, came to be expressed less in the PLD in the light of three developments in early Modern English.

First, the modal auxiliaries (*can, could, may, might, shall, should, will, would, must*), while once instances of verbs that could raise to I, were recategorized such that they came to be base-generated as instances of I; they were no longer verbs, so sentences with a modal auxiliary ceased to include ₁[V] and ceased to express the cue for V-to-I movement. Sentences with a modal auxiliary, *Kim must leave*, are very common in ordinary speech addressed to young children, and the recategorization meant that they no longer expressed the cue. Sentences of this form existed at all stages, of course, but they came to be analyzed very differently after the change in category membership. The evidence for the recategorization is the obsolescence of (19), which follows if the modal auxiliaries are no longer verbs but are generated in I and therefore can occur only one per clause (19a), without an aspectual affix (19b, c), and mutually exclusively with the infinitival marker *to*, which also occurs in I (19d).

19   (a)   John shall can do it.
      (b)   John has could do it.
      (c)   Canning do it.
      (d)   I want to can do it.

This change has been discussed extensively in Lightfoot 1979, 1991; Kroch 1989; Roberts 1985, 1993b; and Warner 1983, 1993. Some of these studies have focused on the initiation of the change, others on its spread, and others on its completion. There is consensus that the change was complete by the early sixteenth century.

Second, as periphrastic *do* came to be used in negatives like *John did not leave* and interrogatives like *Did John leave?*, so there were still fewer instances of ₁[V]. Before periphrastic *do* became available, sentences like *Visited you London last week?* (17a) and *The women visited all London last week* (17b) expressed the ₁[V] cue. Periphrastic *do* began to occur with significant frequency at the beginning of the fifteenth century and steadily increased in frequency until it stabilized into its modern usage by the mid-seventeenth century. Ellegård (1953) shows that the sharpest increase came in the period 1475–1550. For every instance of *do*, there is no verb in I.

Third, in early grammars with the verb-second system all matrix clauses had a finite verb in C, as we just discussed. Therefore, many matrix clauses expressed the cue for V to I, ₁[V] (on the assumption that V could move to C only by moving first to I). As these grammars were lost, and as finite verbs ceased to occur regularly in C, so the expression of the cue for overt V-to-I raising was reduced.

By quantifying the degree to which a cue is expressed, we can understand why English grammars lost the V-to-I operation, and why they lost it after the modal auxiliaries were reanalyzed as nonverbs, as the periphrastic *do* became increasingly common, and as the verb-second system was lost. We can reconstruct a plausible history for the loss of V to I in English. What we are doing here is identifying when grammars changed and how the available triggering experiences, specifically those expressing the cue, seem to have shifted in critical ways prior to the grammatical change.[10]

Our conclusion in earlier work was that V-to-I movement was lost in the seventeenth century, much later than suggested by Kroch (1989), Roberts (1993b), and others. Warner (1997) now argues that the operation may have been lost as late as the eighteenth century. He offers some statistics from Ellegård (1953) and Tieken-Boon van Ostade (1987). Ellegård shows that interrogative inversion with nonauxiliary in positive clauses (i.e. *Came he to London?* as opposed to *Did he come to London?*) occurred 27 percent of the time for 1625–50; 26 percent for 1650–1700. Tieken-Boon van Ostade shows a drop to 13 percent in the eighteenth century. Forms like *Came he to London?* could be generated only by grammars with V to I, so those grammars are still well attested in the seventeenth century, persisting into the eighteenth. The figures show a gradual development at the level of the language, reflecting changes in the PLD and the decreasing use of grammars with V-to-I raising. Negative declaratives with a nonauxiliary (*He came not to London*, as opposed to *He did not come to London*), which are also generated only by V-to-I grammars, show a very different pattern of development. They occur 68 percent of the time in 1625–50, 54 percent in 1650–1700, dropping sharply to 20 percent in the eighteenth century.

These figures show emphatically that V-to-I grammars were still very much in use throughout the seventeenth century and into the eighteenth. The drop in the negative patterns is actually sharper than these figures suggest; Tieken-Boon van Ostade's figures for the later period include a high proportion of recurrent items (*know*, *doubt*, etc.) which tend to be distortingly conservative and which Ellegård omitted for that reason. A particularly interesting feature of these figures is the discrepancy between the interrogatives and the negatives, which lends some support to the hunch (above) that structures like those underlying (16d) and (17a) are a more effective expression of the cue $_i$[V] than structures like those of (16c) and (17b). We see that structures like (17b) were robust and widely attested in the texts of the late seventeenth century and then disappeared rapidly – the kind of bumpiness that the abstractness of the cues leads us to expect. In any case, we also see that V-to-I grammars were prevalent in the seventeenth century and survived into the eighteenth.[11]

The historical facts, then, suggest that lack of rich subject–verb agreement cannot be a sufficient condition for absence of V to I, but it may be a necessary condition. On this view the *possibility* of V to I not being triggered first arose in the history of English with the loss of rich verbal inflection; similarly in Danish and Swedish. That possibility never arose in Dutch, French, and German, where verbal inflections remained relatively rich. Despite this possibility, V to I continued to be triggered, and it occurred in grammars well after verbal inflection had been reduced to its present-day level. However, with the reanalysis of the modal auxiliaries, the increasing frequency of periphrastic *do*, and the loss of the verb-second system, the expression of $_I[V]$ in English became less and less robust in the PLD. That is, there was no longer anything very robust in children's experience which had to be analyzed as $_I[V]$, i.e. which *required* V to I, given that the morphological I-lowering operation was always available as the default. In particular, common, simple sentences like *Jill left* could be analyzed with I-lowering (16a); meanwhile, sentences like (17b) with post-verbal adverbs and quantifiers had to be analyzed with the V in I, but these instances of the cue were not robust enough to set the parameter, and they disappeared quickly, a by-product of the loss of V to I in another domino effect.[12]

This suggests that the expression of the cue dropped below some threshold, leading to the elimination of V-to-I movement. The next task is to quantify this generally, but we should recognize that the gradual reduction in the expression of $_I[V]$ is not crucial. What is crucial is the point at which the phase transition took place, when the last straw was piled onto the camel's back. This can be demonstrated by building a population model, tracking the distribution of the $_I[V]$ cues in the PLD, and identifying the point at which the parameter was reset and V to I ceased to be triggered (differing, of course, from one individual or one dialect area to another). This work remains to be done (see below), but one would expect to find correlations between the changing distribution of the cue and the change in grammars.

So children scan the environment for instances of $_I[V]$. This presupposes prior analysis, of course. Children may scan for this cue only after they have identified a class of verbs and when their grammars have a distinct inflection position, I.

Consequently, very young children may have difficulty in recognizing elements as such which are in fact instances of $_I[V]$ in the adult language. This would explain why young children produce the optional infinitives noted by Ken Wexler (1994): children acquiring grammars with V-to-I movement produce uninflected (infinitival) verbs in base-generated positions despite never hearing such forms from adults – another mystery for a pure input-matching learning model. Wexler cites some Dutch examples found by Mieke Weverink (20). At this "optional-infinitive" stage, children know that finite verbs may not occur (more technically, may not be "checked") in clause-final position in matrix clauses, because they do not produce clause-final inflected verbs: *Pappa schoenen wasst. But they do not consistently know that finite verbs are instances of I.

20   (a)   Pappa schoenen wassen.
            Daddy shoes wash.
     (b)   Pappa nieuwe scooter kopen.
            Daddy new scooter buy.
     (c)   Ik ook lezen.
            I also read.
     (d)   Pappa kranten weg doen.
            Daddy newspapers away do.

The difficulty in recognizing $_I[V]$ also explains the tendency of young Dutch children (noted by Evers and van Kampen 1995) to produce *do* support forms (21).

21   (a)   Ik doe ook praten.
            "I do also talk."
     (b)   Dat doe ik spelen.
            that do I play
            "I am pretending that."

These forms also do not occur in adult speech and do not represent input matching; the adult language uses *do* support only in VP topicalization (22), and the adult equivalents of (21) are (23). That is, (23) is the kind of thing that Dutch children hear, not (21); but there is a stage at which many children are not able to generate the adult forms.

22   $_{VP}$[De roos treffen] doet hij zelden.
      the mark hit does he seldom
      "Hit the mark he seldom does."

23   (a)   Ik $_I$[praat]$_i$ ook e$_i$
     (b)   Dat $_I$[speel]$_i$ ik e$_i$

This grammatical approach to diachrony explains changes at two levels. First, the cues postulated as part of UG which embody the points of parametric variation explain the unity of the changes, why superficially unrelated properties cluster in the way they do. Second, the cues permit an appropriately contingent account of why the change took place, why children at a certain point converged on a different grammar: the expression of the cues changed in such a way that a threshold was crossed and a new grammar was acquired. That is as far as this model goes, and it has nothing to say about why the distribution of cues should change. This may be explained by claims about language contact or socially defined speech fashions, but it is not a function of theories of grammar, acquisition, or change – except under one set of circumstances, where the new distribution of cues results from an earlier grammatical shift; in that circumstance, one has a "chain" of grammatical changes. One example would be the recategorization of the modal auxiliaries (above), which contributed to the loss of V to I.

Notice that this approach to change is independent of any particular grammatical model. Warner (1995) offers a persuasive analysis of parametric shift, using a lexicalist head-driven Phrase Structure Grammar model, quite different from the one assumed here. Interesting diachronic analyses have been offered for a wide range of phenomena, invoking very different grammatical claims (see Fontana 1993; van Kemenade 1987; Pearce 1990; Roberts 1993a, b, 1994; Sprouse and Vance 1998; Vance 1995; etc.).

The cue-based account we have offered here for the loss of verb-second phenomena and the loss of V to I works quite differently from the account offered by Clark and Roberts (1993) for the loss of verb-second and the account offered by Roberts (1998) for the loss of V-to-I movement. Using the learnability model of Clark (1992), Clark and Roberts account for the loss of verb-second in Middle French by having children track data which change somewhat. Given the introduction of XP subject V . . . forms, earlier grammars were no longer as successful in their fit with the input data and were therefore replaced by a new grammar which did not generate a verb-second language. The supposition here is that new forms were introduced for unspecified reasons, and that therefore the child tracking input data in accordance with Clark's genetic algorithm is forced to adopt a new grammar which fits the new data better. This amounts to saying that verb-second was lost because non-verb-second forms were introduced into the language. The nature of this explanation and its circularity are intimately linked to the input-matching nature of the learning model. The problem is that the model, at least in the way it is presently articulated, is crucially an input-matching device. Because input matching plays such an important role, it is difficult to see why there should be bumps and catastrophes, points where children converge on grammars which generate sets of structures and sentences quite different from earlier grammars. One can imagine how the model might be revised, but that would involve reducing the role of input matching, which makes acquisition too heavily data-driven.

Roberts (1998) considers the loss of V to I in English and invokes an elegance condition from Clark and Roberts (1993), "which, *all other things being equal*, favors those parameter-settings which generate relatively simple representations over those which generate relatively more complex ones" (emphasis added). He takes simplicity to be in part a function of movement operations, and therefore movement operations are "marked." This element of UG, for Roberts, is an active, causal factor in the loss of V-to-I movement in English, biasing learners intrinsically against movement operations; to that extent, it is not merely a default option of the type that I invoked earlier (our idea that morphological lowering is a default option did not explain the loss of V-to-I movement). For Roberts, the UG bias explains why V to I is not acquired when *all other things are equal*. This raises two obvious questions: if UG has a bias against V-to-I operations, why and how did V-to-I operations ever develop in grammars? Second, when exactly are "all other things equal"? Presumably the answer to the latter question is that the UG bias is effective when the PLD do not demand a movement operation. But if the PLD do not demand a movement operation, then that is a sufficient explanation for the lack of movement, and the UG bias is unnecessary.[13] We shall return to the explanatory force of these UG biases in chapter 8.

Other historians have accounted for these changes in reverse, claiming that periphrastic *do* was introduced as a function of the loss of V-to-I raising. Since periphrastic *do* first occurred very early and spread most rapidly in the fifteenth–sixteenth century, while V-to-I grammars persisted into the eighteenth century, that story seems to be even more far-fetched than Odysseus's escape from the cave of Polyphemus.

6.4   Creolization and Signed Languages

Roberts (1998) goes on to illustrate the UG bias against V-to-I operations by turning to creoles. He argues that generally creoles have unmarked or default values of parameters, and that specifically they lack V-to-I movement because the movement represents a marked value (a strong feature), and this despite movement in the lexifier language.[14] It is to be expected, of course, that English-based creoles will lack V to I, since English lacks it. Also, it is not surprising that French-based creoles may lack it, because the most robust evidence for V to I in French, namely V in C, is limited to contexts where the subject is a pronoun: *Lisez-vous ces journaux?*, but not **Lisent les ouvriers ces journaux*? If V to I is less common in creoles than one might expect, that might be a function of problems in recognizing the cue, $_I$[V], in the kind of restricted input that early speakers have. We noted at the end of the last section that children have some difficulty in recognizing these structures even in languages where they seem to be somewhat transparent.

On the matter of UG biases and creole evidence for them, consider Berbice Dutch, a better-worked-out example where the debate can be sharpened. A striking property of this Guyanese creole is that it has subject–verb–object order, while its lexifier languages, Dutch and Eastern Ijo, are both underlyingly object–verb and verb-second (as discussed in Lightfoot 1991: ch. 7). Roberts (1998) takes this to illustrate the fact that subject–verb–object order represents an unmarked option, and that creoles generally adopt unmarked parameter settings. A cue-based, degree-0 approach to learnability would tackle things differently.

Dutch and Ijo have underlying object–verb order, but verb–object order often occurs in matrix clauses because of a verb-movement operation that moves the verb to I and then to an initial C position, yielding verb-second order in the way we discussed earlier. Our theory of constituent structure demands that verbs be generated adjacent to their complements, either right-adjacent or left-adjacent. A degree-0 learner resolves the verb-order option on the basis of unembedded data which reveal the position of the verb (as argued in Lightfoot 1991). In Dutch these data are the position of separable particles (24a), negation elements (24b), certain adverbs (24c), and clause-union structures (24d), each of which mark the underlying position of the verb to the right of its complement.

24   (a)   Jan belt de hoogleraar op.
           "John calls the professor up."
    (b)   Jan bezoekt de hoogleraar niet.
           John visits the professor not.
    (c)   Jan belt de hoogleraar soms/morgen op.
           John calls the professor up sometimes/tomorrow.
    (d)   Jan moet de hoogleraar opbellen.
           "John must call up the professor."

Furthermore, there are uninflected, infinitival constructions in colloquial Dutch, which manifest object–verb order directly in unembedded contexts (25).

25 (a) En ik maar fietsen repareren.
         "I ended up repairing bicycles."
    (b) Hand uitsteken
         hand outstretch "signal"
    (c) Jantje koekje hebben?
         "Johnnie has a cookie?"
    (d) Ik de vuilnisbak buiten zetten? Nooit.
         I the garbage-can outside set? Never.
         "Me put the garbage out? Never."

We can understand this in terms of cue-based acquisition: the cue for object–verb order is $_{VP}$[NP/DP V], where the V may be a trace. In each language, children set the verb-order parameter on the basis of evidence in unembedded domains; the evidence may be indirect and show that the *trace* of the moved verb is to the right of the direct object. The verb will necessarily be a trace for a degree-0 learner in a consistently verb-second language, because in simple, unembedded domains verbs are consistently moved to C and are pronounced in that position. The verb is often a trace in a language like Dutch, where verbs generally (but not always) move to C. So (24a) contains the structure *Jan belt$_i$ $_{VP}$[de hoogleraar op e$_i$]*, and the child knows that this is the structure by virtue of knowing that *opbellen* is a phrasal verb and that *belt* must therefore have originated in a position to the right of *op* and moved from there. Similarly, in (24b) the negative *niet* occurs to the right of the direct object and marks the position from which the verb has moved. In this way the child finds instances of the cue for object–verb order in unembedded domains in Dutch. If the evidence for the position of the verbal trace is obscured in some way, the PLD would fail to some extent to express the cue for object–verb order. Lightfoot 1991: 179 noted:

> In the case of Berbice Dutch, if the first speakers did not have robust evidence about the distribution of separable particles, or if negative elements were no longer retained in their D-structure position (marking the D-structure position of the verb), or if the verb-raising (clause union) operation was not triggered in the same way as in Dutch, then there would arise a situation comparable to that of late Old English: there would no longer be adequate data to trigger the object–verb setting. Negation, for example, works differently in Ijo and Dutch. In Dutch the negative element occurs to the right of an object NP, marking the position from which the verb moves, but in Ijo the negative particle "is adjoined directly to the verb in its proposition-negating role" (Smith et al. 1987) and moves with it, as in Old English:

26 Á nimi-γá.
    I know not.

Ijo provided the negative for the creole, *kane*, which is a clitic attached to the verb, and because Ijo provided the basis for negation patterns, one of the Dutch indicators of the position of the verbal trace was obscured.

We lack good records for the early stages of Berbice Dutch; therefore it is hard to be more precise and to show exactly how the PLD failed to express sufficiently the cue for object–verb order. Lack of good records is a general problem for work on the early stages of creoles. However, the negation example is suggestive and shows that one indicator of underlying object–verb order may be nullified if the other language is dominant in the relevant aspect. Conversely, Dutch may have been dominant in an area of grammar that expressed the cue for the position of the verbal trace in Ijo. Of course, if children are not degree-0 learners, then the cue for object–verb order would be expressed robustly, because this is the standard order for embedded clauses in both Dutch and Ijo. In fact, early learners of Berbice Dutch were unaffected by this evidence, as expected if they were degree-0 learners, searching for the cue only in unembedded domains.[15]

So it is not difficult to see how a degree-0, cue-based learner might acquire a verb–object grammar when the lexifier grammars are object–verb and verb-second, and we do not need to say that there is a UG bias or that creoles always manifest unmarked parameter settings.

Creole children, just like all other children, scan their environment for cues. They interpret what they hear, impoverished though it may be, as expressing cues, and they converge on grammars accordingly. They are not subject to any bias built into UG of the type that Roberts has suggested. So new languages may emerge rapidly and fully formed, despite very impoverished input.

Work on creoles is limited by the sketchiness of the data available for the earliest stages, but the view that new languages emerge rapidly and fully formed despite impoverished input receives striking support from work on signed languages. The crucial fact here is that only about 10 percent of deaf children in the USA are born to deaf parents, who can provide early exposure to a conventional sign language like ASL (American Sign Language). This means that the vast majority of deaf children are exposed initially to fragmentary signed systems which have not been internalized well by their primary models. This is often some form of Manually Coded English (MCE), which maps English into a visual/gestural modality and is very different from ASL (which is not English-based). Goldin-Meadow and Mylander (1990) take these to be artificial systems and offer a useful review of work on how deaf children go beyond their models in such circumstances and "naturalize" the system, altering the code and inventing new forms which are more consistent with what one finds in natural languages. Goldin-Meadow and

Mylander show that children exposed to people who use morphological markers irregularly and spasmodically nonetheless regularize the markers, using them consistently and "in a system of contrasts . . . akin to the system that characterizes the productive lexicon in ASL" (p. 341).

Newport (1998) extends these ideas by reporting work on a single child, Simon, showing how he comes to use morphology consistently and "deterministically," where his models used it inconsistently and "probabilistically." She notes that Simon does not create "an entirely new language from his own innate specifications," as the language bioprogram hypothesis of Bickerton (1984) would imply. "Rather, he appears to be following the predominant tendencies of his input, but sharpens them, extends them, and forces them to be internally consistent." Inconsistent input, then, presents no problem for young children, who simply generalize across the board. Newport reports that adult learners, on the other hand, are seriously impeded by inconsistent input and often perform even more inconsistently than their models.

Work by Supalla (1990) on MCE casts more light on this and on themes that I have been addressing in this chapter. MCE systems were invented by educators to teach English to deaf children. They rely on a lexicon borrowed heavily from ASL. However, while ASL morphology is generally "nonlinear," with simultaneous spatial devices serving as morphological markers, MCE morphology is generally "linear," using invented signs which reproduce the morphological structure of English; those signs precede or follow the root word. The English *take–took* alternation is an example of nonlinear morphology, and *walk–walked* is an instance of a linear alternation, where the verb stem precedes the tense marker. Supalla studied Signed Exact English (SEE2), the dominant version of MCE, where all bound morphemes are invented and based on English. For example, the SEE2 suffix representing English -ing involves the single hand-shape "I"; the suffix -S (for singular present tense or plural) is a static upright S hand-shape in the neutral signing space; the -ment, -tion, -ness, and -age suffixes are all syllabic, /M/, /S/, /N/, and /G/ respectively. Of the 49 English affixes that have an equivalent in SEE2, 44 consist of at least one syllable. They are strictly linear and, importantly, phonologically independent of the root.

Supalla cites several studies showing that SEE2 morphology is not attained well by children, who do not use many of the markers that they are exposed to and use other markers quite inconsistently and differently from their models. He focuses particularly on deaf children who are exposed only to SEE2 with no access to ASL, and he found that they restructure SEE2 morphology into a new system. The SEE2 "bound morphemes were rejected and replaced with devised forms. Moreover, in the devised forms, the affixation type was predominantly non-linear in nature . . . not exactly like that of ASL, [but] formationally within the constraints of affixation in ASL" (Supalla 1990: 46). Unlike in Newport's study, children did not simply generalize markers which were used inconsistently in the input. Rather, there were particular problems with inflectional morphemes, and children invented a new system.

Supalla's approach to this was to postulate a Modality–Constraints Model, which limits signed languages to nonlinear morphology, whereas spoken languages tend to have linear morphology. However, this approach seems suspect. First, the correlation does not hold reliably: spoken languages often have nonlinear morphology (e.g. the *take–took* alternation of English above), and nonlinear morphology is comprehensive in Semitic and other languages; and Supalla (ibid. 20) points out that ASL has some linear morphology, e.g. agentive (analogous to the English -*er* suffix) and reduplicative markings. Second, the model fails to account for the fact that SEE2-type morphology does not exist even in spoken languages. What is striking about the inflectional morphemes of SEE2 is that they "are produced in terms of timing and formation as separate signs" (ibid. 52). Supalla shows that they are not subject to assimilation; they are phonologically independent, articulated distinctly, and even emphasized. In general, this kind of phonological independence is characteristic of free morphemes but not of inflectional, bound morphemes, and the system seems not to be learned by children.

Clearly this cannot be modeled by an input-matching learning device of the kind discussed earlier, because the input is not matched. It doesn't even come close. Furthermore, it is not enough simply to say that SEE2 morphology violates UG constraints, because that would not account for the way in which children devise new forms. Nor is it enough to appeal to some UG characterization of functional categories. More is needed from UG. The unlearnability of the SEE2 morphology suggests that children are cue-based learners, programmed to scan for clitic-like, unstressed, highly assimilable inflectional markers. That is what they find standardly in spoken languages and in natural signed languages like ASL. If the input fails to provide such markers, then appropriate markers are invented. Children seize appropriate kinds of elements which can be interpreted as inflectional markers. In signed languages there seems to be at least a strong statistical tendency to reinterpret linear elements in this fashion.[16] It would be interesting to see work that examines how this reinterpretation takes place and how new morphology is devised when children are exposed to unlearnable systems like SEE2. This would flesh out the general perspective of Goldin-Meadow and Mylander (1990) and of Newport (1998).

Deaf children are often exposed to artificial input, and we know a good deal about that input and about how it is reanalyzed by language learners. Therefore, the acquisition of signed languages under these circumstances offers a wonderful opportunity to understand more about abrupt language change, creolization, and cue-based acquisition. One particular case of great interest is the emergence of Nicaraguan Sign Language, as described by Kegl, Senghas, and Coppola (1998).

I submit that work on abrupt creolization, the acquisition of signed languages, and catastrophic historical change shows us that children do not necessarily converge on grammars which match input. This work invites us to think of children as cue-based learners, who scan the environment for certain elements of I-language in unembedded domains. These elements are not explicit in the input, but they are derived from the input, in the mental representations yielded as children understand and "parse" their input. So a cue-based learner acquires a verb-second grammar not by evaluating grammars against sets of sentences, but on exposure to structures commencing $_{SpecCP}$[XP]. This requires analyzing the XP as in the specifier of CP: that is, i.e. knowing that the XP needs to have no fixed grammatical or thematic function and knowing that it is followed by a finite verb. $_{SpecCP}$[XP] is the cue for a verb-second system, and the cue must be represented robustly in the mental representations resulting from parsing the PLD.

The name is new, but the cue-based approach to language acquisition is *implicitly* assumed in some earlier work, and it comports well with work on the visual system, which develops as organisms are exposed to very specific visual stimuli – horizontal lines, for example (Hubel 1978; Hubel and Wiesel 1962; Sperry 1968). Current theories of the immune system are similar: specific antigens amplify preexisting antibodies. In fact, this kind of thing is typical of selective learning quite generally (Piattelli-Palmarini 1986). The cue-based approach has been productive for phonologists concerned with the parameters for stress systems (Dresher 1998; Fikkert 1994, 1995), and a similar approach has been invoked independently for some syntactic problems by Fodor (1998).

Cue-based acquisition is a radical departure from much current work on learnability, which postulates various forms of input matching. It is striking that so much of this work has children dealing with elements of E-language (Chomsky 1986), often requiring that the system in effect perform elaborate calculations. For example, one of the best-known results of work on learnability, the Subset Principle of Berwick (1985), is usually construed as calculating subset relations among sets of E-language and choosing among grammars accordingly. Dresher and Kaye (1990) show that the Subset Principle can be defined intensionally with respect to cues. The model advocated here plays down the centrality of E-language for a good account of acquisition, and postulates children seeking elements of I-language in the input and selecting grammars accordingly; the model makes no reference to elements of E-language or to the output of the grammar.

The cue-based approach assumes (with Lightfoot 1989) that there is a learning path, an order in which parameters are set. We have seen that a child cannot determine whether specifiers precede heads until some analytical vocabulary has been developed. Similarly, the child cannot determine whether the specifier of CP is filled (in a verb-second language) until he or she has identified phrasal categories, learned that initial categories do not have any fixed grammatical or thematic role and (therefore) are followed directly by a finite verb. All of this represents prior stages of acquisition. Representations are elaborated step by step in the course of acquisition, and the cues needed become increasingly abstract and grammar-internal. On this model the learning path is part of linguistic theory, a function of the way in which the parameters and their cues are stated.

Gibson and Wexler's TLA and Clark's genetic algorithms are learning algorithms quite distinct from the grammars assumed. However, the cue-based approach suggests that there is no relevant learning algorithm beyond the information provided specifically by UG.

Cue-based learning is "deterministic" in the sense of Berwick (1985): the learner may not backtrack or undo parameter settings that have already been set. This represents a strong and testable claim about how acquisition proceeds. Of course, there is no theory of cues yet: that is, no theory of what constitutes a possible cue. But then we also have no very substantive theory of parameters. These are topics for ongoing research.

On this view, one would expect there to be grammatical changes which are abrupt, and also that languages would differ from each other in bumpy ways. We may seek to quantify the degree to which cues are represented in the PLD, showing that abrupt, catastrophic change takes place when expression of those cues falls below some threshold of robustness.

If we devise productive models for historical change along these lines, relating changes in simple cues to large-scale grammatical shifts, our results will have consequences for the way in which we study language acquisition. In particular, we shall not be surprised that changes sometimes occur abruptly. With the development of computer corpora, Niyogi and Berwick's results, and an explicit cue-based theory of acquisition, we have all the ingredients for success in the historical domain, synthesizing work on language change, acquisition, and variation.

Notes

1   This chapter incorporates material from Lightfoot 1997a, which was a cue-based rendering of some similar material in 1997b (first published in 1994, in the University of Maryland Working Papers in Linguistics). I received helpful comments on that earlier paper from Stephen Crain, Michel DeGraff, Norbert Hornstein, Ceil Lucas, Jairo Nunes, and Juan Uriagereka.

2   Clark's Fitness Measure has a serious technical problem. There is no reason to suppose that a grammar with more parameters set correctly will be more successful in parsing/generating incoming data. Dresher (1998) illustrates this by considering the settings needed to generate the phonological stress system of Selkup, computing the relative score which the Fitness Measure would give them when applied to eight representative words. It isn't obvious what criterion the Fitness Measure should use, so he tried three different criteria: words correct, syllables correct, and main stress correct. Some results are shown in table 6.2.

Table 6.2   Fitness of grammars for Selkup stress

	Parameters correct		Words correct		Syllables correct		Main stress correct	
(a)	4/10	40%	2/8	25%	7/20	35%	3/8	37.5%
(b)	6/10	60%	1/8	12.5%	7/20	35%	5/8	62.5%
(c)	7/10	70%	4/8	50%	12/20	60%	4/8	50%
(d)	8/10	80%	5/8	62.5%	14/20	70%	5/8	62.5%
(e)	9/10	90%	5/8	62.5%	14/20	70%	5/8	62.5%
(f)	9/10	90%	3/8	37.5%	10/20	50%	3/8	37.5%

Candidates (e) and (f) are each correct in all but one (different) parameter, but they are very different in their apparent fitness. (e) scores high, but no higher than (d), which has fewer correct settings. Candidate (f), with only one parameter wrong, scores worse in every category than (c), which has three parameters wrong. And (a) does better than (b) in one category, despite having only four correct parameter settings. Dresher also points out that these results can be influenced in unpredictable ways by the chance occurrence of various types of words. As a result, there is no simple relationship between success and the number of parameters set correctly, which is a problem for Clark's Fitness Measure.

3   The UG condition that lexical material in the specifier of CP needs a lexically filled C entails that in constructions where a wh- phrase is moved to the front of a clause but the finite verb does not move to second position, the wh-phrase occurs not in the specifier of CP, but rather in some adjoined position or in the specifier of some other functional category: Brazilian Portuguese *O que a Maria comeu?*, "What did Maria eat?"; colloquial French *Où il est parti?*, "Where did he go?" Jairo Nunes (personal communication) points out

that Brazilian Portuguese also allows a fronted wh- element with an overt complementizer: O *que que a Maria comeu?* But the complementizer may not occur if there is no wh- fronting: *Que a Maria comeu?* This suggests that Brazilian Portuguese fronts wh- items by adjunction and by movement to the specifier of CP, the latter requiring the C position to be filled.

4   I do not adopt the details of Kroch and Taylor's analysis, for reasons discussed in Lightfoot 1997b, particularly in the Appendix.

5   (11d) (verb–object and I-final) probably does not exist as an actual option. Nothing in the texts seems to require it. This suggests that (10a, b) do not represent two independent parameters.

6   Van Kemenade reported 73 instances of subject-initial clauses, where the subject was followed by a finite verb, 32 instances of verb-third (i.e. XP-subject-Vf), 6 wh- questions, and 23 instances of Vf preceded only by *þa* or the negative particle *ne*. Of the 26 cases of XP-Vf-subject, 19 involved a full noun in subject position, and 7 a subject pronoun.

7   There is an extensive literature now on "exploded inflectional systems," involving agreement phrases, tense phrase, aspect phrase, etc.; but happily this is not relevant to our concerns here, and I ignore it.

8   Swedish is sometimes analyzed as lacking the V-to-I operation. So Vikner (1994) has verbs moving directly to C, because negatives precede finite verbs in embedded clauses: . . . *om Jan inte köpte boken*, "if John didn't buy the book." But this indicates that *inte* "not" and other such adverbs occur to the left of I and does not provide evidence against the application of V to I. Presence of verbs in C is strong evidence of movement through I, given almost any version of the proper government condition on traces. Also, Swedish allows VP fronting, and a dummy finite verb, analogous to English *do*, occupies the position of I (i).

(i)   [läser boken] kanske Allan inte gör
       reads the book maybe Allan not does

This provides direct evidence that the negative marker is left-adjacent to I even in matrix clauses.

In addition, Roberts (1998) invokes V-to-I movement for the Kronoby dialect of Swedish, citing work by Platzack and Holmberg (1989). Holmberg (1986) and Platzack (1986) argued that mainland Scandinavian has V-to-I raising, and that negatives and adverbs are adjoined to I'. Kyle Johnson (1997) argues something similar.

9   I ignore here the very plausible suggestion of Iatridou (1990) that infinitival counterparts to (16c) may not be direct evidence for movement of V across an intervening adverb, if French allows complex verbs of the form [V Adv].

10   Warner (1995) also adopts this methodology explicitly.

11   In fact, Kroch's own figures from Ellegård show several sentence types (positive intransitive questions, negative declaratives, and positive wh- object questions) with *do* less than 40 percent of the time at the very end of the sixteenth century, showing that V-to-I grammars were still very much in use.

12   Some readers balk at the notion that sentences like (17b) were too subtle and not robust enough to trigger a V-to-I operation. However, the fact of the matter is that these forms did not trigger V to I or anything else, because they dropped out of the language – compelling evidence, it seems to me. And they dropped out of the language at the same time as other putative reflexes of the V-to-I operation. This shows not only that they had no triggering effect, but also that they were incompatible with the grammatical operations that *were* being triggered – hence their disappearance. I know of no alternative account of this particular change.

    Furthermore, it also seems reasonable to take the periphrastic *do* forms as robust enough to act as a trigger for grammatical development. They appear in interrogative and negative statements and imperatives. There are several statistical studies showing that *most* of the speech directed at young children consists of interrogatives and imperatives (see Newport et al. 1977).

13   Norbert Hornstein (personal communication) points out that an input-matching model of language acquisition might incorporate an analogue of our notion of a threshold for the expression of a cue by requiring the child to match the input to, say, 70 percent. In fact, Clark and Roberts's learner ignores triggers which fall below a frequency threshold. However, if the partial match is not keyed to specific parameters, this would predict random oscillation in grammars. By contrast, our thresholds are keyed to specific cues.

    It is worth noting that our account would allow a single grammar to have both V-to-I movement and periphrastic *do*, while other accounts do not, notably those within Optimality Theory. Since V-to-I movement and periphrastic *do* coexisted for several hundred years in the history of English, it is implausible that these structures were incompatible and were manifested in separate, competing grammars; competition between grammars is generally more short-lived (see section 4.5).

14   Bickerton (1998: n. 13) notes that he "briefly adopted" the position that creoles have unmarked values for parameter settings, but "rapidly rejected" this viewpoint. Roberts claims that my objection to this position (Lightfoot 1991: 175–7) disappears, but he does not address the point made there: that Saramaccan allows wh- movement out of embedded clauses, and that possibility represents a marked parameter setting.

15   My account of Berbice Dutch is based largely on Smith et al. 1987, but Silvia Kouwenberg (1992) has followed this up with interesting results.

16   Supalla (1990: 50–1) hints at a possible explanation for this tendency to nonlinear morphology. He points to studies showing that individual ASL signs take about 50 percent longer to produce than English words, but comparable propositions take about the same amount of time. This is achieved by having signs with more morphemes per sign and nonlinear morphological structure. This could be explained if there is a particular rhythm to natural language, if language processing takes place naturally at a certain speed, and if a language with ASL-type signs and a linear, affixal morphology is just too slow.

7

Equilibrium and Small Punctuations

7.1 Equilibrium

If a healthy individual tries to stand still, she is not at rest. The center of gravity of her body and the center of pressure under her feet continually move around in tiny adjustments. Maintaining an erect stance involves a complex sensorimotor control system and many small muscle movements. Much goes on in our bodies to keep us upright and stable, and a small malfunction may have bruising consequences.

In the normal course of events, grammars are stable while much is in flux. In communities, speech varies significantly from one person to another, but grammars tend to be uniform and do not differ structurally from one generation to another. Even though they have somewhat different experiences, children often end up saying the same kinds of things as their parents from a structural point of view. They may not have the same content or use the same words, but, as we saw early in the book, there is plenty of scope for variation among people who have the same grammar: they may use words and constructions differently and with different frequencies, and lexical items may vary substantially. None of this entails that they have different grammars, and if that is the extent of the variation, their grammars will be structurally uniform, in equilibrium. The fact that grammars may be in equilibrium for long periods requires explanation, in the same way that one needs to explain the punctuations, the structural changes, when they happen.

We know why there is flexibility in the system, which yields this structural stability. Children are not trigger-happy, attaining a different grammar if they have a different experience. Every child's experience is different from every other's: they are exposed to many different varieties of speech; they hear different things, and the same things in different orders. Experiences may vary indefinitely but still trigger the same grammar. We can understand this to a degree, because we know that the crucial experience, the triggering experience, is a subset of total experience. On our cue-based model of acquisition, what exactly a child hears, as such, is not important for the acquisition of grammars. What the child hears is important only insofar as it expresses the cues which trigger the growth of grammars. When a child has the relevant equipment, knowing what a finite verb is and what thematic roles are, she scans for $_{SpecCP}$[XP] structures. If she is in the Netherlands, in the town of Breukelen, she is likely to find them robustly, and so she attains what we call a verb-second grammar. If she is raised in Brooklyn, New York, she is unlikely to find them, and so a different grammar grows in that child. If the family in Breukelen talks only about soccer games, bicycles, and vacations in the mountains, that has no consequences for the child's grammar. Much of the variation in experience is irrelevant to grammatical development. We can understand the equilibrium that grammars have, if the triggering experience is a set of abstract structures and not sets of sentences.

In the last two chapters we have examined some punctuations – structural changes which reflect a new grammar. These were not grand "parameters" which determine whether a grammar is topic-prominent or subject-prominent (Li and Thompson 1976), "configurational" or not (Hale 1983), polysynthetic or not (Baker 1996). In fact, on the parameter approach, it is not obvious that single parameters reflect such fundamental variation. On the cue-based approach, it is hard to imagine that there could be a single cue for what Li and Thompson call "subject-prominence." Rather, the changes we examined were smaller-scale and involved whether or not verbs move to an inflection position, whether or not there is a morphological means of realizing inherent Case, and so on. In all instances, postulating the right grammatical property enabled us to relate the cluster of superficial changes which occurred at the same time. And we *explain* the grammatical shift if we can show how there was a prior shift in the distribution of the cue, such that the cue came to be expressed at a different level of robustness, rising above or falling below some threshold.

On this view, grammatical changes are contingent, and our explanations are keyed to changes in children's trigger experience; those changes interact with the general demands of grammatical theory. We explain a change only if we can point to prior changes in the distribution of the relevant cues. In the next chapter, we shall compare some different approaches which downgrade the importance of the trigger experience and appeal exclusively to internal acquisition strategies. To lead up to that, I want to continue in the vein of the last two chapters, illustrating the kinds of explanations available on our contingent view of history. I shall examine some intriguing new work on some changes in the history of English and

French. As always, God, the devil, and truth in general lie in the details, and we want a theory which enables us to understand the equilibrium that we observe and the various punctuations in the history of a language that we understand relatively well.

What is striking about the changes discussed in this chapter is that they are manifested in the context of one specific lexical item. In that sense, they are still smaller-scale than the changes discussed earlier. Even so, these changes require explanation, and we shall see that matters of great generality are involved. By looking at small-scale variation, we may come to understand more about equilibrium. We may learn about the lowest levels at which variation in the input actually shapes grammatical properties. Variation below those levels has no consequences for emerging grammars. Children may have different experiences but converge on the same grammar. In those contexts, we have the structural stability which yields grammatical equilibrium. A slightly different kind of variation in the input may produce grammars which differ structurally, and structural differences may affect only one lexical item, as we shall now see.

7.2   English Auxiliary Verbs in the Eighteenth Century

It was in the early 1970s that I first became interested in syntactic change and the way in which it related to work on grammatical theory and language acquisition. There was a popular theory at the time, due to a young, charismatic man who was willing to go anywhere to argue at any time that English modal auxiliary verbs like *can, could, may, might, will, would, shall, should,* and *must* were ordinary verbs at a deep level of analysis. Well, not really just ordinary verbs, but verbs with various exceptional features which accounted for the way in which they behaved differently from real verbs like *grab* and *understand*. So a modal auxiliary may be fronted in a question, but a verb like *understand* may not (1); a modal may occur to the left of a negative particle, unlike a verb (2); a modal may not occur with a perfective (3) or progressive (4) marker, unlike a verb; a modal may not occur in the infinitival complement to another verb (5), nor as the complement of another modal (6), unlike a verb like *try*; and no modal may occur with a direct object, whereas some verbs may (7).

1   (a)   Can he understand chapter 4?
     (b)   *Understands he chapter 4?

2   (a)   He cannot understand chapter 4.
     (b)   *He understands not chapter 4.

3   (a)   *He has could understand chapter 4.
    (b)   He has understood chapter 4.

4   (a)   *Canning understand chapter 4, . . .
    (b)   Understanding chapter 4, . . .

5   (a)   He wanted to try to understand.
    (b)   *He wanted to can understand.

6   (a)   He will try to understand.
    (b)   *He will can understand.

7   (a)   *He can music.
    (b)   He understands music.

According to Haj Ross's theory, the differential behavior was allegedly due to features attached to lexical items: one feature would specify that some verbs (the modals) could move around a subject NP/DP in an interrogative; others would specify that modals had no perfective or progressive forms, and so on.

This theory struck me as implausible for a variety of reasons. However, the facts on which it was based were clearly peculiar to modern English. For example, in French the verb *pouvoir* "can" behaves in the same way as a regular verb like *comprendre* "understand" with respect to movement in a question (8) and negation (9). Unlike *can, pouvoir* may occur as a complement to another verb (10), even to another modal verb (11), and may take a clitic direct object (12); to that extent it behaves like ordinary, common-or-garden verbs in French. In French grammars, the words which translate the English modals, *pouvoir, devoir,* etc., walk like verbs, talk like verbs, and are verbs, just like *comprendre.*

8   (a)   Peut-il comprendre le chapitre?
          "Can he understand the chapter?"
    (b)   Comprend-il le chapitre?
          "Does he understand the chapter?"

9   (a)   Il ne peut pas comprendre le chapitre.
          "He cannot understand the chapter."
    (b)   Il ne comprend pas le chapitre.
          "He doesn't understand the chapter."

10 Il a voulu pouvoir comprendre le chapitre.
    "He wanted to be able to understand the chapter."

11 Il doit pouvoir comprendre le chapitre.
    "He must be able to understand the chapter."

12 Il le peut.
    "He can it" (i.e. understand the chapter).

Furthermore, not only may languages differ in this regard, but also different stages of one language. Sentences along the lines of the ungrammatical utterances of (1)–(7) would have been well-formed in earlier English. In that case, if the differences between Old and Modern English were a function of several exceptional features with no unifying factor, we would expect that these features came into the language at different times and in different ways. On the other hand, if the difference between Modern and Old English reflected a single property, a categorical distinction, then we would expect the trajectory of the change to be very different. If the differences between *can* and *understand* in (1)–(7) were a function of the single fact that *understand* is a verb while *can* is a member of a different syntactic category, auxiliary or inflection, then we would expect (1b), (2b), (3a), (4a), (5b), (6b), and (7a) to have dropped out of people's language in parallel, at roughly the same time.

If we attend just to changing phenomena, the change consisted in the *loss* of various forms, not in the development of new forms; people ceased to say some things which had been said in earlier times. Before the change, all the utterances in (1)–(7) might have occurred in a person's speech, but later only those forms not marked with an asterisk. There were no new possibilities after the change, nothing which could not have been said earlier. That fact alone, although not emphasized in the early work, shows that there was a change in some abstract system. People might start to use some new expression because of the social demands of fashion, or because of the influence of speakers from a different community, but it would be quite a stretch to claim that people ceased to say certain things for that sort of reason. There might be an indirect relationship, of course: people might introduce new expressions into their speech for external, social reasons, and those new expressions might entail the loss of old forms. However, when we find changes involving no new expressions, only the loss and obsolescence of some forms, then that needs to be explained as a consequence of some change in an abstract system. This methodological point is fundamental and arose in the last chapter.

The early work focused on the final disappearance of the relevant forms, showing that they were lost at the same time. The most conservative writer in this regard seems to have been Sir Thomas More, writing in the early sixteenth century. He used many of the asterisked forms in (1)–(7) and had the last attested uses of several constructions. This means that his grammar treated *can*, etc. as verbs in the old fashion, and the fact that he was using all the relevant forms and that his heirs did not suggests that his grammar differed from theirs in one way, and not that the new grammars accumulated various unrelated features, as would be expected in a Ross-style account. The uniformity of the change suggested uniformity in the analysis.

In focusing on the final disappearance of the obsolete forms from the speech community and showing that they disappeared together, the early work did not examine the loss of the old grammar across the population, in the way that we discussed towards the end of chapter 4. That kind of work came later. However, the change in category membership of the English modals was taken as a paradigm case of diachronic change for a long time. It was taken to indicate the catastrophic nature of change, not in the sense that the change spread through the population rapidly (as many changes do), but in the sense that phenomena might change together in a way which required explanation. The notion of reanalysis of an abstract grammar and, later, of resetting grammatical parameters was a way of unifying disparate phenomena, taking them to be various surface manifestations of a single change at the abstract level. The details of this story are in Lightfoot 1979: ch. 2, with a somewhat revised account in Lightfoot 1991: ch. 6.

The cause of the change was taken to be other changes which preceded the change in category membership, notably the fact that the modal auxiliaries became a distinct inflectional class, the sole surviving members of the preterite-present class of verbs. There were many verb classes in early English, and the antecedents of the modern modals were preterite-presents. What was distinctive about the preterite-presents (so-called because their present tense forms had past tense, or "preterite," morphology) was that they never had any inflection for the third person singular, although they were inflected elsewhere: *þu cannst* "you can", *we cunnan* "we can", *we cuðon* "we could". Nonetheless, they were just another class of verbs, and the future modal auxiliaries belonged to this class, along with a number of other verbs which either dropped out of the language altogether or were assimilated to another more regular class of verbs. For example, *unnan* "grant" was lost from the language, and *witan* "know" simply dropped out of the preterite-present class, coming to be treated like a nonpreterite-present. After the simplification of verb morphology, verb classes collapsed, and the only inflectional property of present tense verbs eventually came to be the -s ending for the third person singular, a property that the preterite-present verbs had always lacked.[1] The preterite-presents did not change in this regard, but a great mass of inflectional distinctions had disappeared, and now the preterite-presents were isolated; they looked different from other verbs in lacking their one morphological feature, that -s ending.

The morphological distinctiveness of the surviving preterite-presents, the new modals, was increased by the general loss of a separate subjunctive mood. The past tense forms of the preterite-present verbs were identical in many instances to the subjunctive forms, and as a result, some old past tense forms like *could*, *should*, and *might* survived with subjunctive-type meanings rather than tense indications. While *loved* is related to *love* pretty much exclusively in terms of tense in present-day English, the relationship between *can* and *could* is sometimes one of tense (13a) and sometimes has nothing to do with tense (13b). And *might* is never related to *may* in terms of tense in present-day English (14a, b); in earlier times, however, *might* did serve as a past tense – the thought of (14c) would need to be expressed as *might not have intended* in present-day English. So *might, could, should,* etc. came to take on new meanings which had nothing to do with past time, residues of the old subjunctive uses.

13　(a)　Kim could understand the book, until she reached page 56.
　　(b)　Kim could be here tomorrow.

14　(a)　*Kim might read the book yesterday.
　　(b)　Kim may read the book today.
　　(c)　These two respectable writers might not intend the mischief they were doing. (1762, Bishop Richard Hurd, *Letters on Chivalry and Romance,* 85)

As a result of these changes, the preterite-present verbs came to look different from all other verbs in the language, and the evidence is that the surviving verbs from this class were assigned to a new grammatical category, and that change was complete by the early sixteenth century.

There has been an enormous amount of subsequent work on this topic and, as we would hope, some revisions and refinements. For example, Denison (1989) and Warner (1993) looked at the beginning of the change and argued that we find grammars beginning to distinguish *can*, etc. from regular verbs as early as in Old English. They did not argue for full auxiliary status and did not claim that there was a category change this early: only that we find some of the relevant forms ceasing to be attested as early as in Old English. Later work showed that (1b) and (2b) were lost later than the other changes, and that there were two stages to the history of English modal auxiliaries: first, a change in category membership, whereby *can*, etc. ceased to be treated as verbs and came to be taken as manifestations of an inflection category; this change affected some verbs before others, but it was complete by the sixteenth century. Consequently, for a sentence like *Kim can sing*, early grammars had structures like (15), where *can* is an ordinary verb; but later grammars had structures like (16), where *can* is a modal, generated as an instance of I.

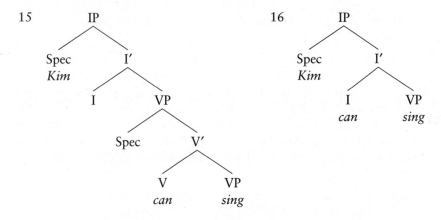

Second, English lost the operation moving verbs to a higher inflection position (e.g. in (15)). We discussed the later change in chapter 6 and argued there that this change was completed only in the eighteenth century, later than is generally supposed.

This much seems to be fairly uncontroversial at this point, although there will probably be more debate on the dating of the loss of the V-to-I operation. I have argued (Lightfoot 1991) that there was less controversy than there appeared to be, and there is now general agreement that something significant happened by the sixteenth century with regard to the category membership of the modal auxiliaries, and that something else happened in the seventeenth or eighteenth century affecting the movement possibilities of all verbs except *be* and *have*. The two changes are, presumably, interrelated in ways that we do not entirely understand: first, the inflection position was appropriated by a subclass of verbs, the modal auxiliaries and *do*, and the V-to-I operation no longer applied generally to all tensed clauses. Somewhat later, the V-to-I movement operation was lost for all verbs other than the exceptional *be* and *have*, and I was no longer a position to which verbs might move.

Now an intriguing paper by Anthony Warner (1995) shows that there is a further stage to the history of English auxiliaries, involving changes taking place quite recently, and this turns out to be of great theoretical interest. It has often been observed that VP ellipsis is generally insensitive to morphology. So one finds ellipses where the understood form of the missing verb differs from the form of the antecedent (17).

17 (a) Kim slept well, and Jim will [sc. sleep well] too.
    (b) Kim seems well-behaved today, and she often has [sc. seemed well-behaved] in the past, too.
    (c) Although Kim went to the store, Jim didn't [sc. go to the store].

There is a kind of sloppy identity at work here. One way of thinking of this is that in (17a) *slept* is analyzed as [*past* + $_V$*sleep*], and the understood verb of the second conjunct accesses the verb *sleep*, ignoring the tense element. However, Warner noticed, first, that the verb *be* works differently. *Be* may occur in elliptical constructions, but only under conditions of strict identity with the antecedent form (18). In (18a, b) the understood form is identical to the antecedent, but not in the nonoccurring (18c, d, e).

18 (a) Kim will be here, and Jim will [sc. be here] too.
    (b) Kim has been here, and Jim has [sc. been here] too.
    (c) *Kim was here, and Jim will [sc. be here] too.
    (d) *If Kim is well-behaved today, then Jim probably will [sc. be well-behaved] too.
    (e) *Kim was here yesterday, and Jim has [sc. been here] today.

This suggests that *was* is not analyzed as [*tense* + $_V$*be*], analogously to *slept*, and *be* may be used as an understood form only where there is precisely a *be* available as an antecedent; not *was* or *is*, but just *be*, as in (18a). Similarly for *been*; compare (18b) and (18e). And similarly for *am, is, are, was, were.*[2]

Earlier we noted evidence that words are stored differently in the mental lexicon. Irregular words are stored individually, but words formed by a regular, productive process are not stored individually. In forming compounds, one accesses lexical entries. So, for example, one may access irregular plurals (*mice eater, men hater*) but not regular plurals (*rats eater, *boys hater*); instead, one has *rat eater* and *boy hater*. The idea here is that the various forms of *be* are listed individually in the lexicon, like *mice* and *men*, and they are not composed by productive lexical processes.

If the various forms of the verb *be* occur in the lexicon unanalyzed, this, in turn, provides a way of addressing an old puzzle: why does one find imperatives like (19c) and not (19a, b)?

19   (a)   *Not be crazy.
     (b)   *Be not crazy.
     (c)   Do not be crazy.

Imperatives are best analyzed with an abstract imperative inflectional morpheme, involving structures like Imp *not leave*. In English, verbs do not move to a higher inflectional position, nor to Imp, at least not after the eighteenth century, so (20b) does not occur. The nonoccurrence of (20a) may then be explained by the stranded affix filter: the affix Imp is stranded. Lack of adjacency blocks the lowering of Imp onto *leave* – see below. Periphrastic *do* saves the structure and yields (20c).

20   (a)   *Not leave.
     (b)   *Leave not.
     (c)   Do not leave.

The same analysis carries over to (19), but we need an extra assumption. In general, forms of *be* may move to a higher inflectional position (yielding *Kim is not here*, *Is Kim here?*, etc.), and this would lead us to expect that (19b) would be grammatical, and that periphrastic *do* (19c) would not be needed to save the structure. We can now understand this in the light of our discussion of the ellipsis facts. If forms of the verb *be* are listed atomically in the lexicon, we can say that modern English lexicons contain no distinct imperative form of *be*, just as no verb in English has an imperative form of any shape or form – unlike, say Latin, which shows specific inflections for imperative forms. Therefore, there is no imperative feature to be checked in the position of Imp, hence no reason for movement, and (19b) does not occur. (19a) does not occur for the same reason as (20a): intervening *not* blocks lowering of Imp onto *be*. And *do* is required to save the structure (19c).[3]

Our tentative conclusion, then, is that *was*, *been*, etc. have no internal structure and occur in the lexicon as unanalyzed primitives. However, there is no imperative *be* in the lexicon.

Warner goes on to note that the ellipsis facts of modern English were not always so, and one finds forms like (18c, d, e) in earlier times. Jane Austen was one of the last writers to use such forms, and she uses them in her letters and in speech in her novels, but she does not use them in narrative prose (21a, b). These forms also occur in the work of eighteenth-century writers (21c), and earlier, when verbs still moved to I (21d).

21 (a) I wish our opinions were the same. But in time they will [sc. be the same]. (1816, Jane Austen, *Emma*, ed. R. W. Chapman (London: Oxford University Press, 1933), 471)

    (b) And Lady Middleton, is she angry?
         I cannot suppose it possible that she should [sc. be angry]. (1811, Jane Austen, *Sense and Sensibility*, ed. R. W. Chapman (London: Oxford University Press, 1923), 272)

    (c) I think, added he, all the Charges attending it, and the Trouble you had, were defray'd by my Attorney: I ordered that they should [sc. be defrayed]. (1740–1, Samuel Richardson, *Pamela* (London, 3rd edn 1741), vol. 2, 129)

    (d) That bettre loved is noon, ne never schal. (ca. 1370, Chaucer, *A Complaint to his Lady*, 80)
         "So that no one is better loved, or ever shall [sc. be]."

These forms may be understood if *were* in (21a) was analyzed as *subjunctive* + *be*, and the *be* was accessed by the understood *be*. In other words, up until the early nineteenth century, the finite forms of *be* were decomposable, just like ordinary verbs in present-day English. So the ellipsis facts suggest.

Warner then shows that there are other differences between present-day English and the English of the early nineteenth century. Present-day English shows quite idiosyncratic restrictions on particular forms of the verb *be*, which did not exist before the late eighteenth or early nineteenth century. For example, it is only the finite forms of *be* which may be followed by *to* + infinitive (22); only *been* may occur with a directional preposition phrase (23); and *being* is subcategorized as not permitting an -*ing* complement (24).

22 (a) Kim was to go to Paris.
    (b) *Kim will be to go to Paris.

23 (a) Kim has been to Paris.
    (b) *Kim was to Paris.

24 (a) I regretted Kim reading that chapter.
    (b) I regretted that Kim was reading that chapter.
    (c) *I regretted Kim being reading that chapter.

Restrictions of this type are stated in the lexicon, and these idiosyncrasies show clearly that *been*, *being*, etc. must be listed as individual lexical entries. However, these restrictions are fairly new in the language, and we find forms corresponding to the nonoccurring sentences of (22)–(24) through the eighteenth century:

25 (a) You will be to visit me in prison with a basket of provisions . . .
          (1814, Jane Austen, *Mansfield Park*, ed. J. Lucas (London: Oxford
          University Press, 1970), 122)

    (b) I was this morning to buy silk. (1762, Oliver Goldsmith, *Cit W*:
          158) (meaning "I went to . . . ," not "I had to . . .")

    (c) Two large wax candles were also set on another table, the ladies
          being going to cards. (1726, Daniel Defoe, *The Political History
          of the Devil* (Oxford: Talboys, 1840), 336)

    (d) . . . he being now going to end all with the Queene . . . (1661,
          Samuel Pepys, *Diary*, ii 129.1 (30 June))

    (e) One day being discoursing with her upon the extremities they
          suffered . . . (1791, Daniel Defoe, *Robinson Crusoe*, vol. 2, 218)

    (f) . . . and exclaimed quite as much as was necessary, (or, being acting
          a part, perhaps rather more,) at the conduct of the Churchills, in
          keeping him away. (1816, Jane Austen, *Emma*, 145)

    (g) Their being going to be married. (1811, Jane Austen, *Sense and
          Sensibility*, ed. R. W. Chapman (London: Oxford University Press,
          1923), 182)

    (h) The younger Miss Thorpes being also dancing, Catherine was
          left to the mercy of Mrs Thorpe. (1818, Jane Austen, *Northanger
          Abbey*, ed. R. W. Chapman (London: Oxford University Press,
          1923), 52)[4]

Warner concludes that, after the change,

> *was* continues to carry the information that it is third singular past finite
> indicative. The point is that it does not do so as a consequence of inflection
> or inflectional relationships, but is essentially monomorphemic. The relation-
> ship *was:be* becomes fundamentally different not only from regular verbs
> *loved:love*, etc. but also from that of irregular or suppletive verbs (*slew:slay*,
> *went:go*), which are in some sense essentially compositional, as the contrast
> of behavior in ellipsis shows. (Warner 1995: 538)

So there were several nineteenth-century changes in the distribution of
be, which related to ellipsis possibilities and subcategorization restrictions
on specific forms. Another change taking place at the same time was the

appearance for the first time of the progressive in *is being*. Until this time, we do not find forms like (26), as often noted. This is discussed by Jespersen (1909–49: vol. 4, 225–6), Mossé (1938: vol. 2, §266), Visser (1973: §§1834–5), and, very usefully, by Denison (1993: ch. 13); Warner (1995: n. 8) joins Denison (1993: 395–6) in noting that some purported earlier examples are more apparent than real.

26   (a)   You are being naughty.
     (b)   You are being a bore.

The first examples of *being* progressives were with passives. Until the late eighteenth century, the progressive passive was expressed by the *-ing* form of a regular verb (27), and these forms continued to occur in the nineteenth century.

27   (a)   At the very time that this dispute was maintaining by the centinel and the drummer, was the same point debating betwix't a trumpeter and a trumpeter's wife. (1759–67, Laurence Sterne, *Tristram Shandy*, 179)
     (b)   She only came on foot, to leave more room for the harp, which was bringing in the carriage. (1818, Jane Austen, *Persuasion*, ed. R. W. Chapman (London: Oxford University Press, 1923), 50)
     (c)   The clock struck ten while the trunks were carrying down. (1818, Jane Austen, *Northanger Abbey*, 155)

Warner finds the first examples of the *is being* passives in the late eighteenth century:

28   (a)   I have received the speech and address of the House of Lords; probably, that of the House of Commons was being debated when the post went out. (1772, *A Series of Letters of the First Earl of Malmesbury*, ed. Earl of Malmesbury (London: R. Bentley, 1870), vol. 1, 264; letter from Mr Harris, Jun., to his mother, 8. xii. 1772)
     (b)   The inhabitants of Plymouth are under arms, and everything is being done that can be. (1779, *Letters of the First Earl of Malmesbury*, vol. 1, 430; letter from Mrs Harris to her son, 22. viii. 1779)
     (c)   A fellow whose uttermost upper grinder is being torn out by the roots by a mutton-fisted barber. (1795, Robert Southey, *Life and Correspondence*, ed. C. C. Southey (London: Longman, 1849), vol. 1, 249)

The form *being* occurs before the eighteenth century, but as a nonprogressive. One may distinguish the nonprogressive (29a) from the progressive (29b).

29   (a)   Crossing the Rubicon, Caesar marched into North Italy.
     (b)   What, Caesar crossing the Rubicon!

Warner treats the nonprogressive *-ing* forms (29a) as nonpredicational [–PRD] and the progressives (29b) as predicational [+PRD]. Prior to the eighteenth century *be* (and *have*) was subcategorized to be followed by a predicational phrase, and *be* (and all auxiliary verbs) was itself [–PRD] by default (i.e. specific, positive evidence is needed for a child to list an item as +PRD) – consequently, no progressives in *is being*. This is a perfectly normal kind of subcategorization restriction.

> Since *being* was regularly formed, it had the properties of *be* and *-ing*; *-ing* had the potential to mark forms as either progressive [as in *Kim was washing*] or nonprogressive, but the only result which complied with the default was nonprogressive *being*. (Warner 1995: 540)

So, what happened to *being* in the eighteenth century? We have noted that forms of the verb *be* ceased to be decomposable in the eighteenth century, being stored in the mental lexicon as distinct, atomic entries with no morphological relationship parallel to *love:loved*, etc. So *was* is listed as a past tense form, but it is not related to *is* by any productive process; it doesn't look like a past tense in the way that *loved* is related to *love*, or even as *took* is related to *take*. In that case, the analysis of *being* had to change. *Being* differs from *was* in that it has some obvious internal structure, *be* + *ing*; but now this has to be specified in the lexicon as some kind of redundancy statement; it is no longer generated by a general rule affecting all verbs, because *be* has come to have a different morphosyntax. All forms of *be* now need to be specified separately as individual and irregular forms, even *being*, which looks regular. Warner claims plausibly that

> such individual specification is sufficient to have priority over the default. Hence as soon as *being* requires a special statement, it becomes available as a progressive form, and *is being* appears. Thus, paradoxically, it is the irregularity of *being* as an auxiliary that requires a statement about it that is capable of reflecting the properties of the verbal affix *-ing*. (Ibid. 540)

Eighteenth-century children heard *being* forms, which were previously analyzed as [−PRD], and listed them as irregular items containing *-ing*. In that event, since *being* was no longer formed by general rule, it was no longer subject to default requirements identifying it as [−PRD], and could be used as if it were [+PRD]. So it could follow another *be*. In this way, we may understand the introduction of progressive passives as a function of the same new property which yielded the new subcategorizational restrictions on various forms of *be*, manifested by the obsolescence of (25a, b) and the *being verb+ing* forms of (25c–h): *be* ceases to be a verb with the usual internal morphological structure.

Warner shows that there was an analogous change with *have*, but that argument involves some complexity that I will dodge here. It is worth noting that the auxiliary verb *have* works in the same way as *be* in elliptical constructions, although the facts are less crisp. Interestingly, the main verb *have* may sometimes be used like an auxiliary for some speakers, occurring to the left of a negative (30a), moving to the left of a subject (30b).

30 (a)   Kim hasn't a lot of experience.
    (b)   Has Kim a lot of experience?

When *have* behaves like an auxiliary in this regard, then it also behaves like an auxiliary with respect to ellipsis (31a): strict identity is needed for an understood auxiliary *have*. The main verb *have* does not require strict identity for ellipsis (31b).

31 (a)   *Kim hasn't a lot of experience, but Jim should [sc. have a lot of experience].
    (b)   Kim was having a good time, and Jim did [sc. have a good time] too.

Whether the change in the representation of the forms of the verb *be* also affects the verb *have*, it is clearly restricted to a very narrow class of lexical items. The analysis, however, reflects quite general properties, and the change relates to the matter of category membership. Forms of *be* cease to be analyzed as a verb with the usual morphological structure.

Grammars have quite small sets of categories, and individual lexical items are assigned to one or other of these categories. Evidence suggests that items are assigned to grammatical categories on the basis of their morphological properties. If a given item becomes morphologically distinct from other items in its category, then it is liable to be assigned to a new category. This is what was involved in the earlier changes involving the modal auxiliaries, formerly preterite-present verbs. As a result of changes affecting the preterite-present class of verbs and the subjunctive mood, these items became morphologically distinct from other verbs and were assigned to a new category, inflection (I). Similarly with the changes affecting *be* in the eighteenth century.

If we ask why the change took place, we get some insight into the grammatical property involved. The change in the internal structure of *be* forms was preceded by two other changes.

First, the operation moving verbs to an inflection position, V to I, was finally lost in the eighteenth century, as I argued in section 6.3. At this point, sentences with a finite verb moved to some initial position or to the left of a negative became obsolete (*Understands Kim this chapter? Kim understands not this chapter*) and were replaced by equivalent forms with the periphrastic *do*: *Does Kim understand this chapter? Kim does not understand this chapter*, etc. Also, sentences with an adverb between the finite verb and its complement became obsolete: *Kim reads always the newspapers*. The loss of V-to-I movement further distinguished the modal auxiliaries from main verbs, with *be* patterning with the modals in continuing to occur in the old positions, initially and to the left of a negative: *Is she happy?* and *She is not happy*.

Second, Warner shows that the pronoun *thou* and the accompanying inflectional forms in *-(e)st* were lost from informal spoken English in the eighteenth century. *Thou* was used like the French *tu*, directed to children, intimates, and inferiors. It was lost for social reasons, as speakers abandoned a linguistic manifestation of these social distinctions. The obsolesence of *Thou shalt*, *Thou shouldest*, etc. removed the last inflectional property of modal verbs which was shared with ordinary verbs.

Modals had become very different from verbs in the course of changes that we have linked to their change in category, completed by the sixteenth century. They ceased to have nonfinite forms, ceased to have mood and tense forms, ceased to have complements, etc.; this showed that they were recategorized as inflection elements, generated in the I position. The loss of the second person singular forms constitutes a further step: the last remaining inflectional commonality shared by modals and ordinary verbs was lost. This last change also affected the verb *be*, which had shown no symptoms of the category change affecting the modals: *be* did not lose its nonfinite forms in the way that *can* did; nor did it lose its mood and tense forms, nor its ability to be followed by a complement. Now, however, *be* became distinct from ordinary verbs in that it continued to move to I and onto C, while main verbs lost this ability; nor did it look like a verb any more in terms of its finite inflectional properties.

The first of these changes affected all verbs – they ceased to move to I – and the second change affected all verbs and (modal) elements generated in the inflection position. Neither change affected *be* in particular, but their effect was to single out *be* and make it less like a verb. As a result of these changes, *be* came to differ from verbs in that it could occur in high functional positions like I and C, and it lacked the only morphological properties characteristic of verbs, the universal third person singular marker in -*s* and the usual past tense -*ed* marker.

It is plausible that these were the changes which led children to treat *be* differently. Now it ceased to look like a verb and ceased to have the internal structure of a verb. *Be* did not undergo the category change that the modals underwent by the sixteenth century: *be* was never associated intrinsically with the (finite) inflection position in the way that modals are, and *be* continues to occur in nonfinite contexts (*I want to be happy*, *Being happy is a good thing*, *Be happy*, etc.). This shows that the finite forms of *be* move to I and are not base-generated there like the modals. In the eighteenth century main verbs ceased to move to I, but the finite forms of *be* continued to do so. As a result, *be* no longer walks like a verb and no longer talks like a verb. The evidence suggests that, in addition, in the nineteenth century *be* ceased to show the paradigmatic properties of verbs; instead, its inflectional paradigm was individually specified as a series of lexical items, stored individually in the mental lexicon.

Warner formulated this change in the terms of head-driven Phrase Structure Grammar, but one can also think of it in terms of ideas in the Minimalist Program. Chomsky (1995) adopts a strict lexicalist view: verbs, all verbs, are taken from the lexicon fully inflected. Inflected forms of a verb have an internal structure resulting from lexical operations; they are drawn from the lexicon and then need to be *checked* against the relevant features of abstract functional heads. For example, the form *loves* has a third person singular feature, which is checked in an inflection position; so *loves* must move to the I position. For Chomsky, the checking may take place in the overt syntax (in French) or covertly at logical form (in English); this distinction corresponds to the idea discussed in section 6.3 that a V moves to I in the syntax in French, while I lowers onto V in the morphology in English.

However, there are problems with this approach. For example, it does not account for the fact that both the sentences of (32) reflect ungrammatical forms.

32 (a) *Kim not understands the chapter.
    (b) *Kim understands not the chapter.

The ungrammaticality of (32a) suggests that checking may not be "procrastinated" until logical form and therefore must take place in the syntax. However, the ungrammaticality of (32b) shows that checking does not take place in the syntax in English and that the inflectional feature is not "strong."

Lasnik (1995) offers a hybrid approach: the inflection position may contain an affix or strong features. Features must be checked in the syntax, whereas an affix must "merge" with a verb at phonological form. Because merger takes place at phonological form, it is a phonological operation and requires adjacency. This is essentially the same idea as was adopted in section 6.3, that I-lowering is a morphological operation. On this view, a verb with features raises overtly to an I position with features, and the verb's features are thereby checked. A bare verb with no features, on the other hand, has an affix lowered onto it from an adjacent position at phonological form.

This entails that a finite French verb and *have* and *be* in English are pulled fully formed from the lexicon and move to an appropriate functional position in which their features may be checked. Main verbs in English, on the other hand, have no features in the lexicon, and an affix lowers onto them at phonological form. Now the reason for the ungrammaticality of (32) is that the inflected *understands* is not in the lexicon, since main verbs in English generally are bare and acquire their inflectional properties through lowering at phonological form. (32b) does not occur, because *understands* does not exist in the lexicon and therefore may not move in the syntax to check its features in I. Nor may an affix lower onto an uninflected *understand* to yield (32a), because of the intervening *not*. *Be* and *have*, however, move to functional positions and therefore are featural, each form fully inflected in the lexicon, like French verbs.

Here we distinguish affixal and featural verbs. *Be* and *have* are featural, fully formed in the lexicon, whereas regular verbs in English are bare, acquiring affixes at phonological form. Before that affix lowering takes place, the abstract *sleep* of *slept* is identifiable as a distinct unit and therefore is an appropriate antecedent for ellipsis in (17a) *Kim slept well, and Jim will [sc. sleep well] too.* This reveals how elements are stored in the mental lexicon: *is* is stored in just that form, whereas *slept* is not stored as such but is created in the course of a derivation. If all verbs were treated the same way, as in Chomsky 1995, there would be no obvious way to make the distinction between those which may be antecedents for ellipsis under conditions of sloppy identity (*sleep*, etc.) and those which may not (*is, are,* and other forms of *be*).

Lasnik keyed the distinction between affixal and featural verbs to whether the verb moves, but there is more to the story than this. Modal elements are featural and are generated in I, rather than moving there. Finite *be* clearly moves to I, because *be* may also occur in other, nonfinite positions if I is filled with a modal (33).

33   Kim might still be reading that chapter.

So forms of *be* and *have* move to I but they are featural. They have always moved to I at all stages of their history, but it was only in the late eighteenth century that they came to be stored atomically and developed the odd properties discussed here. We conclude that if a verb is featural, it moves to I. However, a featural item may be base-generated in I (modern modals) and may or may not be stored atomically: *was* is stored atomically in modern grammars but was not stored atomically in grammars of the early modern period.

What is important about this story is that, while the changes we have discussed only involve the verb *be*, they have the hallmarks of grammatical change. There are several surface changes, all involving *be*, which can be attributed to one analytical notion. The changes reflect quite general properties of the grammar, here relating to category membership. One can identify the structural property which is relevant and tell a plausible, rather elegant story about why and how the grammatical change might have come about. We distinguish how items are stored in the lexicon.

We see, as we have seen elsewhere, that morphology has syntactic effects. It is particularly important in defining category membership; children assign items to categories on the basis of their morphology. We have been able to explain the change by pointing to changes in the trigger experience which led to the new morphological structure of *be* forms. Those changes in the trigger are a function of prior grammatical shifts, relating to the change in category membership of the modal auxiliaries and the loss of V-to-I movement; there are links among the changes, and we have another domino effect. Again we have a sufficient explanation, and we do not need to appeal to internal motivating factors. As Warner notes, "the shift in the primary linguistic data caused by the decline of *thou* seems substantial enough for there to be no reason to suppose that internal strategies should be assigned a major determining role" (Warner 1995: 543).

While morphology clearly influences category membership, one finds a stronger claim in the literature. It is sometimes argued that richly inflected languages differ in a fundamental way from poorly inflected languages like English and Chinese. In this context, it might be argued that grammars with rich inflectional systems, like those of French speakers, list forms individually in the lexicon and do not form them by general operations. On the analysis offered here, this would entail that no bare forms were available to syntactic operations, and one would find various lexical restrictions on particular forms, as we saw for *be* in present-day English in (22)–(24) above. In grammars like those of present-day English speakers, on the other hand, there are fewer individual listings. Plural nouns in *-s* and third person singular forms of verbs in *-s* are composed derivationally through phonological lowering, and they are not listed in the lexicon fully formed. As a result, the bare forms of the noun and of the verb, shorn of its affixal ending, are available to various grammatical operations, and it is not possible to state lexical restrictions on particular third person singular forms.

However, the material of this section shows that this is not correct and suggests that how items are stored in the lexicon is neither a function of movement nor a simple function of morphological richness. Main verbs and *be* could occur in ellipses without strict identity with their antecedent up until the nineteenth century. This suggests strongly that their forms were not stored atomically, even though they were richly inflected in the early stages of the language. Instead, they were stored bare, and individual forms were generated by operations applying internal to the lexicon. Consequently, we conclude that the way in which elements are stored in the lexicon has many syntactic consequences, but the distinction represents variation which is independent of whether an item moves to an inflection position and independent of whether an item is richly inflected.

In affecting a narrow class of words, the change described here is certainly small-scale. It can be understood in terms of prior changes, including the highly contingent loss of *thou* forms, and it reflects ways in which items may be stored in the mental lexicon.

7.3   French *chez*

In this section I shall sketch Pino Longobardi's account of a change in French which is limited to one word. In that respect, the change is similar to the change involving English *be* forms in the late eighteenth century. The kind of explanation which Longobardi (1996) offers depends heavily on the theory of Universal Grammar, but it differs somewhat from the explanation offered in the last section.

Longobardi notes that French *chez* derives etymologically from the Latin noun *casa* "house", but the development is odd in a number of ways. The phonetic development is that shown in (34a), not the expected bisyllabic (34b); ordinarily /a/ is the only Latin short vowel to be preserved in final syllables in Old French.

34 (a)   casa > OF chies > chez
    (b)   casa > OF chiese > *chèse

Furthermore, there was a category change: the noun came to be used as a preposition, and it acquired an abstract, locative meaning which has nothing to do with "house" (35).

35 Chez Platon, Socrate nous apparaît comme l'homme le plus sage.
    "In Plato, Socrates appears to us as the wisest man."

These changes are idiosyncratic, but Longobardi shows that matters of some generality are involved, which provide some explanation for the changes.

The general matters relate to an operation which raises a noun to the higher functional position D (for "determiner") normally occupied by articles, as argued by Longobardi (1994). In the modern Romance languages, this operation affects proper names, some common nouns indicating kinship, and the word for "home". Alongside (36a) in Italian, one finds (36b), and the latter sentence involves the N-to-D operation, as indicated in (36c).

36 (a)   La mia casa è più bella della tua.
          the my home is more beautiful than the yours
    (b)   Casa mia è più bella della tua.
          home my is more beautiful than the yours
    (c)

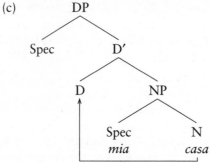

The semantics of all these raised nouns show an individually referential interpretation, and the raised common nouns have an oddity: they are always interpreted as having an overt or understood possessor.

37 (a) Casa è sempre il posto migliore per rilassarsi.
         "Home is always the best place to relax." (= "one's home")
    (b) Casa era ormai vicina.
         "Home was eventually nearby." (= "my/your home")
    (c) Maria pensa che la madre di Gianni abbia ripulito casa.
         "Maria thinks that Gianni's mother has cleaned up home."
         (= "Gianni's mother's home")

The sentences of (37) do not have the simple, possessor-less interpretation of unraised phrases like *La/quella casa era ormai vicina*, "The/that house was eventually nearby," in which a specific house is indicated with no implication that it belongs to anybody in particular.

Longobardi notes that these forms in Romance languages are reminiscent of the "construct state" constructions of Semitic languages, which are subject to the same N-to-D analysis. For example, the most typical raising noun in Italian, *casa*, when raised as in (38a), has possessors without the usual preposition *di*; when it does not raise, *di* must be present (38b, c). And likewise for Semitic (39).

38 (a) Casa Rossi è qui vicina.
         home Rossi is nearby
    (b) *La casa Rossi è qui vicina.
         the home Rossi is nearby
    (c) La casa di Rossi è qui vicina.
         "The home of Rossi is nearby."

39 (a) Beyt ha-more (ha-gadol).
         home the teacher (the big)
    (b) *Ha-beyt/bayit ha-more
         the home the teacher
    (c) *Beyt šel ha-more.
         home of the teacher
    (d) Ha-bayit (ha-gadol) šel ha-more.
         the home (the big) of the teacher

As in Semitic, adjectives may not be interpolated between the two nouns in a raised construction:

40 (a)   *Casa nuova Rossi.
          home new Rossi
    (b)   Casa Rossi nuova.
    (c)   *Beyt ha-gadol ha-more.
          home the big the teacher

Longobardi goes on to argue that precisely the same common nouns, kinship terms, and *home*, raise to D in English, although covertly at logical form. These determiner-less elements do not move overtly to D across adjectives or genitive phrases (41a, b), but they are interpreted in the same way, displaying an individual reference and requiring an overt or understood possessor (41c–e).

41 (a)   *I always regret home old sweet.
    (b)   *He visited home John's.
    (c)   Home is always the best place to relax.
    (d)   Home was eventually nearby.
    (e)   John's friend was heading home.

In addition, unlike all other place nouns, *home*, when raised to D at logical form, may have the distribution and meaning of a locative PP or adverb (41e). The phenomenon of a noun being interpreted as if it were a locative PP occurs elsewhere: Longobardi notes that modern Veneto dialects omit the preposition *a* which normally introduces locative and directional complements, precisely before a raised *casa*: *Vago casa (mia)*, "I-am-going home (my)." Locative and directional prepositions are also deleted in Latin and Classical Greek not only before the word for "home" but also before the proper names of cities and small islands: *Veni domum/Romam*, "I came home/to Rome." It is necessary to analyze these structures with an empty locative preposition and plausible to claim that the P incorporates into the noun. In order for this to happen, the N must move to the intervening D position, because in general heads may not move across an intervening head – this restriction, which we invoked in chapter 6, follows from the Head Movement Constraint, or the Minimality Condition of Rizzi (1990). This, in turn, predicts that these locative/directional interpretations occur only with proper names and the common nouns which raise to D, like Italian *casa*, English *home*, etc.[5]

So the N-to-D operation occurs quite generally, and it often affects words meaning "home" in various languages. With this in mind, let us return now to French *chez*. *Chez* has a locative meaning, and it has the distribution of a locative PP (42a), never occurring as a subject or direct object, positions generally restricted to NP/DPs or CPs (42b, c); and it does not appear with the internal structure of a NP/DP, preceded by a determiner or followed by a PP (42d).

42 (a)   Je vais chez Pierre.
         "I am going to Pierre's."
    (b)   *Chez Pierre est très joli.
         "Pierre's is very beautiful."
    (c)   *J'ai vu chez Pierre.
         "I saw Pierre's."
    (d)   *Je vais à la chez de Pierre.
         "I am going to the home of Pierre."

So in modern French *chez* is clearly a preposition, despite the fact that it is derived historically from a Latin noun, *casa*.

Longobardi notes that in certain stylistic varieties *chez* has some properties of a raised noun. Certain dialects allow sentences like (43), where *chez* has the meaning of "family, household" and requires a plural verb.

43   Chez (les) Meillets sont partis.
     "The Meillets left."

A raised noun analysis is still more plausible for Old French, where *chies* has nominal qualities. *Chies* does not yet have the abstract reading of *Chez Platon, Socrate nous apparaît comme l'homme le plus sage* (35), and it occurs with an independent preposition *a/en ch(i)es* "at home" and sometimes has a very obvious nominal interpretation (44).

44   La place de terre ou Florence siet fu jadis apelee chiés du Mars, ce est a dire maisons de bataille.
     "The piece of land where Florence lies was once called *chiés* of Mars, that is to say home of battle."

It appears that the N-to-D raising operation applied to *casa* early on in the history of the Romance languages, perhaps in Latin or perhaps at a very early stage of the Romance languages, since there are reflexes in many of the modern languages.

Longobardi observes:

> ... the resulting picture is a familiar one in the historical-comparative frame-
> work: a group of related languages displays a phenomenon with partially but
> significantly similar properties and, furthermore, the similarities increase the
> more one goes back toward the past. (1996: 13)

In early French, *chies* raised to D and was then available to be incorporated into a higher locative preposition. In later grammars *chez* (< *chies*)
came to occur as a preposition and was not treated as a noun at any level
of analysis; no N-to-D raising is involved in expressions like (42a), which
is analyzed with *chez* base-generated as a preposition. UG plays an important role in explaining this development, in that if a common noun raises to
D, then the resulting DP lacks an overt article (*le*, *la*) and the noun is not
followed by a preposition; moreover, it is only a raised noun which may be
interpreted as a locative PP (**John went the home of Kim*), and therefore,
only a raised N is susceptible to recategorization as a preposition.

Longobardi adds a further (informal) theorem: every DP has one and only
one phrasal stress, which falls on the rightmost noun of the DP. Since,
apart from kinship terms, *casa* is the only common noun raising to D
in early Romance, we can now understand why it alone was subject to
an apparently irregular phonological development. By virtue of moving
to D, *casa* could not receive phrasal stress when followed by another
(prepositionless) NP/DP, as in, say, *casa Rossi* (38a); in this example *Rossi*
received phrasal stress. Consequently, *casa* was subject to reduction, yielding Italian *ca'*, Catalan *ca'*, Spanish (dialectal) *ca/cas*, and Old French
monosyllabic *chies* (> *chez*), in a way that other, nonraised nouns with a
short /a/ in final syllables were not.

Despite the commonalities and the fact that several grammars raise the
noun meaning "home" to a higher D, French is the only language to show
a change in the category of *casa*. The fact that this development took place
in French but not in, say, Italian or any other set of grammars with N-to-
D raising, needs to be explained. Longobardi argues that, since *casa* raised
to D, then it was liable to be incorporated with a higher locative preposition. Then, in turn, early French children would have been susceptible to
analyzing *chies* as a preposition.[6]

Children need evidence to establish the category that a lexical item belongs to. That evidence might be distributional, inflectional, or paradigmatic.

After raising of *chies* had triggered the possibility of incorporating with an empty locative preposition, the distributional evidence favoring a nominal analysis would be occurrences of *chies* in an unmistakably NP/DP position (subject and object – cf. (42b, c) or the co-occurrence of *chies* with determiners, inflected possessives (42d), or attributive adjectives (cf. Italian *casa mia* in (36b)). So, for example, this kind of evidence is available for English *home* – e.g. (41c, d) and usage as a direct object: *Kim loves home*. In Old French, however, the comparable evidence was apparently slender. Since *chies* raised to D, it could never co-occur with an overt determiner; and attributive adjectives occur very rarely with raised nouns. So, if *chies* became less commonly used in subject and object position, then there would have been very little distributional evidence for a nominal analysis.

The second kind of evidence for a nominal analysis might be inflectional. Romance prepositions are uninflected and do not vary in form, while nouns were inflected for number, gender, and case. A particular noun does not vary in gender, so we may put this aside. Longobardi shows that N-to-D raising affects only singular nouns, so *chies* never varied for number. And the relevant case distinctions were present only for masculine nouns. So no inflectional variation could distinguish the feminine *chies* from a preposition: it was formally invariant and, to this extent, preposition-like.

The third possibility is that a child might recognize that *chies* is a regular allomorph of some unequivocal noun. The other Romance languages do provide such evidence by virtue of alternating *ca/cas* with *casa*; similarly, English *home* has clear nominal uses: *The home of the Washington Redskins*. However, French *chiese* disappeared from regular usage very early, so the French child did not have the kind of paradigmatic evidence to treat *chies* as a noun, unlike what was available in the other Romance languages for the reduced derivatives of *casa*.

So Longobardi offers an explanation for the recategorization of *chez* as a preposition, and the explanation is based on the nature of the N-to-D raising operation: only nouns which undergo that raising are susceptible to the recategorization, and the recategorization takes place when there is no longer sufficient evidence for the nominal character of the word. He notes that "the success of this research is not really complete, in the sense of failing to attribute the primitive change to some grammar-external factor" (p. 16). Nonetheless, there is a significant level of explanation. The explanation is based on (a) the idea that specific evidence is needed for assigning items to the N category and (b) the analysis of N-to-D raising for certain common nouns. Then the assumption that common Romance *casa* underwent N-to-D raising and that the unreduced *casa* (> *chiese*) was lost in early French effectively makes *chez* susceptible to recategorization. Loss of sufficient distributional or inflectional evidence for the nominal character of *chez* is what leads to its specific development in French.

So UG provides the channels for the change. Longobardi's account is incomplete, in that he does not demonstrate the reduction in the evidence for the nominal nature of *chez*, and to that extent, his explanation differs from Warner's explanation of the changes affecting English *be*.[7] Nonetheless, the account is plausible, and it provides a good transition to a discussion of nineteenth-century style historicism and the abuse of Clio.

In this chapter, we have discussed changes which affected the forms of *be* in nineteenth-century English and *chez* in early French. Because the changes are so restricted, they constitute small punctuations, but they nonetheless require explanation, and, indeed, interesting explanations seem to be available on certain reasonable assumptions about UG. The explanations offered are highly contingent; they depend on very particular circumstances, including the nongrammatical circumstances of the loss of *thou* forms. It is hard to imagine that changes as restricted as this could follow from general principles about language types or the nature of linguistic change. Let us turn now to explanations of that type.

Notes

1   There was an interim period, after the change in category membership, in which verbs and modals showed second person singular form in *-(e)st*, as we shall see below in the main text.

2   The distinction is parallel to the ability to access *Chomsky* in (i), but not in (ii), where *Chomsky* is embedded within an adjective.

(i)   Chomsky's analysis got him into trouble with modals.

(ii)   *The $_A$[Chomskyan] analysis got him into trouble with modals.

3   If there is no imperative form, then the structure of *Be good* is: Imp $_{VP}$[be good]. Similarly for *Read this book*: Imp $_{VP}$[read this book]. Imp lowers onto *be* and onto *read*. Presumably the fact that there is no imperative form of any verb in English is related to the fact that verbs used as imperatives always occur in their stem form.

4   This kind of construction, which does not occur in present-day English, has led modern commentators to decry Jane Austen's English: "It is not good writing – it is not even grammatical writing" (Garrod 1928).

5   Mark Hale reminds me that the "accusative of goal" is fully productive in Classical Greek and Sanskrit. This raises the question of whether N-to-D raising was more widespread in those grammars.

6 At this point Longobardi invokes a markedness explanation in dubious fashion.
   He appeals to a principle which encourages children to "minimize feature
   content." Categories are composed of the features +/–N, +/–V, and Longobardi
   takes prepositions, which are [–N, –V], to be the most contentless category, as
   if minus values do not count for content. A category with one + feature has
   more content, and adjectives, which are [+N, +V], are the most contentful. "In
   these terms, a shift from N to P instantiates a classical case of feature simplification or grammaticalization (loss of lexical content)" (Longobardi 1996: 14).

7 Longobardi argues that there is no parameter resetting in the history of the
   categorial change that he sketches. He goes on to speculate that we may be able
   to achieve "a near 'ideal' theory of diachronic change" in which "syntactic
   change does not exist as a primitive . . . but can be reduced to independent
   changes in the phonology or semantics interfaces of individual lexical items"
   (ibid. 17). Such an "ideal" theory would entail reanalyzing the changes that we
   have discussed in the last few chapters.

8

Historicism: The Use and Abuse of Clio

The last three chapters have offered some analyses which contribute to the innovative core of this book. There I argued for a cue-based theory of acquisition, claiming that children scan their linguistic environment for certain grammatical structures, and that when they find these cues with a sufficient degree of robustness, they converge on a grammar accordingly. They do not search for a grammar which generates the set of sentences that they are exposed to, as in other learnability models. Then, by making certain claims about the nature of UG, I was able to develop *contingent* accounts of various changes. The principles of UG provide the channels within which change may take place. So a grammar changes like a billiard ball on an undulating surface. The ball needs to be set in motion, and then it may move along the channels of the surface, coming to rest at some point, but certainly not at the top of any of the undulations.

The case study of French *chez*, for example, illustrates the influence of those channels very clearly. Children have quite limited options; but if the triggering experience shifts just a little, then sometimes a new option arises. The structural change may affect just one lexical item, but we saw in the last chapter that we may learn a lot even from changes whose effects are limited to a very small number of lexical items. Restricted changes of that type need explanation in the same way as bigger changes which affect the distribution of all the verbs in some system.

8.1 Principles of History

All of the accounts I have given have involved claims about UG, the cues, and distributional shifts in the trigger experience, but nothing more. At no point have I invoked an independent "theory of change," and that makes this work different from the work of many historical linguists. People have been working on language change since the beginning of the nineteenth century, and much work in this area is "historicist," in the sense that analysts invoke principles of history. This is very much a nineteenth-century approach, as I discussed in chapter 2, and was subjected to a famous critique by Sir Karl Popper (1957). Biologists, political historians, and linguists in the nineteenth century expected to find principles of history, as if there were a Newtonian-style, deterministic, predictive theory of change to be found. Give us a full, detailed, accurate description of an organism or a political organization or a language, and, armed with our theory of change, we will give you a prediction of what that organism, society, or language will be like in 200 years. Not only were there theories of organisms, societies, and languages to be found, but in addition there was an independent theory of change. So Clio, the muse of history, had work to do, prescribing the ways in which things could change.

For us, Clio is free to play idly with her water clock. A good thing too, because I'm not sure we would want to give too much responsibility to somebody who was reputed to be both a virgin and the mother of the beautiful Hyacinthus. Grammatical, structural changes need explanation; but there is no theory of why trigger experiences should change, except insofar as they change as a result of earlier structural changes. That is, if the V-to-I operation is lost, then that grammatical change affects the triggering experience for the next generation, because the new grammars with no V-to-I raising generate different sentences and structures. If we ask why the cue for V-to-I raising, $_I$[V], became less robust, then to some extent that was a function of prior grammatical shifts, as outlined in section 6.3: the category change affecting the modal verbs, the loss of the verb-second system, and the rise of periphrastic *do*. To some extent, $_I$[V] became less robust as a function of periphrastic *do* becoming more pervasive in the speech community, and at base there is no theory which explains that. There may be a theory which explains why periphrastic *do* was more prevalent earlier with transitive verbs than with intransitives; that would be a function of grammatical theory, but grammatical theory has nothing to say about why *do* became more widely used first in the southwest, and why this usage then spread to the rest of the country. Similarly, grammatical theory has nothing to say about why the Middle English of northeast England was subject to Scandinavian influence which affected verb-second patterns, or about why early modern speakers dropped the familiar *thou* forms. This simply falls beyond the purview of grammarians. There is an interaction, of course, between the demands of grammatical theory and the nongrammatical factors which lead one speech form to be influential when languages are in contact. The grammarian may as well regard those nongrammatical factors as "chance" elements, and usually it is not appropriate to shape grammatical theory to explain them.

Let us now contrast this general approach with other work which is more historicist and which perpetuates that distinctive, nineteenth-century, predictive view of history, which we identified earlier. In chapter 2, we discussed the outcome of the nineteenth-century research paradigm initiated by Sir William Jones's claim about the historical relationships among the Indo-European languages. We saw that by the end of the century there was an enormous body of work on sound correspondences between historically related languages and vast compendia of changes which had taken place in many Indo-European languages. However, there were few ideas about why those changes had taken place. The notion that there was a directionality to change, that languages tended to become simpler/more natural/easier to pronounce, collapsed in its own circularity, partly because linguists of the time were pretty much exclusively concerned with language change (before the development of phonetics at the end of the century), and because they had no notion of a grammar, a system more abstract than a language, and certainly no notion of a biological grammar.

By the early twentieth century the data of linguistics seemed to be a compendium of sound changes occurring for no good reason and tending in no particular direction. The historical approach had not brought a scientific analysis of language that withstood scrutiny, and there was no predictability about changes. The study of language change became less dominant during the structuralist era, partly because the study of language broadened and began to deal with dimensions other than historical change. There was a strong anti-historicism in the writing of many of the major figures, who objected to the notion of historical laws and principles. There has been a revival in work on change over the last few decades, but the nineteenth-century teleological ideas about history have reappeared in the modern work.

Again the search has been for diachronic generalizations. In the 1970s much work focused on the notion of "drift," originally due to Sapir (1921: ch. 7). A drift for Sapir represented the unconscious selection of those individual variations that are cumulative in some direction. So he attributed the replacement of English *whom* by *who* to three drifts: the leveling of the subject–object distinction, the tendency to fixed word order, and the development of the invariant word. He was concerned that in positing a "canalizing" of such "forces" one might be imputing a certain mystical quality to this history. Certainly the modern work invoked mysticism. Robin Lakoff (1972), for example, examined changes in various Indo-European languages which yield a more "analytic" surface syntax, and she sought to combine Sapir's three drifts into one. The phenomenon cannot be described, she pointed out, by talking about individual changes in transformational rules or whatnot.

> Rather, it must be described as a metacondition on the way the grammar of a language as a whole will change . . . Speaking metaphorically, it instructs the language to segmentalize where possible . . . It is not at all clear where this metacondition exists: neither as part of a grammar nor as a universal condition on the form of grammars. It is not clear how a constraint on change within one language family, a constraint which is not absolute but which is nevertheless influential, is to be thought of. But there is no other way to think of these things: either there is such a metacondition, whatever it is, or all the Indo-European languages have been subject to an overwhelming series of coincidences. (Lakoff 1972: 192)

If the explanation is admittedly incoherent, then maybe the fallacy is in requiring a principled explanation for such a large-scale change taking place over such a long period. What's wrong with a series of coincidences or a series of independent events? Why should we believe that this is the only way that history could have progressed?

Only slightly less mystical is the approach to drifts based on Greenberg's word-order typologies. This distinguishes transitional and pure language types, which are defined universally in terms of hierarchically ranked word-order phenomena. Languages change from one pure type to another by losing/acquiring the relevant orders in the sequence specified by the hierarchies. A pure subject–verb–object language, for example, has verb–object order, auxiliary–verb, noun–adjective, and preposition–NP/DP, and these orders are ranked in some hierarchy. A subject–object–verb language is essentially the mirror image and has the opposite orders: object–verb, verb–auxiliary, adjective–noun, and NP/DP–preposition, etc. If a language changes from the object–verb type to the verb–object type, it acquires all the new orders in the sequence prescribed by the hierarchy: first verb–object, then auxiliary–verb, and so on.

This raises the question of how a child attains a language which is exactly half-way between the subject–verb–object and subject–object–verb types; how does she know whether this is a subject–verb–object language changing to subject–object–verb, or vice versa? How does she know that her generation must push the language a little towards, say, an subject–verb–object type? It seems that the only conceivable answer is to postulate a racial memory of some kind, such that the child knows that this is a subject–verb–object language changing towards subject–object–verb. This is presumably what Robin Lakoff had in mind in postulating a "metacondition on the way the grammar of a language as a whole will change."

Whether or not an individual change is part of a larger drift, its cause must be found locally. Sapir knew this. While claiming that the replacement of *whom* by *who* is part of the general drift towards invariable words and the loss of the case system, he nonetheless isolated four reasons for this particular change: first, *whom* was felt not to belong to the set of personal pronouns, which have distinct subject/object forms, but to a set of interrogative and relative pronouns, which show no such distinction; second, the emphatic nature of interrogative pronouns militates in favor of their invariableness; third, an objective form rarely occurs in initial position; and fourth, [hu:m] was alleged to be phonetically clumsy before the alveolar stops of *do* and *did*. I am less interested here in the validity of this account than in the form that Sapir felt an explanation should take. This is very different from the ideas of the 1970s typologists, who argued that notions like the subject–object–verb to subject–verb–object continua constituted diachronic explanations; for them, the drift was the explanatory force, rather than being something which required explanation, as it was for Sapir.[1]

The typologists remained faithful to the methods of the nineteenth century. They retained the same kind of determinism, and they dealt with the products of the language capacity rather than with the capacity itself, like their nineteenth-century predecessors. In recent terminology, they dealt with E-language, and not with I-language or with biological grammars (Chomsky 1986). Other modern approaches have been less conservative. They have formulated change in terms of changes in grammars, abstract systems of some kind, but they have retained the commitment to a nineteenth-century, deterministic, predictive history.

These approaches compare the grammars of various stages of a language and identify tendencies at the grammatical level. So some people have argued that, whatever happened superficially, changes in grammars were essentially gradual. Others argued that grammars tended to simplify over the course of time. So grammars changed in specifiable ways, even if languages were harder to pin down. The goal remained one of finding what Roger Lass called "straight-line explanations for language change," i.e. generalizations which would hold of history (see chapter 2). And they were not successful.

One approach of this type was to appeal to notions of Universal Grammar – some set of constraints on language acquisition – and to locate historical explanations there. But still the fundamental errors remain. Keyser and O'Neil (1985) argued that English has changed in a direction such that "surface allomorphy which exists at a prior stage is eliminated at the subsequent historical change" (p. 3). They found a tendency whereby "rules generalize and optional rules become obligatory," and they went on to explain this through UG: "wherever possible the language acquisition device reduces the level of optionality, either by change of status or by rule loss" (ibid.). Their strategy was to identify a historical tendency whereby optional rules are lost. They explained this tendency by framing the evaluation metric so that grammars with optional rules are not as highly valued as those without such rules.

Nowhere do Keyser and O'Neil justify optional rules for stem allomorphy, and this vitiates their central claim. The fact that some people say "tomeyto" and others say "tomahto" does not motivate optional rules, if one acknowledges that there is no such thing as a "grammar of English" codifying such alternations, but only various grammars of different English speakers, which differ to some extent (section 4.5). Even in the case of an Englishman living in the USA, who may use both forms of *tomato*, depending on circumstance, it does not follow that his grammar has a rule relating the two forms. It is even harder, of course, to claim that grammars of some English speakers 600 years ago had such rules. Mere occurrence of multiple forms in a single text does not force the conclusion, unless one shows that those multiple forms do not represent the usual effects of textual transmission, different spelling conventions, etc. These questions are worth raising, because if Keyser and O'Neil are right in assuming that rules may be optional or obligatory, then one must ask how language learners acquire such distinctions without access to negative data. If rules may be optional, a linguist might postulate an *obligatory* rule to prevent *over*generation, i.e. to block the generation of nonoccurring items. Since children are generally supposed not to have prior information about what does *not* occur, it is hard to imagine how a child could learn that a rule should be obligatory. Precisely this issue arose in sections 4.5 and 6.2.

Even if it were shown that some optional rules applied obligatorily in later grammars, this would not justify adding a statement to the evaluation metric that optional rules are of lower value and so are gradually eliminated. What would be needed would be a demonstration that some generation of speakers had an obligatory rule, despite exposure to the *same* childhood experience as earlier speakers for whom the rule applied optionally. Failing such a demonstration, we are free to attribute the new grammar to a different childhood trigger experience. Then the question becomes: why did the childhood trigger experience change for the two generations? A very different question. New forms can be introduced for various reasons, and they might include novel allomorphs. It is then likely that one or other form will eventually spread and supplant the other; that follows from Aronoff's Blocking Effect (section 4.5). Surely there is no reason to suppose that this process reflects a genetic principle which predisposes us to eschew optional rules where possible. If alternative forms are robust in a child's environment, then multiple forms will be attained.

If some general tendency is observed historically, there is no reason to attribute it to the effects of UG – least of all to maintain that UG should incorporate essentially a summary statement of the historical facts. There is no reason to believe that this is a reliable mode of discovery for principles of grammar.

Lamarckism has exercised a powerful hold over biologists, who are often trapped into explaining evolutionary developments by taking acquired features to be inherited. Similarly, historical linguists often succumb to the temptation to see a general directionality to change and to explain this either by invoking laws of history or by attributing historical effects to genetic predispositions. The particular case offered by Keyser and O'Neil is especially strange. They believe that "the elimination of optionality constitutes a contribution to a phonology's simplification" (ibid. 86), and they build a statement into UG predisposing us against optional rules. But for optional rules to be lost, they must first be introduced; if we are predisposed not to attain optional rules, one wonders how they would be triggered in the first place.

8.2   Clio Working through Biology

Languages change over time, and historical linguists, who study the phenomenon and fancy themselves as scientists, seek to explain what they observe. However, this work has to be conducted with a broad view, with an appropriate theory of UG and of acquisition. Historical linguists who limit themselves to phenomena of language change are prone to offer pseudo-explanations which lose touch with reality and which create mysteries where there is nothing mysterious. This feature was one of the problems of nineteenth-century work and is found in modern historical work. It is illustrated recently and graphically by a book by Brigitte Bauer (1995), which I reviewed a few years ago (Lightfoot 1996). The book is worth looking at in some detail, because it offers a historicist approach in a novel guise, appealing to biological factors which predict historical developments.

Bauer's book needs to be set in the context of the "typological" approach to change, which flourished in the 1970s and which I just discussed. Language types were defined in terms of the harmonic properties of Greenberg's universals. One could then distinguish "pure" and "transitional" types, and a particular pure type, say a subject–object–verb language with several of the features of Latin, might change into a fairly pure subject–verb–object type like French, by changing the various ordering features in accordance with a universal "diachronic continuum" (e.g. Lehmann 1974; Vennemann 1975). The explanation for any particular change, therefore, lay in the notion that the language was taking another step along the universal continuum. The continuum, which existed presumably in some theory of history, was the explanatory engine, or *explanans*, for these progressive changes in languages. It had this status despite the fact that comparable notions of drift had been the *explanandum* for Sapir and earlier writers, the thing to be explained. Since the continuum was essentially a diachronic notion, it could not exist as part of a theory of acquisition, or as part of the theory of language types, and such a theory of history was the essential mystery concocted by these typologists.

Bauer adapted the work of the typologists and avoided postulating principles of history. Like the typologists, Bauer was interested in big, comprehensive changes. But rather than thinking in terms of a language moving from one pure type to another, via various transitional types, Bauer argued that Latin (like other early Indo-European languages) was a thoroughgoing left-branching language, which changed into a thoroughgoing right-branching system in French. We'll get to the explanation for this comprehensive shift later.

She offered examples of Latin left-branching structures, along with the equivalent right-branching structures of French: table 8.1.

These structures make sense only if the rightmost item in the Latin list and the leftmost item in the French list are *heads* of the phrases to which they project and which contain the other item: thus $_{VP}[exercitum \; _Vduxit]$, etc. Bauer's definition of a head raises several analytical problems, which I discussed in the review, but they are not important for present purposes.

There are several differences in branching structure between the grammars of Latin and French. In fact, right-branching structures emerged at very different times and at different rates. Those details, if they could be established, might enable us to track changes in primary linguistic data, which is what we need for an explanation of the grammatical shifts, as I have shown in earlier chapters.

That, however, is not Bauer's view of how the changes should be explained. Rather, she views the change in direction of branching as irreversible and adopts an "evolutionary concept of language change," under which general and irreversible language changes are viewed as analogous to evolutionary change at the phylogenetic level. On this view, general, linear, irreversible, unidirectional changes are due to a natural selection process: "languages

Table 8.1   Bauer's left/right-branching structures

Latin		French	
object	verb	verb	object
exercitum	*duxit*	*il conduisit*	*l'armée*
PP	verb	verb	PP
in partes	*discindere*	*diviser*	*en parties*
adverb	verb	verb	adverb
leniter	*ridere*	*rire*	*doucement*
adjective	copula	copula	adjective
avidus	*est*	*il est*	*avide*
noun	adposition	adposition	noun
me	*-cum*	*avec*	*moi*
temporis	*causa*	*à cause*	*du temps*
adjective	noun	noun	adjective
longissimus	*truncus*	*un tronc*	*très allongé*
genitive	noun	noun	genitive
deorum	*munus*	*le présent*	*des dieux*
noun	adjective	adjective	noun
pecuniae	*avidus*	*avide*	*d'argent*
referent	comparative	comparative	referent
Paulo	*grandior*	*plus grand*	*que Paul*
adjective	degree	degree	adjective
grand	*-ior*	*plus*	*grand*
noun	ending	preposition	noun
leg	*-ibus*	*avec*	*des lois*
verb	ending	aux/pronoun	verb
am-	*-av-erit*	*il aura*	*aimé*
noun	conjunction	conjunction	noun
populus	*-que*	*et*	*le peuple*

evolve in the direction of features that are acquired early" (Bauer 1995: 170). She speaks repeatedly of the "advantages" of a right-branching system, and she implements these ideas by arguing that the switch from left branching to right branching represents evolutionary progression, because left-branching languages, at least as manifested in Latin (with nonagglutinating morphology), were hard for children to acquire – hence the progression to right-branching structures. "Latin must have been a difficult language to master, and one understands why this type of language represents a temporary stage in linguistic development" (ibid. 188). So she explains her diachronic change not in a mysterious theory of history, along the lines of the earlier typologists, but rather in terms of human biology: our brains work in such a way that complex structures in left-branching languages without agglutinative morphology are hard to acquire. This is more sophisticated, but of course it immediately raises the question of why early Latin would have been left branching. Bauer devotes section 7.2 to this question: "If left-branching structures are less recursive and are acquired with greater difficulty, it is indeed legitimate to wonder why languages, in an early period, exhibit this kind of structure" (ibid. 216). She concludes that this "still remains to be explained" (ibid. 217).

One can explain the change by saying that human biology required it, but human biology must also allow an account of how Latin was acquired, unless one has evidence that it was not acquired in the usual way. Bauer's error is precisely comparable to that of a linguist who explains a property of English or a creole language by saying that it manifests some otherwise unmotivated property of Universal Grammar, which in fact makes other grammars unlearnable willy-nilly. This is quite unsatisfactory and is a kind of Lamarckism with a twist: truly acquired properties are given a biological explanation. Properties of UG have been postulated successfully by arguments from the poverty of the stimulus, and so far only on that basis. There is an increasing tendency to invent properties of UG in order *only* to explain the direction of certain diachronic changes. The fallacy is widespread, which is why I have discussed Bauer's book in some detail.

8.3   Diachronic Reanalyses

Consider now a very different kind of work, far more useful analytically, but of a kind which also appeals to deterministic views of history. Notice that in the last three chapters we did not postulate rules or formal operations which account for the changes in trigger experiences or relate sets of primary linguistic data (1).

1   $PLD_1 \rightarrow PLD_2$

In fact, it is a fallacy to think that there could be formal operations that relate sets of PLD: the adaptive rules of Henning Andersen (1973) or the "peripheral rules" of Weerman (1993). This fallacy is part of a more widespread problem, the view that for any "language" there must be some recursive device or a grammar which will generate its sentences. Chomsky has discussed this problem in the introduction to the published version of his dissertation (1975) and in *Knowledge of Language* (Chomsky 1986) and elsewhere, but the distinction between E-language and I-language has not been properly absorbed. There need not be any single recursive device which generates a given set of PLD, and we have seen in our case studies here that sometimes there cannot be such a device: as the verb-second system was lost in northern England, there was no single recursive device to generate what children were hearing – namely, the output of their parents' grammar plus more expressions from people with southern, non-verb-second grammars. Similarly, the statistical shifts which seem to have given rise to split ergative systems (section 5.4) could not have been represented in any recursive device.

The notion of a formal device operating on sets of PLD has reappeared in the recent work of Ian Roberts, and it is linked to an attempt to explain some changes entirely through UG, independently of changes in trigger experiences. This is the same idea as occurred in Keyser and O'Neil's (1985) book and in a strikingly strong form in the work on "drift" undertaken by the typologists in the 1970s. I believe that there is some confusion here which is worth unpacking.

Roberts (1993b) developed a theory whereby English children ceased to postulate what he called AGR^{-1} (a "negative projection" which yields a position for an affixal morpheme), because the morphological distinctions had been simplified appropriately. This links to changes affecting the modals, because only with the loss of AGR^{-1} could modals (or other free morphemes) be inserted into AGR, as opposed to V, and thus have the distribution of nonverbs (§ 3.3). The link with the new periphrastic *do*, which emerged in the Middle English period and spread enormously during the sixteenth century, is less obvious. Roberts (§ 3.2) analyzes *do* and makes its introduction a *result* of the loss of V to AGR, rather than a precondition for it, unlike what we did in section 6.3. Here he invokes a new technical device, what he calls a Diachronic Reanalysis (ibid. 23), taking place in the sixteenth century (ibid. 295, 315). Modal verbs and periphrastic *do* originally moved to a tense position (T) (2a) but came to be base-generated there (2b).

2   (a) $NP_i \ _T[do/M_j \ T^{-1}] \ e_j \ [e_i \ VP] \Rightarrow$
    (b) $NP \ _T[did/M] \ VP$

This is the clearest invocation of a Diachronic Reanalysis, although they are alluded to at several points in the book. Roberts distinguishes three notions in what he calls a "theory of language change" (ibid. 158ff): (a) a step, which might be the appearance or change in frequency of a new construction; (b) a new parameter setting, as discussed above; and (c) a Diachronic Reanalysis. Roberts (1993a) is devoted to explicating the notion of a Diachronic Reanalysis; he puts it forward as the "formal correlate of the informal notion of grammaticalization" (p. 219). There he describes Diachronic Reanalyses as relations between the E-language of one generation and the I-language of a subsequent generation. Diachronic Reanalyses are seen as the causes of parametric shifts, and for any given phenomenological change one needs to ask whether it manifests a new parameter setting or a Diachronic Reanalysis. He also says that "Parametric Changes can trigger Diachronic Reanalysis" and that "Parametric Changes are usually observable as clusters of Diachronic Reanalyses" (1993a: 253).

This is where the confusion lies. Diachronic Reanalyses are said to be provoked by principles of acquisition, often by the "Least Effort Strategy", which led children to reanalyze (2a) as (2b) in the sixteenth century. So early grammars had structures like (2a), and later grammars had structures like (2b). But then what is the role of a Diachronic Reanalysis? Roberts clearly thinks of Diachronic Reanalyses as formal devices, but what do they relate? (2a), containing structures and indexed empty elements, is not a piece of E-language but a *grammatical* representation. So Diachronic Reanalyses relate grammatical representations. They do not relate "the grammars of successive generations," as he claims in Roberts 1993b: 154; nor do they relate the E-language of one generation to a later grammar. If Diachronic Reanalyses relate grammatical representations of successive generations, then they occur where grammatical shifts have already taken place. Roberts notes that "the notion Diachronic Reanalysis may also prove to be epiphenomenal. All Diachronic Reanalyses may turn out to be instances of Parametric Change" (ibid. 159) and therefore to have no reality of their own; but he insists that the notion has real utility and is necessary for a theory of syntactic change.

But why? Apart from the notion of parameter setting needed to account for language acquisition, and therefore needed independently of an account of change, Roberts's "theory" of change consists of two things: steps and Diachronic Reanalyses. He calls a "step" the traditional, "observationally adequate" (p. 259) notion of change; and a Diachronic Reanalysis is an epiphenomenon, really a particular type of parametric shift which involves different analyses for given strings of morphemes. This is not a theory, and Diachronic Reanalyses gain no credibility for being part of a coherent theory of change.

It has always seemed to me that historical linguistics is more concerned with explanations than our other subdisciplines. But sometimes the concern with explanation is excessive, and seeking a *theory of change* as such shows the weak part of the pedigree. There is no theory which accounts for why people speak French in France and Japanese in Japan, and no theory of grammar or acquisition will predict that people in a certain location talk somewhat differently from the way people there spoke a generation previously. Such things happen for various reasons, which are often of no particular interest to grammarians. The facts, where they can be established, are crucial, for without these shifts in usage there would be no systematic change, no changes in grammars. This is the point of connection between traditional work on change and work on grammatical change; the traditional work is describing changes in the primary linguistic data, which affect the cues, which, in turn, entail the grammatical changes. The grammarian needs the decriptivist. Nonetheless, the fact is that not all changes are explainable by grammatical factors, nor should they be.

In reality, Roberts's Diachronic Reanalyses and parametric shifts more generally are *not* provoked by the Least Effort Strategy, or by the Transparency Principle (Lightfoot 1979), or by any "endogenous" tendency towards "optimization." Specifically, the Least Effort Strategy cannot be "the sufficient condition for the move from one step to the next" (Roberts 1993b: 159). If there were no changes in trigger experiences, there would be no changes in grammars. If representations like (2a) disappeared, it was because they ceased to be triggered; the children who did not acquire them must have had different experiences from earlier generations; it wasn't because they were more sensitive to the demands of the Least Effort Strategy or the Transparency Principle.

In the case studies I have examined here, one can plausibly reconstruct shifts in the input such that the relevant grammatical changes were forced. These shifts consisted in changes in frequencies – that is, changes resulting from the way in which grammars were used, rather than changes in the grammars themselves – and changes in trigger experiences resulting from population movements. For these cases, the notion of a Diachronic Reanalysis with the formal properties of (2) is irrelevant and, in fact, inadequate; the relevant changes cannot be represented in schemata like (2).

Irrespective of the validity or usefulness of Diachronic Reanalyses, I have not yet seen a persuasive argument for a change motivated entirely by internal factors, by economy or another element of UG. It seems to me to be axiomatic that there can be no change in grammars without change in trigger experiences. Something has to set the billiard ball in motion. Similarly, there will be no variation in grammars independent of variation in triggers, . . . apart perhaps from possible cases of indeterminacy. In cases of indeterminacy, the variation would be random and could not be systematic enough to be manifested in new grammatical properties.

Paul Kiparsky is also impressed by what he takes to be long-term tendencies and by asymmetries like the prevalence of object–verb systems changing to verb–object and the rarity of the reverse development (Kiparsky 1995, 1996, 1997). Like Roberts, he also appeals to internal causal factors, forces of "endogenous optimization." Kiparsky (1996) examines the shift from object–verb to verb–object, which took place in several, but not all, Germanic languages; and he argues that it manifests a bias toward harmonizing the direction of head–complement relations: in the new grammars which underwent the change, "all complements of all heads, lexical and functional, are licensed uniformly on the right" (p. 152). This bias, in turn, is explained by Kayne's (1994) claim that specifier–head–complement order is the universal underlying order, and that surface object–verb languages have extensive leftward-movement derivations. In that case, the change to a surface verb–object system would consist in a loss of those leftward movements.

Kiparsky's position is different from Roberts's. He does not rely exclusively on these endogenous forces, and he requires other, external factors to interact with the internal forces. He recognizes that his approach raises the same kind of question that we discussed in the context of work by Keyser and O'Neil, Bauer, and Roberts: if there is a bias built into UG, then why should there ever be nonoptimal systems? His answer is that there might be other structural or functional constraints which compete with the harmonization requirement, or historical processes which work against them. He does not tell us what these competing factors were for early Germanic syntax, which was object–verb, but he does show how the early system was undermined.

He argues that the "enabling cause" of the change to verb–object syntax in certain languages was verb-fronting in embedded clauses. Yiddish, for example, shows general verb-fronting, where verb-fronting appears in all types of embedded clauses, while German grammars show verb-fronting only in matrix clauses and in embedded clauses with no complementizer. Yiddish has sentences like those of (3), where the equivalent in German would be (4).

3   A jidisch mejdl hot sech barimt, as efscher hundert mol *hot* men si schojn gebetn, as si *sol* chassene hobn.
    "A Jewish girl bragged that she had already been asked perhaps a hundred times to marry."

4   Ein jüdisches Mädel hat sich gerühmt, dass man sie vielleicht hundert
    Mal schon gebeten *hat*, dass sie heiraten *soll*.

Dutch, Frisian, and modern mainland Scandinavian behave like German
in restricting verb movement to certain clauses, while older mainland
Scandinavian and Icelandic behave like Yiddish in extending verb movement to all clause types (this was also an option in Faroese, Old English,
and Old Yiddish). The generalization is that "the shift from a head-final
base to a head-initial base took place in exactly those languages which
developed general verb-fronting in embedded clauses" (Kiparsky 1996: 155).
    So Kiparsky's claim is that the change to verb–object order is an endo-
genous optimization, but one which is "enabled" by certain verb-movement
operations. Crucially for our discussion here, Kiparsky recognizes that
grammaticalization or, more generally, any optimization account does not
by itself address the actuation problem; nor does it explain why a change
takes place in one language but not in another closely related one. His
account motivates the change to verb–object syntax through environmental
factors, and to that extent the account is not historicist, even though he
invokes optimization effects. Such a story raises empirical questions about
how much influence the internal and external factors each had, but it does
not raise the methodological problems of historicism.

8.4   Trajectories

So far I have been quite skeptical about work offering principled explanations for purported, long-term historical tendencies, because the historicist
principles strike me as implausible. I do not see how a historical law can
be anything other than an epiphenomenon, an effect of other aspects of
reality. I realize that this skepticism is at variance with a more general
enthusiasm for these approaches. More generously, we could treat these
historicist accounts of long-term tendencies as interim analyses, generalizations for which future work will seek explanations based on changing triggering experiences, changes in cues, or what Kiparsky calls the "enabling
causes."

This is the stance taken by Olga Fischer (1997) in her reanalysis of
grammaticalization approaches to the development of *have to* in English.
Grammaticalization is taken to be a semantic tendency for an item with a
full lexical meaning to be bleached over time and to come to be used as a

grammatical function (Hopper and Traugott 1993; Traugott, forthcoming). Fischer reports work by Adrienne Bruyn (1995), who has shown that

> the grammaticalization processes which are said to be so typical for pidgins developing into creoles are not at all so straightforward in Sranan, when looked at in more detail. It could be the case, as Bruyn shows painstakingly, that a particular process was aborted before it was completed . . . or that it was heavily supported or even instigated by substratum features . . . or that it does not develop in the way it is expected to, or that the development is much more abrupt than is usual in grammaticalization cases. Her investigation shows that it is important at each stage to take into account the synchronic circumstances, which will ultimately decide what will happen. In other words, there may not be such a thing as an *in*dependent process of grammaticalization. (Fischer 1997: 180)

Some recent work by Partha Niyogi and Bob Berwick (1997) may suggest other sympathetic ways of thinking about these long-term tendencies, which do not fall into the traps we have discussed. They have developed a very interesting computer simulation of language change.

As is natural, and as in earlier chapters of this book, Niyogi and Berwick take the problem of language acquisition at the individual level as leading logically to the problem of language change at the group or population level. If it is possible that children may not converge on the target grammars, then, over several generations, this could drive language change, in much the same way as speciation occurs in the population biology sense. If one has an adequate grammatical theory, then there are two means by which the linguistic composition of the population might change over time.

First, there are the factors that we have discussed: the primary data presented to the child may change in some critical way which affects the distribution of the cues. This may happen because of contact with another speech community, the presence of foreigners, or just because the speech community has taken to using some construction more or less frequently than in a previous generation or with a special kind of pragmatic force. As a result, the sentences presented to children may no longer be consistent with a single target grammar, and the children may converge on some other grammar or may converge on that new grammar with some probability and on some other grammar with some other probability. Once one child converges on some new grammar, then the linguistic composition of the population will change, because the child with the new grammar produces and works with different sets of structures; and this may have domino effects.

Second, even if the PLD comes from a single target grammar, the actual data presented to the learner are truncated, some finite subset of what the grammar is capable of generating. After a finite (truncated) sample sequence, children may arrive at a grammar different from that of their parents. This can again lead to a differing linguistic composition in succeeding generations.

> In short, the diachronic model is this: individual children attempt to attain their caretaker grammar. After a finite number of examples, some are successful, but others may misconverge. The next generation will therefore no longer be linguistically homogeneous. The third generation of children will hear sentences produced by the second – a different distribution – and they, in turn, will attain a different set of grammars. Over successive generations, the linguistic composition evolves as a dynamical system. (Niyogi and Berwick 1997: 2)

Niyogi and Berwick then develop a toy language learner. This consists in a computer simulation which contains precise assumptions about a set of relevant parameters, a learning algorithm, and the primary linguistic data.[2] If these items are specified appropriately, then the system computes the linguistic composition for the next generation. By repeating the process, Niyogi and Berwick compute the evolving composition of the population from generation to generation and arrive at a dynamical system.

The first version of their toy learner incorporates the three-parameter syntactic subsystem of Gibson and Wexler (see table 6.1 above), their Trigger Learning Algorithm, and a uniform distribution of degree-0 sentences generated by the subsystem.

First, they consider the case of a homogeneous population, with no noise or confounding factors like foreign target languages. They exposed each learner to 128 degree-0 sample sentences, having shown in earlier work that 128 sentences suffice to ensure convergence to the target grammar with high probability. "Some small proportion of the children misconverge; the goal is to see whether this small proportion can drive language change – and if so, in what direction" (Niyogi and Berwick 1997: 6). Table 8.2 shows the language mix after 30 generations. +V2 refers to a grammar with the verb-second property, and the grammars may or may not be specifier-final or complementizer-final, yielding the eight language types listed in table 6.1 above.

This model generates some striking patterns. First, we see that homogeneous populations may split into different groups, and they may split at different rates. For example, a population of Language 7 speakers splits

Table 8.2 Language change and misconvergence: variation 1

Initial language	After 30 generations
1 (−V2)	2 (0.85), 6 (0.1)
2 (+V2)	2 (0.98); stable
3 (−V2)	6 (0.48), 8 (0.38)
4 (+V2)	4 (0.86); stable
5 (−V2)	2 (0.97)
6 (+V2)	6 (0.92); stable
7 (−V2)	2 (0.54), 4 (0.35)
8 (+V2)	8 (0.97); stable

over five to six generations to one with 54 percent speaking Language 2 and 35 percent speaking Language 4 and remains that way with no further shifts through 30 generations. On the other hand, Language 1 eventually gravitates to Language 2; but very little happens over the first six or seven generations, and then the population changes at a much faster rate.

Second, all the verb-second languages are relatively stable, and the linguistic composition did not vary significantly over 30 generations, each succeeding generation converging on the same parameter settings. On the other hand, the non-verb-second languages all drift to verb-second. So a population of Language 1 speakers winds up speaking mostly Language 2.

What is remarkable about this is that Niyogi and Berwick have a model which generates diachronic trajectories; there are long-term tendencies for certain language types to change to certain other types. Some of the actual tendencies that they find in their initial model are surprising. Their model, as we have discussed it so far, shows verb-second languages to be quite stable; but we know that both English and French lost their verb-second properties, an observation that needs to be explained.

> Immediately then, we see that our dynamical system does not evolve in the expected manner. The reason could be due to any of the assumptions behind the model: the parameter space, the learning algorithm, the initial conditions, or the distributional assumptions about sentences presented to learners. Exactly which is in error remains to be seen, but nonetheless our example shows concretely how assumptions about a grammatical theory and learning theory can make evolutionary, diachronic predictions – in this case, incorrect predictions that falsify the assumptions. (Ibid.)

Niyogi and Berwick then proceed to change their assumptions and to derive different trajectories. For example, they drop one particular constraint

Table 8.3　Language change and misconvergence: variation 2

Initial language	After 30 generations
1 (−V2)	2 (0.41), 4 (0.19), 6 (0.18), 8 (0.13)
2 (+V2)	2 (0.42), 4 (0.19), 6 (0.17), 8 (0.12)
3 (−V2)	2 (0.40), 4 (0.19), 6 (0.18), 8 (0.13)
4 (+V2)	2 (0.41), 4 (0.19), 6 (0.18), 8 (0.13)
5 (−V2)	2 (0.40), 4 (0.19), 6 (0.18), 8 (0.13)
6 (+V2)	2 (0.40), 4 (0.19), 6 (0.18), 8 (0.13)
7 (−V2)	2 (0.40), 4 (0.19), 6 (0.18), 8 (0.13)
8 (+V2)	2 (0.40), 4 (0.19), 6 (0.18), 8 (0.13)

from Gibson and Wexler's Trigger Learning Algorithm (the "Single Valued Constraint"), and the dynamical system yields very different results, as shown in table 8.3.

On this scenario, all initially homogeneous populations eventually drift towards the same composition mix after 30 generations. As on the earlier scenario, all populations drift to a population mix of only verb-second languages, and again there is a tendency to gain verb-second systems, contrary to the facts of the history of French and English.

This work opens up the possibility of revising the model in such a way that the diachronic trajectories generated correspond most closely to those that are actually attested, and this introduces an exciting new criterion for the success of a grammatical model. We saw in section 4.6 that Niyogi and Berwick were able to derive the S-curves of certain diachronic changes, whereby a change begins slowly, proceeds much more rapidly, and then tails off in a slow, gradual completion, while also deriving very different trajectories for changes which show no S-curve. In their paper, they show some effects of changing the maturation time, so that learners may have access only to eight sample sentences; they discuss the potential effects of changing the set of sample sentences to put more emphasis on certain word forms, of entertaining nonhomogeneous initial populations, etc. They ask what the conditions are for the kind of stability that some verb-second systems have and how many stable fixed points there might be. They examine the loss of null subjects in French, which involves a richer, five-parameter system, and they find that verb-second properties are less stable in these richer systems.

The general point relevant to our discussion of historicism is that Niyogi and Berwick have provided a formal means to derive from theories of grammar models of emergent, global population behavior. The key point is that whenever somebody proposes a new grammatical or learning theory, this implies a particular evolutionary theory. So one seeks a class of grammars and learning theories which yields a dynamical system which matches that of the true evolution of human languages.

This, in turn, suggests that maybe one day work on long-term tendencies may not be as mysterious as I have suggested here, that one will be able to find explanations for long-term diachronic tendencies in terms of the shape of the learning mechanism. To be sure, progress will come only through the precise kind of work that Niyogi and Berwick exemplify, not through the anecdotal generalizations which have typified some of the work discussed earlier. Also, Clio will remain free to play with her water clock. There will be no historicist principles nor any primitive principles of change. Rather, the explanation for the long-term tendencies, if they emerge, will be a function of the architecture of UG and the learning procedure and of the way in which populations of speakers behave. In this way the historical tendencies will turn out to be epiphenomena, derived in an interesting fashion, not stipulated by brute force.

Language change is fascinating, because it represents an interaction between chance oscillations in the trigger experience and the biological necessities of the human language acquisition device. I have suggested in chapters 5–7 that if one looks in the right places, one can show with some plausibility that shifts in the distribution of cues caused some of the grammatical shifts that have interested us. Change may be chaotic and flukey, but it is explainable to a degree. Nongrammatical factors may shift the distribution of cues. The shifts in the cues may require the billiard ball to move, and the theory of grammar defines the undulations in the available surface area and therefore predicts the points, finite in number, at which the ball might come to rest.

To explain language change, it seems to me that one needs nothing more than (a) an account of how trigger experiences have shifted and (b) a theory of language acquisition that matches PLD with grammars in a deterministic way. I tend to think that people seeking a substantive theory of change are too ambitious, too principled, and seek to explain too much, and that they fail to come to grips with the essentially contingent, flukey nature of language change. However, I also note the intriguing work of Niyogi and Berwick, which provides a new way of thinking about long-term diachronic trajectories in terms of the kind of primitives that we have used in earlier chapters, without committing historicist errors and appealing to the intervention of Clio.

Notes

1 See Lightfoot 1979: ch. 7 for further discussion.
2 Niyogi and Berwick adopt the framework of Gibson and Wexler (1994). So their simulation involves not only claims about the parameters of UG and the primary linguistic data, but also about a "learning algorithm," which instructs the child what to do when the current grammar is faced with unanalyzable data. As we discussed in chapter 6, a learning algorithm does not play a central role in a cue-based approach to acquisition and may, in fact, play no role whatsoever. We shall return to this point in the last chapter.

9

The Evolution of the Language Faculty

So far we have been discussing changes in people's grammars over the course of time, changes in phenotypical properties. Languages change from generation to generation, and some language change is a function of change in grammars, but none of this represents biological innovation. The issues which arise in work on phenotypical change are different from those which arise in asking how genotypical systems might change.

This difference, however, is not self-evident. One line of thought among some historical linguists has been that language change, phenotypical change, is subject to the same principles as those which guide the evolution of species. In effect, this has meant natural selection. So languages with certain new properties are fitter for our communicative needs, better, and therefore more likely to flourish. This was a common view in the nineteenth century, when historians sought a general direction to change, as discussed in chapters 2 and 8.

Darwin himself thought that languages tended to change in the direction of having shorter, "easier" forms, and that this could be explained by natural selection (Darwin 1874: 88–92). Contemporaries of Darwin thought that languages become simpler, more natural, or easier to pronounce, and these ideas continued into the twentieth century. Brigitte Bauer (1995) thinks that right-branching languages are easier to learn than left-branching languages, hence fitter; and this is offered as an explanation for why left-branching Latin developed into right-branching French. For her, evolutionary principles guide this kind of language change, and children eventually come to select fitter languages (see section 8.2).

However, we have seen that quests for a general direction to change have not been successful. Present-day English is not fitter than Old English in any general way; nor is French fitter than Latin. As far as we can tell, languages have always been about as complex as they are today. When we look at our earliest records, we conclude that there never were any simple languages. Never. So we assume a kind of "uniformitarianism": as far back as records take us, all grammars have been acquired on the basis of the same relevant genetic inheritance, the same UG. Change in grammars turns out to be more contingent than Darwin and Bauer expected, and natural selection is not a useful notion to explain how languages change. Nonetheless, I shall suggest that our approach to grammar change has interesting points of contact with questions about the evolution of the language faculty.

Many people have speculated about how language as we know it came to emerge in the species, and how the present genotype developed. There is the bow-wow theory, that human language has evolved from animal cries; the heigh-ho theory, that language developed from grunts of socialized effort (along the more sophisticated lines of sea chanteys); and the ouch theory, that it all developed from cries of pain. Very little evidence is offered for such proposals, and it is difficult to see the relation between cries of pain and the very specific properties of UG that we have identified – its compositional and algebraic nature, its plasticity, the defining features of clitics, and so on.

Another idea is that the crucial element in the emergence of language was physiological. It is sometimes claimed that the throat of Neanderthal man was constructed in such a way that it was not possible to articulate a variety of vowel sounds, as would be necessary for human language. If that were so, it is hard to know why Neanderthals didn't develop a language with just one vowel, or why they didn't use another modality, perhaps a form of sign language.[1] One wonders why the language faculty would have lain idle and unexploited until the throat changed shape. This strikes me as a most unlikely history, but, whatever the fossil evidence, such a view would not be helpful for somebody who views language as the product of a mental organ with a rich structure provided by the genotype. We want to know how that mental organ evolved in the species.

9.1   Bumpiness

On the perspective that we have taken, what has evolved in the species is not a set of languages, or grammars, but the language faculty itself – the linguistic genotype, UG. If we are to investigate "the evolution of language" in the species, we must ask about the evolution of UG. I want to speculate here on the origin of the language faculty, because there are two points of similarity between phenotypical and genotypical change which emerge from the approach we have taken in earlier chapters: at both levels, change takes place in fits and starts, in a kind of bumpy "punctuated equilibrium," and change takes place within structural limits imposed by more general theories. These points of similarity bear on recent, lively discussion about the role of natural selection in explaining evolutionary developments.

Traditional approaches to the evolution of cognitive functions have involved ethological analyses comparing observations of the typical behavior of living animals and psychological studies testing and measuring the abilities of various species. These analyses seek to compare living animals in such a way as to hypothesize an evolutionary history, rather as historical linguists hypothesized the prehistory of Greek, Latin, and Sanskrit by comparing the internal structure of those languages and hypothesizing what must have happened before our records began: the variety of present patterns of behavior is projected backward to likely ancestral patterns. It is in this context that people study the communication of chimpanzees, dolphins, or bees.

A problem is that although many animals can communicate danger, anger, fear, information about food sources, and the like, communication is not the same thing as language. Even in the case of the chimpanzee, whose internal world is fairly similar to man's (Premack and Woodruff 1978), there is very little remotely comparable to the principles of UG. Chimpanzees do show analogues to the human capacity to label items (Premack 1980, 1990); but they don't use anything like human words, and they seem to be incapable of "displaced reference" – that is, reference to something not in the sensory field. There seems to be nothing in other species remotely comparable to the kind of computations and compositionality made available by the human UG.

The traditional methods for establishing an evolutionary history are not very helpful for considering the emergence of language, because there is no close analogue of the human language capacity in other species. Unlike most animals, we have no close cousins, and our evolutionary space is too sparsely populated for evolutionists to be able to connect the points sensibly.

However, there is a novel approach to the evolution of functions: the approach of paleoneurology. If a human mental organ evolved, investigators might be able to identify a physical correlate of the mind that is manifested in the fossil records. Harry Jerison has tried to trace the "index of encephalization," a measure of actual brain size relative to the size of the brain that can be expected for a certain species, given a certain body weight and size. It is known that the human being's most distinctive anatomical feature is the central nervous system, and that human evolution has been marked above all by progressive increase in cranial capacity. Jerison aimed to establish the brain and body sizes of fossil vertebrates and identified periods where there was a four- and fivefold increase in relative brain size for the average mammal.

Major evolutionary changes may take place without significant advances in relative brain size. Jerison reports that, according to paleoneurological evidence, the advance from fish to amphibian around 350 million years ago took place without an increase in encephalization. This was possible because there were only minor changes in the neurological and behavioral organization of the earliest amphibian as compared to its immediate ancestor among the bony fish.

> Although the step from reptiles to mammals required a certain amount of encephalization (approximately a fourfold increase in relative brain size . . .), mammalian encephalization did not progress immediately but remained at a steady level for at least 100 million years . . . That stability for such a long period of time suggests a successful response to the selection pressures of a stable new ecological niche. Progressive evolution of encephalization within the mammals came late in their history, in the last 50 million years of a time span of about 200 million years. That evolution transformed the archaic mammalian map into the map of living mammals by another four- or fivefold increase in relative brain size for the average mammal. (Jerison 1976: 95)

The picture that emerges is that the brain may have increased in relative size in a series of explosions.

> The evolution of hearing and smell to supplement vision as a distance sense is sufficient reason for the evolution of an enlarged brain in the earliest mammals. The reason is to be found in the way neural elements are packaged in vertebrate sensory systems. In the visual system many of the circuits are in the retina, which contains an extensive and complex neural network that allows elaborate analysis of visual information. The corresponding neural elements of the auditory and olfactory systems of living vertebrates are in the brain proper. . . .
> An auditory system analogous to the visual system would presumably have to have about as much integrative circuitry as there is in the retina . . . There is no space for this in the middle and inner ears; the obvious place to package the additional material is in the brain itself, and solving the packaging problem would therefore require the enlargement of parts of the brain involved in audition. (Ibid. 98–9)

Visual information may be encoded at the retina, but no such encoding is possible for sounds and smells. The introduction of finely tuned hearing and smelling required encephalization as a means to encode the neural information. Another of the explosions may have been associated with the development of upright posture, which correlated not only with specialization

of the foot but with many changes in muscle and bone structure, particularly in the vertebrate column and the position of the skull in relation to it.
Man's evolution, as often noted, must have been greatly spurred when he
stood erect and his hands became free as he walked and ran. Jerison claims
that the hominid brain evolved to its present size in relatively recent
times, having been completed only within the last million years, long after
the development of erect posture. This would involve at least one further
explosion. There is no evidence of a change in encephalization in any other
mammals in the last five million years.

If the vertebrate brain was enlarged in this way, then intelligence and
language may have evolved as an incidental consequence as one of these
explosions. Once language emerged, it brought with it the means for communicating traditions and a new kind of evolution, a cultural evolution. At
that point, the whole emphasis of human development moved into a different mode. Cultural change rests on the passing of acquired characteristics
to subsequent generations. Whatever we invent, we may pass on by our
writing and teaching. This kind of Lamarckian change proceeds much
more rapidly than the effects of natural selection and involves a very different modality. A Darwinian evolutionary process requires genealogical
descent (one cannot make a new species by mixing 50 percent rat, 30 percent sparrow, and 20 percent mackerel), but cultural change does not.
Much of the Japanese class system was imported from England in the
nineteenth century; Italians eat pasta because Marco Polo visited China.
As Gould (1997) notes, "If we want a biological metaphor for cultural
change, we should probably invoke infection rather than evolution."

Jerison's work suggests that the brain may be viewed as evolving in a
series of explosions and qualitative changes, and not as a gradual development. Presumably something like this happened for most physical features,
since evolution typically is a discontinuous process, prizing only those
innovations which are big enough and effective enough to be adaptive.
Even if relevant facts are in short supply, it can be speculated that perhaps
something similar happened in the evolution of the mental genotype in the
species. As with the emergence of the heart or upright posture, so with
language. Nobody has any idea of how this happened with physical or
mental organs; there are no principles which allow us to predict that from
some organism some particular property must evolve. This is not to say
that these developments are inexplicable, only that they are unexplained at
the present state of knowledge. From that perspective the evolution of the
human heart and mental organs are on a par.

If the evolution of the human brain progressed in a series of explosions,
then it resembles phylogenetic change in grammars: it manifests punctuated

equilibrium and is bumpy. However, it differs in that the novel systems were different in kind. An organism with finely tuned hearing and smelling is substantially different and has different fundamental properties from one that lacks these functions. Such organisms are likely to flourish under different circumstances and to have different ecological niches and different evolutionary futures. Grammars are not like this. Grammars with and without V-to-I raising, say, are not different in kind nor likely to be spoken in different ecological niches; neither one of these grammars is "adaptive."

We have depicted grammar change as proceeding through a narrow range of options, defined by the parameters of UG. Minor changes in environmental factors may stimulate the growth of a grammar with different properties. I shall argue that our notion of change being guided by the intrinsic properties of UG has an analogue at the evolutionary level, and that this accounts for the bumpiness of change in both domains. The argument relates to the role of natural selection and the possibility of other factors shaping evolutionary developments. It is often claimed that the human capacity for language, UG, was shaped by natural selection. Here I want to ask to what extent this might be true. I shall argue that it can be true only to a very limited extent and perhaps not at all; other factors must be involved.

9.2 Explaining Evolution

In asking how the language faculty may have evolved in the species, we are faced with some immediate problems. First, there is no useful comparative data from other species with some form of "primitive language," as we have noted. Second, we have no real substantive data on the neural architecture which subserves the operation of our grammars, at least not beyond very gross notions (unenlightening so far, for our purposes) about brain localization; in fact, this point is true of all cognition, except for some aspects of low-level vision. Perhaps it was these difficulties which led the Société de Linguistique in Paris to issue a ban in 1866 on all papers on the evolution of language. Furthermore, we have no idea whether there was one big, homogeneous mutation yielding UG in all its present glory, with all the individual principles and parameters emerging at the same time.[2]

Nonetheless, there have been several papers and books in recent years on the evolution of language, and it is worth revisiting the matter in the context of the perspective I have sketched and in the context of recent discussions about natural selection. It is useful to distinguish two positions.

The *singularists* invoke just one factor to explain evolutionary development: natural selection. The result of natural selection is adaptation, the shaping of an organism's form, function, and behavior to achieve enhanced reproductive success, the Darwinian *summum bonum*. In the context of the evolution of UG, the singularists say that selective forces shaped individual components of UG, such as the Subjacency Condition, which permits elements to move only very locally, and Principle B of the Binding Theory, which requires pronouns not to be co-indexed locally (section 3.2). For the singularists, these items are adaptive. The idea is that various principles of UG evolved by selective demands in a kind of "mosaic evolution." Newmeyer (1991) and Pinker and Bloom (1990) have adopted stances which we can lump together under the rubric of singularism, abstracting away from many details and subtleties.

The *pluralists*, on the other hand, appeal to more than natural selection in explaining evolution. In particular, they try to understand the limits to the variation on which natural selection works. They assume that natural selection plays a limited role. Natural selection may explain the development of some central characteristics of language, but other factors narrow the range of options. For example, Brandon and Hornstein (1986) argued that the general algebraic character of the language faculty was selected for, but not, say, the Subjacency Condition. A species able to convey and understand an unbounded number of stimulus-free messages would presumably have had a reproductive advantage in a fluctuating and variable environment. It would have been able to give and receive warnings about a wide range of dangers and predators, and engage in abstractions – for example, abstractions about predators which *might* be present, although not currently visible or audible. This would be a more effective way of responding to predators than by genetic tracking. So the fact that the organism has a language faculty allowing unbounded, stimulus-free messages may be explained by selection. But there is no discernible selective advantage for an organism whose grammars permit elements to move only locally, in accordance with the Subjacency Condition.

The physicist Freeman Dyson takes a similar view. He speculates that a fundamental aspect of the language faculty was adaptive: namely, its plasticity (1979: 220). He notes that a world with a universal, common language would be a simpler world for bureaucrats and administrators to manage and control. The plasticity of our faculty, however, is what enables us to invent new words and express new ideas. This very adaptability makes human language very different from a fixed system and a fixed set of words, and it also allows for the variation and change which has led to our current differences. To say that the plasticity of UG may have been adaptive does not entail that each of its principles were adaptive in the mosaic evolution of Newmeyer, Pinker, and Bloom.

The linguistic singularists have flourished at a time when Richard Dawkins, Daniel Dennett, and others have articulated a conviction that every evolutionary change of any importance is due to the shaping effects of natural selection, and that adaptation emerges as a universal result and proof of the selective forces (e.g. Dawkins 1995; Dennett 1995). They have been joined in recent years by proponents of the much-ballyhooed "evolutionary psychology" (Barkow et al. 1992; Wright 1994).

Evolutionary psychology, itself evolving from 1970s-style sociobiology, insists that developments may turn out to be maladaptive, but that they all arose as functional adaptations. Aggressivity may be maladaptive for human beings in a nuclear age, but it arose, they say, as a progressive adaptation when aggressivity would have been prized among the hunter-gatherers on the African savannas. So evolutionary psychologists seek the so-called EEA, "environment of evolutionary adaptation," operating in prehistoric times. An argument about *modern* usefulness can be tested by looking at the reproductive success induced by a certain feature. By pushing their claims into prehistory, evolutionary psychologists have rendered their claims untestable. As Gould (1997) remarks:

> How can we possibly know in detail what small bands of hunter-gatherers did in Africa two million years ago? These ancestors left some tools and bones, and paleoanthropologists can make some ingenious inferences from such evidence. But how can we possibly obtain the key information that would be required to show the validity of adaptive tales about an EEA: relations of kinship, social structures and sizes of groups, different activities of males and females, the roles of religion, symbolizing, storytelling, and a hundred other central aspects of human life that cannot be traced in fossils?

Testability aside, Robert Wright has a deep faith in the power of natural selection:

> The thousands and thousands of genes that influence human behavior – genes that build the brain and govern neurotransmitters and other hormones, thus defining our "mental organs" – are here for a reason. And the reason is that they goaded our ancestors into getting their genes into the next generation. If the theory of natural selection is correct, then essentially everything about the human mind should be intelligible in these terms. The basic ways we feel about each other, the basic kinds of things we think about each other and say to each other, are with us today by virtue of their past contribution to genetic fitness. . . . (Wright 1994: 28)

Natural selection has now been shown to plausibly account for so much about life in general and the human mind in particular that I have little doubt that it can account for the rest. (Ibid. 383)

Returning to the evolution of UG, we might ask what would be involved in showing that some property is in fact due to the effects of natural selection. It is not enough to point to desirable functions that are served by that property, for that is to commit the "Panglossian fallacy" identified in Gould and Lewontin's (1979) discussion of spandrels and by-products. Voltaire's Dr Pangloss held that "Things cannot be other than they are.... Everything is for the best purpose. Our noses were made to carry spectacles, so we have spectacles. Legs were clearly intended for breeches, and we wear them." He would have held that the spandrels of San Marco (tapering, triangular spaces formed by the intersection of two rounded arches at right angles, a necessary architectural by-product of mounting a dome on rounded arches) must have been designed to accommodate the mosaics which seem to require just such triangular spaces, which they fit so perfectly. He would hold that anything that performs a function well must have been selected for that purpose.

Modern Panglossians show that the Subjacency Condition, the Binding Theory, etc. constrain speakers to produce forms which can be understood ("parsed") in accordance with our apparent parsing capacity.

> Given the reasonable assumption that verbal interaction was as important in prehistory as it is today, one can easily imagine that populations whose communicative abilities were honed by having grammars that more effectively allowed such abilities to be realized would have had an edge over those that did not. (Newmeyer 1991: 15)

But this is not enough. If the emergence of the Subjacency Condition limited traces of movement operations to those that are local enough to be parsed (1a), one wants to know why *this* solution was adopted. The problem that Newmeyer raises a little later is substantial in this regard: why was the relevant limitation not made by using a resumptive pronoun in place of a trace (1b)?

1 (a) *who$_i$ did you meet the woman who knew e$_i$?
  (b) ?who did you meet the woman who knew him?

Alternatively, why did the parsing capacity not evolve in such a way as to make the trace of (1a) comprehensible?

In order to approach the question of *why* the Subjacency Condition evolved, one needs to have a notion of *how* it evolved. Assuming that the Subjacency Condition is a condition on the distribution of traces of movement operations, one might show that organisms with traces constrained by Subjacency "had an edge over" similar organisms which lacked Subjacency, other things remaining constant. Or did the condition evolve along with the possibility of movement operations? This makes a substantial difference for what is being attributed to adaptation. Needless to say, nobody has the faintest idea of what properties the organism had when the Subjacency Condition evolved, and it is therefore hard to see how we can address the question of why it arose.

Furthermore, to say that an organism with some property "has an edge over" a similar organism without that property entails claiming that it had a better chance of having descendants, if one intends to offer an argument that the property is due to natural selection. That is, one would need to show that an organism that solved its parsing problem by evolving a Subjacency Condition was more likely to reach puberty than an organism which could not parse deeply embedded traces. I am willing to believe that a general ability to comprehend unbounded and stimulus-free messages may have had survival value. These messages might include "Get out of the way," "Look left," "There might be a dragon behind that rock," etc. But an ability only to move elements locally, and thus not to use unparsable forms like (1a) (as opposed to forms like (1b)), is unlikely to have increased the chances of reproduction. The Subjacency Condition has many virtues, but I am not sure that it could have increased the chances of having fruitful sex. The claim that the Subjacency Condition was selected for does not amount to much.

To say that the Subjacency Condition was selected for suggests that the elements of UG evolved gradually in a piecemeal fashion, in the same way that some argue that language change progresses gradually (section 4.3). It also suggests that evolutionary development is highly data-driven, largely dependent on external circumstances. But we don't have to believe that every organism, every cell, every molecule, has been refined down to the last detail by the adaptation process, even though it has been in action incessantly over millions of years and millions of generations. Furthermore, Jerison's work suggests that the Subjacency Condition may have evolved as one component of a large-scale mutation, involving a package of new properties. In that case, the whole package may have been adaptive, but there would be no reason to seek adaptive accounts for each of the subparts.

The pluralists allow that forces other than natural selection may be at work in guiding evolutionary developments. Despite the attempts of the singularists to cloak themselves with the mantle of true Darwinism, Darwin closed the Introduction to his *Origin of Species* by saying, "I am convinced that natural selection has been the main but not the exclusive means of modification." There *are* alternatives. The fundamental properties of all physical systems surely play some role in determining the kinds of mutations that organisms and specific organs might undergo – for example, the fact that organisms cannot transfer themselves instantaneously from Maryland to Cornwall or become invisible on demand (surely a property which would convey selective advantage, if it were possible). Similarly, complex biological systems may be subject to particular principles. One thinks, for example, of the nature and behavior of cells, the properties of exons and introns, and other fundamental aspects of the biological world which were not specifically selected for. In 1917 D'Arcy Thompson discussed constraints on the shape and functioning of biological forms, finding certain geometric forms recurring in many unrelated organisms: hexagons, spirals following the Fibonacci series, etc. (Thompson 1961). It is reasonable to believe that constraints yielding these repeated forms hold independently of the effects of natural selection. There are, in fact, some sophisticated physical models which explain the Fibonacci series effects.

Therefore it is, in principle, an empirical matter whether any particular property of an organism evolved because it was selected for. It might have arisen as a by-product of something else that was selected for, perhaps induced by physical or biological principles, or perhaps as an accidental consequence of some other change. For example, Lewontin points out that hemoglobin was adaptive, because natural selection would have favored the acquisition of a molecule which would carry oxygen from our lungs to the rest of our body and carbon dioxide on the reverse route.[3] However, the redness of our blood is an accidental epiphenomenon of the structure of hemoglobin, and lobsters and other animals have green blood. It is, therefore, a mistake to seek an adaptive account for why our blood is red. After all, a gene might not be selected but might be dragged along on the same chromosome as some quite unrelated gene which *is* selected.

Since organisms are often complex and highly integrated, any adaptive change must automatically spin off structural by-products. Those by-products may later be co-opted for useful purposes, but they were by-products and didn't arise as adaptations. The human brain is a good example of a complex organ, and it may have evolved to its large size for adaptive reasons – for some set of activities that our ancestors could perform only with bigger brains. But this doesn't entail that all attributes of universal human nature must be adaptations. We can read and write, and these capacities are now highly advantageous for humans, but the mental machinery for them must have originated as a spandrel that was co-opted later.

Some properties of organisms are not selected for and are not accidental by-products, but they emerge because of deep, physical principles which affect much of life. For example, organisms as diverse as robins, redwoods, and rhinos obey exactly the same mathematical laws governing the way size affects structure, physiology, and life history. Those laws – the "scaling relations" that dictate how thick bones must be in animals of different weights – are a near-universal feature of life. They reflect fundamental limits on the kinds of things that evolution can make, and they arise from the interaction of a few simple physical principles.

Living things, from microbes to whales, vary in size by a factor of a billion trillion, 21 orders of magnitude; they come in a profusion of body designs, and inhabit quite different environments – earth, air, and water. Despite this stupefying complexity, organisms obey remarkably simple scaling laws. Across thousands of species, the rules mandate that the larger the animal, the slower its metabolism. Similar relationships have been found for variables such as respiration rate, heart rate, life span, proportion of body weight devoted to skeleton, length of pregnancy, and more. Try to make a mouse the size of an elephant, and it wouldn't last a day, because it wouldn't have enough surface area to dissipate the heat generated by the super-active mouse metabolism, and it would cook itself to death in short order.

Scaling follows precise mathematical relationships. Three "power laws" have turned out to have widespread effects. The *Three-quarter power law* describes, for example, metabolic rate (a body's total energy consumption per unit of time): this varies as the three-fourths power of an animal's mass. So, a creature that is 10,000 (10^4) times more massive than another – say, the difference between a mouse and a large hog – will have a metabolic rate only 1,000 (10^3) as large: the mouse uses energy at about 0.2 watts, the hog at around 200 watts. The *One-quarter power law* applies to life span, which generally varies as the $\frac{1}{4}$ power of weight. So an animal that is 10^4 more massive than another typically lives only ten (10^1) times longer. Elapsed times for blood circulation and gestation scale by the same factor. So does the cross-sectional area of mammalian aortas and tree trunks: a tree with a mass 1,000 times that of a sapling will have a trunk cross-section only 5.6 times larger. Heart rate scales as a negative $\frac{1}{4}$ power under the *Minus one-quarter power law*: the larger the animal, the slower its heartbeat. A 110-pound human has a pulse of about 70 beats per minute, and creatures 10,000 times smaller (around 5 grams, like shrews or a hummingbirds) have heartbeats 10 times faster.

What has been mystifying about these three laws is the appearance of $\frac{1}{4}$ as the common factor in all these relationships. Now West, Brown, and Enquist (1997) have proposed a model which generates accurate scaling equations from three principles. First, the organism's energy supply network has to be a branching "fractal" system (like blood vessels in animals or vascular conduits in plants), in which the sum of the area of all daughter branches is equal to the area of the parent. Second, the smallest branch (such as a capillary in animals) has the same dimension, no matter how large the organism. And third, the organism is assumed to employ the minimum energy necessary to distribute resources around its volume. The model – a unique combination of the dynamics of energy transport and the mathematics of fractal geometry – has produced results that conform well with observations of living systems, including the enigmatic $\frac{1}{4}$-power scaling. West et al. derived the $\frac{3}{4}$ power law for metabolism, along with many other relations. It may seem remarkable that equations apply to organisms at all, but now there is a theoretical basis for understanding the central role of body size in all aspects of biology.

Physical laws of this type describe the limits to evolutionary change, in the same way that the principles of UG prescribe the limits to grammatical change at the phenotypical level. They define the undulating terrain on which natural selection works, and they illustrate the pluralists' multi-factored approach to evolution, which goes beyond the working of natural selection. The physical laws shape the way in which evolutionary changes take place, and they are quite independent of the workings of natural selection.

If evolutionary change takes place in explosive, catastrophic developments within the channels defined by physical and biological laws, then one expects complex changes which are, in certain respects, maladaptive. In the next two sections, I shall offer a new kind of argument that UG is not shaped entirely by the workings of natural selection. I shall claim that certain features of UG are to some extent dysfunctional, hence maladaptive, hence spandrels in the sense of Gould and Lewontin (1979), a by-product of something else (cf. Lass 1990 for a similar argument from morphology).

9.3   A UG Condition on Movement Traces

English grammars have an operation whereby complementizers may be deleted (2). So we have structures like (3), where the *that* may or may not be present ("0" for zero, an absent complementizer).

2   Delete *that*

3   (a)   It was apparent [that/0 Kay left].
    (b)   The book [that/0 Kay wrote] arrived.
    (c)   It was obvious [that/0 Kay left].

This operation does not apply in languages like Dutch and French, where complementizers like *dat* and *que* are invariably present. Nonetheless, this English-specific operation is learnable, because children are likely to hear sentences in both forms, sometimes with the complementizer present, sometimes not. Therefore an operation like (2) meets the basic requirements for inclusion in English grammars.

However, as with virtually every grammatical operation, we find that many aspects are not determined by normal childhood experience. Certain instances of *that* may not be deleted. Consider (4), where only the structure with *that* actually occurs in speech.

4   (a)   It was apparent yesterday [that/*0 Kay left].
    (b)   The book arrived yesterday [that/*0 Kay wrote].
    (c)   [that/*0 Kay left] was obvious to all of us.
    (d)   Fay believes, but Kay doesn't, [that/*0 Ray is smart].

This is a standard poverty-of-stimulus problem. Since children are not told that *Kay left was obvious to all of us* does not occur (corresponding to (4c) with no *that*), principles of UG must be implicated. Various linguists have argued that complementizers may be deleted only where they are governed by an overt, lexical item. We introduced the structural notion of government in section 3.2: in nontechnical terms, this means that *that* is deleted only where it heads the complement of some adjacent overt word (see Hornstein and Lightfoot 1991 for one account). In (4a–d), each instance of *that* fails to be appropriately governed, because the clause indicated is not the complement of the preceding word; consequently it may not be deleted.

It was discovered that the same condition applies to the traces of movement. In a sentence like *Who did Jay see?*, *who* leaves a trace when it moves from the complement of *see* (5a). In more complex movement, where *who* is understood in an embedded clause, *who* moves first to the front of its clause (CP), then to its final position, leaving a co-indexed trace with each movement (5b).

5   (a)   Who$_i$ did Jay see e$_i$?
    (b)   Who$_i$ did Jay say $_{CP}$[e$_i$ that Fay saw e$_i$]?

This entails that alongside *Who was it apparent that Kay saw?*, we do not find **Who was it apparent yesterday that Kay saw?* in normal speech. The structure would be (6) and, because of the intervening adverb *yesterday*, the clause is not a complement of the adjacent word, and the trace at the front of the embedded CP (bold) fails to be governed. If *yesterday* is not present, then the clause is the complement of *apparent* and the trace is governed: *Who was it apparent that Kay saw?*

6   **Who$_i$ was it apparent yesterday $_{CP}$[**e$_i$** that [Kay saw e$_i$]]?

The nature of government is of great interest to linguists, who debate its exact definition. Indeed, on the Minimalist Program (Chomsky 1995), government cannot be a primitive; it is too derivative a notion to meet minimalist requirements. We need not be concerned here with these debates; suffice it to say that there can be no doubt that UG conditions are implicated in these data.

Consider some other contexts where government has been invoked. (7a) illustrates a common-or-garden conjunction, and the second verb may be unpronounced (7b). In cases like (7b), we say that there is a "gapped" verb, which is understood to be present in the position indicated but is not pronounced. This means that the trace of a wh- word to the right of the gap (boldface) (7c, d) fails to be governed by an overt word, and sentences corresponding to these structures fail to occur: **Which man did Jay introduce to Ray and which woman (did) Jim to Tim?* (7c), **Jay wondered what Kay gave to Ray and what Jim to Tim* (7d). Similarly with the illicit traces of non-wh- words, which are moved in (7e, g).

7   (a)   Jay introduced Kay to Ray and Jim introduced Kim to Tim.

     (b)   Jay introduced Kay to Ray and Jim GAP Kim to Tim.

     (c)   **Which man$_i$ did Jay introduce e$_i$ to Ray and which woman$_j$ (did) Jim GAP **e$_j$** to Tim?

     (d)   **Jay wondered what$_i$ Kay gave e$_i$ to Ray and what$_j$ Jim (did) GAP **e$_j$** to Tim.

     (e)   **Jay admired e$_i$ greatly [his uncle from Paramus]$_i$ but Jim (did) GAP **e$_j$** only moderately [his uncle from New York]$_j$.

     (f)   Jay gave his favorite racket to Ray and Jim GAP his favorite plant to Tim.

     (g)   **Jay gave e$_i$ to Ray [his favorite racket]$_i$ and Jim (did) GAP **e$_j$** to Tim [his favorite plant]$_j$.

The same point holds for a deleted *that* to the right of a gapped verb (8b) and a trace at the front of an embedded clause (8c). The deleted *that* and the trace at the front of the CP fail to be governed by an adjacent overt word; consequently the structures do not occur.

8 (a) Jay thought Kay hit Ray and Jim GAP $_{CP}$[that Kim hit Tim].
  (b) *Jay thought Kay hit Ray and Jim GAP $_{CP}$[0 Kim hit Tim].
  (c) *Who$_i$ did Jay think Kay hit e$_i$ and who$_j$ (did) Jim GAP $_{CP}$[e$_j$ (that) [Kim hit e$_j$]]?

More subtleties hold of the speech of every mature speaker of English, which follow from this particular condition of UG, requiring movement traces to be governed by an overt word. The simple expression *Jay's picture* is three ways ambiguous. Jay might be the owner or agent of the picture, or the person portrayed – that is, the object. For various reasons that we need not go into here, linguists say that the structure for the reading in which Jay is the object, the person portrayed, is (9): *Jay* moves from the complement position to the possessive position, leaving a trace in the usual fashion. The trace is governed by the noun *picture*.

9 $_{DP}$[Jay$_i$'s $_{NP}$[picture e$_i$]]

But now consider an expression like *The picture of Jay's*. Here Jay is the owner or the agent of the picture, but not the object – the expression does not refer to a picture in which Jay is portrayed. This is something that most untrained linguists are not aware of and something which is not imparted explicitly to children. Again, a condition of UG must be involved, and it is the condition that traces of movement must be lexically governed. The intended structure is (10a), and the trace (indexed) is the complement of another empty element, understood as "picture," but no overt lexical element governs it (cf. (9)). Similarly for *The picture is Jay's* (10b) and *The picture which is Jay's* (10c), which also lack the objective reading for *Jay*, and whose structures have an illicit trace.

10 (a) *the picture of $_{DP}$[Jay$_i$'s $_{NP}$[e e$_i$]]
   (b) *the picture is $_{DP}$[Jay$_i$'s $_{NP}$[e e$_i$]]
   (c) *the picture which is $_{DP}$[Jay$_i$'s $_{NP}$[e e$_i$]]

For a further illustration, the deviant (11b) has an illicit trace right-adjacent to the gapped verb. Because the verb is a gap, the trace fails to be lexically governed, as is now familiar. That is the only relevant difference from (11a), which is perfectly comprehensible and straightforward, involving no ill-formed traces.

11 (a)   It is known that Jay left but it isn't GAP that he went to the movies.

   (b)   *Jay$_i$ is known [e$_i$ to have left] but he$_i$ isn't GAP [e$_i$ to have gone to the movies]

As a final illustration of the utility of this UG condition, consider the sentence corresponding to (12a), *The crowd is too angry to organize a meeting*. This is ambiguous: the understood subject of the embedded clause, written here as "PRO," may refer to *the crowd* (the "anaphoric" reading), or it may be arbitrary in reference, meaning "anybody".

12 (a)   The crowd$_i$ is too angry $_{CP}$[PRO$_{i/arb}$ to organize a meeting]
   (b)   What$_i$ is the crowd$_j$ too angry $_{CP}$[e$_i$ [PRO$_j$ to organize e$_i$]]

However, the sentence corresponding to (12b), *What is the crowd too angry to organize?*, allows only the anaphoric reading, in which the understood subject is *the crowd*. This is because the trace of *what* at the front of the embedded clause must be governed by *angry*, and as a result the PRO must also be governed.[4]

The UG condition that traces must be governed overtly does a lot of work; it enables us to distinguish many well-formed from deviant structures of English, and to do so in such a way that we can offer plausible stories about what is learned and what is not learned by children acquiring English. Now I want to show that this condition, despite the work it does, is actually maladaptive in well-defined ways. This demonstration concerns a sub-case of the general condition that traces must be governed lexically, whereby subjects of tensed clauses are immovable; they are immovable because, in general, their traces would not be licit, not heading the complement of an adjacent overt word.

9.4   The Condition is Maladaptive

We noted earlier that English embedded clauses are introduced by a complementizer which may or may not be pronounced; the unpronounced (or "deleted") complementizer occurs only where it is governed lexically (see discussion of (3)–(4) above). So sentences corresponding to (13a) occur with and without the *that*. This is also true if a wh- item moves from the embedded object position (13b).

13 (a) I thought [that/0 Ray saw Fay]
   (b) Who$_i$ did you think [e$_i$ that/0 Ray saw e$_i$]?
   (c) *Who$_i$ did you think [e$_i$ that **e**$_i$ saw Fay]?

However, a *who* may not move from an embedded subject position if *that* is present (13c), and the reason is that the subject trace (bold) would not be licit: *Who do you think that saw Fay?* The same is true of indirect questions introduced by a word like *how*: subjects cannot move (14a), but objects can (14b).[5]

14 (a) *Who$_i$ do you wonder [e$_i$ how [**e**$_i$ solved the problem]]
   (b) Which problem$_i$ do you wonder [e$_i$ how [John solved e$_i$]]

A wh- word also may not move from a subject position if the indirect question is part of a relative clause. In (15b) the wh- word has been moved from an underlying object position (where the trace is the complement of *bought*), and the result is a normal sentence. However, (15a) is impossible, for the trace is in subject position and is not a complement; [e$_i$ bought e$_j$] is not the complement of *what*. The sentence corresponding to (15a) would be *This is the student who I wonder what bought.

15 (a) *This is the student who$_i$ I wonder [what$_j$ **e**$_i$ bought e$_j$]
   (b) This is the sweater which$_i$ I wonder [who bought e$_i$]

English has an operation whereby a "large" DP may occur in a displaced position at the far right of its clause, leaving a trace as usual. In (16a) the trace of the moved element, *All the students from LA*, is the complement of the verb *introduced*. In (16b) the trace is in a subject position, but the subject of a nontensed, or "infinitival," clause, and it is governed by the verb *expect*. However, (16c) sounds very un-English, and the problem is that the subject trace is not governed by anything overt.

16 (a) I introduced e$_i$ to Mary [all the students from LA]$_i$
   (b) I expect [e$_i$ to be at the party] [all the students from LA]$_i$
   (c) *[e$_i$ are unhappy] [all the students from LA]$_i$

So the UG condition on traces has a negative effect and blocks the movement of wh- items from the subject of tensed clauses. To this extent, the UG condition is maladaptive. It apparently conflicts with an overwhelming desire/need to ask questions about subjects of tensed clauses, just as one may ask questions about entities in other structural positions. The evidence for this claim is that individuals adopt strategies to circumvent the effects of this UG principle in certain contexts, and these strategies are manifested quite differently in individual languages. Because they vary so much, the individual strategies cannot directly reflect genetic principles. There are three classes of strategies used in different languages, and each strategy permits an *ad hoc*, learned device which licenses extraction from a subject position. They are:

(a)   Adjust the complementizer to license the extraction.
(b)   Use a resumptive pronoun in the extraction site.
(c)   Move the subject first to a nonsubject position and then extract.

English exploits strategy (a) and permits extraction of a subject if the complementizer *that* is not present: *Who do you think saw Fay?*, which has the structure (17). Here the lowest trace (the subject) is governed by the higher trace at the front of the CP (through co-indexing[6]), and that trace is governed by the verb *think*. In the comparable (13c) and (14a), the subject trace was illicit. In other words, subjects of tensed clauses in English are movable only if the complementizer is unpronounced; that permits the subject trace to be governed appropriately.

17   Who_i did you think $_{CP}[e_i [e_i$ saw Fay]]?

Consider now French, where complementizers like *que* are never deleted. Again we see that objects may be extracted freely (18b), but a subject is not extractable in a comparable way (18c). French speakers can adjust the complementizer to the "agreeing" form *qui*, if it is followed by a trace. This effectively licenses the trace, governing it (18d).

18   (a)   Je crois $_{CP}[$que Marie a vu Jean].
            "I think that Mary has seen John."
      (b) Qui_i crois-tu $_{CP}[e_i$ que Marie a vu $e_i]$?
            who think you that Marie has seen
            "Who do you think Marie has seen?"
      (c)   *Qui_i crois-tu $_{CP}[e_i$ que e_i a vu Jean]?
      (d) Qui_i crois-tu $_{CP}[e_i$ qui e_i a vu Jean]?

Again we see a very specific, *ad hoc* device, in this case an operation changing *que* to *qui*, whose sole motivation is to permit extraction of a subject DP.

Luigi Rizzi (1990) identified similar devices in a variety of languages, which permit extraction of subjects. West Flemish behaves similarly to French: the usual form of the complementizer is *da* (19a), but a special "agreeing" form *die* occurs where a subject is extracted (19b).

19 (a)   Den vent da$_i$ Pol peinst [e$_i$ da Marie e$_i$ getrokken heet]
the man that Pol thinks that Marie photographed has
"The man that Pol thinks that Marie has photographed."

   (b)   Den vent da$_i$ Pol peinst [e$_i$ die e$_i$ gekommen ist]
the man that Pol thinks that come is
"The man that Pol thinks has come."

Hebrew also does not allow extraction of a subject DP (20a), in accordance with the condition that traces must be lexically governed. Objects extract freely (20b). But subjects are extractable only if a special device applies adjusting the complementizer, in this case cliticizing the complementizer *še* on to an adjacent head (20c). In (20c) the complementizer cliticizes on to *lo*, vacating the complementizer position and permitting the subject trace to head the complement clause and to be lexically governed. Shlonsky (1988) offers a careful analysis, which would take us too far afield.

20 (a)   *Mi$_i$ ein- ex joda'at ['im e$_i$ mešaret ba-milu'im]?
who not you know whether serves in reserves?

   (b)   Et mi$_i$ ein- ex joda'at ['im ha-milu'im me'aifim e$_i$]?
Acc + who not you know whether the reserves tire?

   (c)   Mi at ma'mina [še-lo ohev salat xacilim]?
who you believe that not likes salad eggplants

Norwegian shows a special complementizer *som* only in embedded questions with a subject extracted (21a); its function seems to be to license a trace which otherwise would violate our UG condition. It never occurs with an extracted object (21b).

21 (a)   Vi vet [hvem$_i$ som/*0 e$_i$ snakker med Marit]
we know who that talks with Mary
"We know who talks with Mary."

   (b)   Vi vet [hvem *som/0 Marit snakker med e]
we know who that Mary talks with
"We know who Mary talks with."

The second general strategy we observe is to replace the illicit trace with a "resumptive" pronoun (b). Swedish exploits this strategy: (22a) shows that if a wh- word moves from an embedded subject position to the right of a complementizer, the resumptive pronoun *det* is required. On the other hand, if no complementizer is present, no resumptive pronoun is allowed (22b) (Engdahl 1985).

22 (a) Vilket ord$_i$ visste ingen [hur det/*e$_i$ stavas]?
which word knew no one how it/e is-spelled?
"Which word did no one know how it is spelled?"

(b) Kalle$_i$ kan jag sla vad om e$_i$/*han kommer att klara sig
Kalle can I bet about e/he is going to succeed
"Kalle, I can bet (*he) is going to succeed."

The West African language Vata adopts the same strategy, but here even for local movement in a simple, unembedded clause. Again we see the familiar subject–object asymmetry: an extracted subject has a resumptive pronoun in its underlying position, never a trace (23a); and vice versa for an extracted object (23b).

23 (a) Alo$_i$ *(o$_i$) le saka la?
who he eat rice WH?

(b) Yi$_i$ Kofi le (*mi$_i$) la?
what Kofi eat it WH

Italian, on the other hand, manifests a third strategy: moving the subject first to a nonsubject position and then to the front of the CP (c). Subjects may occur to the right of the verb phrase (24a), where they are governed by the verb, and that is the position from which they are extracted; so (24b) is the structure for a sentence like *Chi credi che abbia telefonato?*, "Who do you think has telephoned?"

24 (a) Credo [che abbia telefonato Gianni].
I-think that has telephoned Gianni
"I think that Gianni has telephoned."

(b) Chi$_i$ credi [che abbia telefonato e$_i$]?
who do-you-think that has telephoned?
"Who do you think has telephoned?"

The Arabic dialect Banni-Hassan employs a similar device. Here there is a morphological distinction between a post-verbal subject *miin* and its pre-verbal counterpart *min*. If the complementizer *innu* occurs (25a), then the post-verbal subject form is required. In other words, if the complementizer is present, a trace in the pre-verbal subject position would not head a complement, and consequently the element must move from the post-verbal position, showing the appropriate morphology. On the other hand, if the complementizer is absent, then the subject position heads the complement, as illustrated by English above (17), and the pre-verbal subject is a possible extraction site, and the pronoun shows the appropriate pre-verbal morphology (25b).

25 (a) Miin/*min$_i$ Fariid gaal [innu *pro* kisar e$_i$ al-beeda]?
         who Fariid said that broke the egg?
         "Who did Fariid say broke the egg?"
    (b) Min/*miin$_i$ Fariid gaal [0 e$_i$ kisar al-beeda]?

We have discussed a bewildering range of data, but the data have become quite comprehensible. UG blocks extraction of subjects. However, for reasons of expressibility, speakers "need" to extract subjects; that is what the evidence from specific languages shows. Because of the constraints of UG, they are forced to adopt *ad hoc* strategies which either eliminate illicit traces (Swedish, Vata), provide a post-verbal, governed alternative to them (Italian, Banni-Hassan), or adjust the complementizer in some way so as to license them in some special fashion (English, French, West Flemish, Hebrew, Norwegian). Each of the devices we have examined is learnable, if children are prohibited genetically from extracting embedded subjects in the normal case. That is, children are exposed to positive, accessible data which demonstrate the language-specific operation that adults use: the deletability of *that* in English, the operation changing *que* to *qui* in French, the need for a resumptive pronoun *only* in subject positions in Swedish and Vata, etc. We therefore have accounts for the specific languages, which meet our basic requirements. We can also see that a condition of the linguistic genotype may be countermanded by the needs of expressivity; to that extent, the condition is dysfunctional and maladaptive.

The restriction on moving subjects is maladaptive, and part of our evidence is that it does not hold transparently at the level of individuals; individuals do extract subjects, in apparent violation of the government condition on movement traces. But we have seen that these individual phenomena make sense only if there is a government condition at the genetic level, which therefore evolved in the species. It evolved in the species despite the fact that it is maladaptive. If maladaptive elements evolve, then we need something other than natural selection to drive evolutionary developments. The restriction on the movement of subjects is a by-product of the more general condition, a spandrel.

The spandrels of San Marco are by-products of the particular architectural design, and the restriction on the movement of subjects is a by-product of the general condition on movement traces. That general condition may well be functionally motivated, possibly by parsing considerations. In parsing utterances, one needs to analyze the positions from which displaced elements have moved, traces. The UG condition discussed restricts traces to certain well-defined positions, and that presumably facilitates parsing.

The same general point is true of "substantive universals." For example, it is generally supposed that UG makes available four lexical categories: nouns, verbs, prepositions, and A-forms (chapter 3). However, some languages do not distinguish verbs from A-forms (adjectives and adverbs), and it is claimed that some languages even lack the noun–verb distinction (Squamish). This raises the question of how the four-way distinction made available by UG could possibly convey reproductive advantage, as required for a natural selection account, if there are viable, reproducing individuals which lack it.

9.5 Conclusion

I have stated the argument in terms of a government condition on movement traces, but the argument does not depend on any details about government or traces. There can be no doubt that UG principles are implicated in the phenomena discussed. If the bewildering range of phenomena of the last section are indeed grammar-specific, then our argument about adaptation is unaffected. If future work provides a more general UG account, which does not use the technicalities invoked here, it must prohibit the movement of embedded subjects. To that extent, any account will be maladaptive.

If the relevant UG principles are dysfunctional over a significant range, blocking expressions that are needed, then it is unlikely that they could have been specifically selected for. In that case, the whole package of UG may have been adaptive as a whole, but the singularists cannot be right: it is not necessary to look for adaptive accounts of the subparts of UG. Specific elements of UG like the government condition on subject traces are spandrels in the sense of Gould and Lewontin (1979), nonadaptive by-products of something else. But then, of course, precisely the same argument could be true of UG as a whole: UG may have evolved as an accidental side-effect of some other adaptive mutation. This means that one may not take as certain even the scenario that the general algebraic character of the language faculty was selected for. Natural selection may have played no direct role in the evolution of UG specifically. We do not know, but natural selection is not the only possibility.

This conclusion will come as no surprise to Stephen Jay Gould, who has speculated that the language faculty as a whole is a spandrel (Gould 1991b), or to Massimo Piattelli-Palmarini (1989). Nor will it surprise molecular biologists who have emphasized the internal forces motivating genetic change. They adapt Francis Galton's image of organisms as perfectly round billiard balls, which are struck at some angle and with some force by a cue, roll over a perfectly flat surface, and come to rest at one of an infinite number of points which can be predicted simply by calculating the angle and force of the cue and the dimensions of the plane on which they roll. They adapt this image and suggest that organisms may instead be thought of as polyhedrons, which will move only if subjected to a significant force; there will be rapid movement, and they will come to rest at one of only a finite number of end points, because of the intrinsic properties of their shape. This view, of course, builds on the early insights of D'Arcy Thompson, who identified forms which recur pervasively in unrelated species, suggesting that there are physical laws – like the scaling laws discussed earlier – which drive species to adopt familiar forms (Thompson 1961). Our conclusions will also not surprise complexity theorists like Waldrop (1992) and Kauffman (1991), who have argued that complex, dynamical systems can sometimes go spontaneously from randomness to order, and that this may be a plausible driving force for evolutionary change.

Modern biologists often see themselves as engaged in a deeply historical science. Shared features among organisms are seen not as expressions of underlying laws, like the scaling laws, but as contingent, useful accidents passed down genealogically. However, Kauffman and the complexity theorists have argued that the forms among which selection chooses were generated by laws of complexity. Dynamical systems follow trajectories that inevitably flow into attractors, which "trap" the system and create order. Kauffman notes that "selection has always had a handmaiden. It is not, after all, the sole source of order, and organisms are not just tinkered-together contraptions, but expressions of deeper natural laws . . . the patterns of life's bursts and burials are caused by internal processes, endogenous and natural" (Kauffman 1995: 8, 15).[7] The task, then, is to find how much work selection does and how effective the underlying physical laws are.

In short, almost 140 years after Darwin's seminal book, we do not understand the powers and limitations of natural selection, we do not know what kinds of complex systems can be assembled by an evolutionary process, and we do not even begin to understand how selection and self-organization work together to create the splendor of a summer afternoon in an Alpine meadow flooded with flowers, insects, worms, soil, other animals, and humans, making our worlds together. (Ibid. 163)

There are alternatives to natural selection, and it is worth the time of linguists to consider some of them. Current understanding suggests that elements of UG are maladaptive, hence spandrels evolving as a by-product of something else, and not the result of adaptive change favoring survival to reproductive age. Therefore, no extreme form of adaptationism is necessary or plausible.

One possibility is that a mental organ evolved with a capacity for "discrete infinity," which manifests itself in grammars, the number system, and music, all of which therefore evolved together. And it is possible that, due to physical laws, a mental organ of that type could only have the properties that the human brain now has. We do not know enough to deny this possibility. In principle, it is an empirical matter to decide to what extent evolutionary development is due to selection by external forces and how much is due to the demands of internal laws. In fact, of course, the empirical work is hampered by a dearth of relevant facts.

Evolutionary change at the genetic level is similar to phenotypical change in grammars, in that both take place in fits and starts, when environmental factors tweak existing systems in some fashion. However, in neither case do environmental factors suffice to shape the changes that result. The principles of UG provide the channels along which grammatical change may proceed, and physical laws define the terrain on which evolutionary change takes place. That is the point of contact between work on grammar change and evolutionary concerns.

Notes

1 It has been argued that some actual languages have just one vowel at an abstract, underlying level, e.g. Kabardian (Kuipers 1960; for discussion see Halle 1970 and Anderson 1978).

2 We do have some evidence which suggests that in pathological cases some individual aspects of UG may be inoperative in individuals. Gopnik (1990) identified a class of dysphasics who seem to lack grammatical "features," and do not use and understand plural and past tense morphemes. She also studied 30 family members over three generations, 15 of whom are dysphasic in the same way, suggesting that the linguistic impairment is associated with a single dominant gene (Gopnik and Crago 1991). This suggests that UG may be impaired in

piecemeal fashion. This, in turn, raises the possibility that UG evolved in piece-meal fashion; but it does not by any means demonstrate it.

3   This is not to say that natural selection is a *sufficient* account for the availablity of hemoglobin. Hemoglobin is indeed adaptive, but it is available because of a highly structured set of options. An ability to become invisible on demand would also be adaptive, but it has not been selected because physical laws make it unavailable.

4   Here we are on the edge of slipping into unnecessary technicalities, but Hornstein and Lightfoot (1987) and others have shown that governed PRO is anaphoric, and only an ungoverned PRO may be arbitrary in reference. In the structure (12a), the embedded clause may be the complement to *angry* or a noncomple-ment, i.e. an adjunct. Where the clause is a complement, a trace at the front is governed by *angry*, and PRO is anaphoric. Where the clause is a noncomple-ment, PRO is arbitrary in reference, and a trace at the front would be not governed, hence illicit.

5   In section 3.5 I discussed the role of this principle in accounting for the course of language acquisition by children who use "medial" wh- items, *What do you think what Cookie Monster eats?* (Thornton 1995). Such children retain medial wh- items longest in contexts where the wh- word is extracted from a subject position and where it acts as a kind of "agreeing" complementizer: *Who do you think who's under there?*

6   Indexed elements are effectively overt. This can be seen in a language where verbs move and leave indexed traces. French *Qui voyez-vous?*, "Who do you see?," has the structure (i), where e_i is the complement of e_j and thereby governed.

(i) $_{CP}[qui_i \ voyez_j \ _{IP}[vous \ e_j \ e_i]]$

By contrast, the English "gapped" verbs in (7) and (8) cannot result from movement and therefore are not indexed.

7   In resisting the claims of the singularists that evolutionary developments are due entirely to the shaping effects of natural selection, and in emphasizing the role of endogenous factors, Kauffman argues that the laws of complexity have lent the evolution of life a certain inevitability (Horgan 1996: 136). Sometimes his passion carries him away to enthuse that particular developments, like the emergence of human beings in our current form, were not accidental but pre-dictable: "Not we the accidental, but we the expected" (Kauffman 1995: 8), and we are "at home in the universe" in the sense that the development of human beings was somehow inevitable.

It may be inevitable that organisms conform to the scaling laws, but virtually no particular development in the history of life was inevitable. Mathematical laws seem to be involved in defining the range of possibilities, but it is a very different matter to suggest that the history of life *unfolds* according to math-ematical laws. Surely contingency plays too large a role for that to be possible.

10

A Science of History

A science of history. These are two heavily loaded terms, and a warning
that we are on the last chapter. Final chapters are occasions for authors'
hubris and times for readers to fasten their seat belts. I plan to avoid the
baggage as much as possible and not to debate "science." Loosely, I mean
some system of principle- or law-based explanations; I don't need more
refined a definition than that for the purposes of these reflections. I shall
argue first that we don't have to be able to predict future events in order to
provide viable explanations. Then I shall argue that if we study language
history in the way that I have sketched, we have a scientific history. At this
stage, linguists can offer more principled histories than those in other, conventional domains of history. If this is true, then work on grammar change
may serve as a model for work on other kinds of history.

10.1 Classical and Chaotic Views of Science

At several points in the book I have contrasted two visions of science. The
classical, Aristotelian-Newtonian view unfolded from theories about the physical universe articulated by Galileo, Bacon, Descartes, and Newton. According to this tradition, the universe functions like a vast machine governed by
unchanging laws.[1] A set of laws explains properties and events and allows
us to deduce predictions about future behavior. In this way, we can predict
the positions of planets and stars long in advance, and chance plays no role.
Chance is an artifact of multiple variables within experiments or environmental intrusions, or it represents our ignorance. For ages, this was a satisfying view. A Tom Stoppard character says: "We were quite happy with
Aristotle's cosmos. Personally, I preferred it. Fifty-five crystal spheres geared
to God's crankshaft is my idea of a satisfying universe" (*Arcadia*, II. v).

The other, "chaotic" view also has laws and allows the deduction of
predictions; it is just as deterministic as the classical view. But it pays more

attention to unpredictable contingencies; systems are more sensitive to contingent factors, and predictions may only be short-term. Tiny changes in a complex system may lead to hugely unpredictable consequences. Researchers in disciplines from weather modeling to theoretical physics to population biology have turned from the regular, orderly behavior of classical science to irregular, disorderly, unpredictable, erratic behavior. New kinds of mathematical tools let them look at the nasty sorts of problems that had long been swept to the backs of drawers, considered (when they were considered at all) as unapproachable exceptions: turbulence in fluids, crashes in financial markets, fibrillation in the human heart. Chaos seems more human. Classical geometry misses out on the intricacies of natural forms: clouds are not spheres, and mountains are not cones. As another of Stoppard's characters says, chaos is about "the ordinary-sized stuff which is our lives, the things people write poetry about – clouds, daffodils, waterfalls, and what happens in a cup of coffee when the cream goes in."

The classical view of science has dominated work on language change now for 200 years, beginning with the earliest systematic work, articulated very clearly throughout the nineteenth century, and persisting in somewhat more confused fashion through to the end of the twentieth century. Many nineteenth-century scholars, particularly before the late-century neogrammarians, believed that they had discovered *laws* of change, and that future research would uncover more general directions to change. A full, accurate description of a language could be fed through these laws to yield predictions about what the language would look like a few hundred years later... in much the same way that Newton's three laws of motion predicted all movement possibilities. We examined these ideas in chapter 2, and in chapter 8 we saw how they had persisted into the late twentieth century. Twentieth-century researchers have sought historical universals, diachronic continua, theories of change, theories of grammaticalization, and whatnot. In all cases, they were looking for straight-line explanations for changes, which would allow long-term predictions, including predictions spanning thousands of years in the case of the 1970s typologists. This desire for a long-term determinist theory, under which there are endogenous reasons for a language to change and to become better in some way, occurs even in recent generative work.

Richard Dawkins says:

> We humans have purpose on the brain. We find it hard to look at anything without wondering what it is "for", what the motive is for it or the purpose behind it . . . Show us any object or process and it is hard for us to resist the "Why" question – that "What is it for?" question. (1995: 96)

We want simple, deterministic reasons for why a language has become what it is.

One feature of classical, mechanistic physical theories is that time is "reversible," so that one can go forwards or backwards at any point, and the same essential laws will be in operation. That notion has also featured in work on language change: proponents of linear, deterministic theories of change also engage in the reconstruction of earlier, prehistoric stages of languages, making claims about the syntax of Proto-Indo-European, etc. The idea is that they have a rich enough theory of change that they can apply its principles to a language and work backwards, hypothesizing about earlier stages. Harris and Campbell (1995) insist on the viability of syntactic reconstruction, and indeed it should be possible if they have the linear, deterministic theory of change that they claim to have.

A traditional view – in fact, the view discussed in the chapter on the nineteenth century – holds that reconstructed systems play a role in comparative work: they express relationships precisely. If Greek and Latin are "related," that relationship is expressed by the properties of the parent language from which they descend and the specification of the changes which led to the two daughter languages. Antoine Meillet (1937) expressed the view forcefully that a reconstruction is not a representation of earlier reality, but rather an abstract representation of similarity:

> *la seule réalité à laquelle elle ait affaire, ce sont les correspondences entre les langues attestées.* Les correspondences supposent une réalité commune, mais cette réalité reste inconnue, et l'on ne peut pas s'en faire une idée que par des hypothèses, et par des hypothèses invérifiables: la correspondence seule est donc objet de science. On ne peut restituer par la comparaison une langue disparue: la comparaison des langues romanes ne donnerait du Latin vulgaire ni une idée exacte, ni une idée complète . . . ce que fournit la méthode de la grammaire comparée n'est jamais une restitution de l'indo-européen, tel qu'il a été parlé: *c'est rien autre chose qu'un système defini de correspondences entre les langues historiquement attestées.* (Meillet 1937, emphasis original)

In the 1970s a different view emerged: that reconstructions do express prior reality and that, furthermore, one can even learn new things about change by investigating changes between a reconstructed system and the daughter languages. That view was often asserted but never, as far as I know, argued for; it always struck me as quite incoherent (Lightfoot 1979). A more conservative claim was that one could apply general principles of change, based on the examination of changes between attested languages, to hypothesize prehistory in cases where the earlier language was not attested. The logic is that this could be successful, if one had a viable theory of change.

In 1976 Cal Watkins provided a devastating critique of efforts of this type to reconstruct the syntax of Proto-Indo-European, the best-supported of the world's major proto-languages. The reconstructions were based on Greenberg's (1966) theory of typological change. Watkins pointed out that almost all Indo-Europeanists agree on the presence and the precise shape of a relative pronoun (*yo*) and a comparative morpheme (*-tero*) in the parent language, because cognate forms are attested robustly in the daughter languages. However, Greenberg's typology prescribes that "pure subject–object–verb languages" lack such forms, and therefore they do not occur in the Procrustean reconstructions that Watkins was criticizing. The theories of change were so weak and the desire for reconstruction was so strong that we witnessed a comical event: within a year around 1975, three studies were published on the syntax of Proto-Indo-European, one arguing that it was "underlyingly" subject–verb–object, one that it was subject–object–verb, and one that it was verb–subject–object.[2]

There are two traditional tools for reconstruction: an internal method and, by far the more important, the comparative method. The internal method (so-called internal reconstruction) involves examining the properties of a single language and eliminating superficial oddities, in the way that Grassmann explained why certain Greek nouns show an alternation between aspirate and non-aspirate consonants in their stem (section 2.2). It is not really a historical method, as is often noted, and it is used mostly as a prelude to the comparative method, to eliminate the effects of recent changes.

Watkins (1976) used the comparative method to examine relative clauses dealing with athletic events in Hittite, Vedic Sanskrit, and early Greek. He concluded that "the syntactic agreements are so striking and so precise, that we have little choice but to assume that the way you said that sort of thing in Indo-European could not have been very different." However, problems arise when the most archaic patterns are not alike in the daughter languages. What can a comparativist conclude from a demonstration that Hittite had an underlying subject–object–verb order, Germanic subject–verb–object, and Celtic verb–subject–object? The answer is nothing, unless one has a rich theory of change which says, for example, that a subject–object–verb language may change to subject–verb–object, but not vice versa. That is why rich, deterministic theories of change go hand in hand with work on reconstruction. If one has no such theory, one's reconstructions will be limited to the kind of similarities discussed by Watkins. That is indeed as far as we can go, in my view.

For us, the kind of reanalyses that occur in catastrophic change constitute cutoff points to reconstruction. A new grammatical property is not caused endogenously but results from exposure to a new triggering experience in which cues are distributed differently. There is no theory of change which enables us to hypothesize beyond that point.

By contrast, I have adopted a chaotic approach to science. I wish there were a different term, which did not offer such a gift to a negative reviewer. Nonlinear dynamics, maybe. From the ancient Greeks to Sir Isaac Newton, people have believed in a predictable universe. Where unpredictable behavior was observed, for example in weather, the unpredictability was attributed to lack of knowledge: if we just knew more, we would have better weather forecasts.

In 1827 Robert Brown observed that pollen grains suspended in liquid move about in an unpredictable fashion. A hundred years later, Einstein explained this Brownian motion in terms of the pollen grains being pushed about by colliding with billions of water molecules. Since it would be impossible to know the position and velocity of each water molecule, we could never tell where the pollen grain would be deflected next. So randomness results from the interaction of forces too numerous to count or to analyze. It is describable statistically but, in principle, not by Newton's laws of motion. We just don't know enough.

Recently, scientists in various fields have found that Einstein's explanation for unpredictable behavior, while perhaps appropriate for Brownian motion, does not apply to some dynamic systems, which are not random in the same way. Such systems are unpredictable, but they do follow courses prescribed by Newtonian mechanics. The key to understanding how systems may be determinate and unpredictable – an oxymoron from the point of view of classical science – lies in the notion of sensitive dependence on initial conditions. The movement of a system depends on the precise nature of all of its elements, no matter how small.

Edward Lorenz's work on fluid motion first described the importance of initial conditions in the 1960s. Lorenz recognized that we will never be able to predict the weather more than a few days in advance because of the impossibility of knowing all the factors which influence weather patterns. He made a simple mathematical model of atmospheric weather flow. He described the mixing (convection) that occurs in terms of three equations. Using these equations, Lorenz plotted a three-dimensional phase-space graph, a diagram which illustrates two or more physical features, in which he plotted the state of the system for each successive moment.

If the convection occurred randomly, the dots on the graph would be spread evenly with no apparent organization. Instead, they traced a distinct

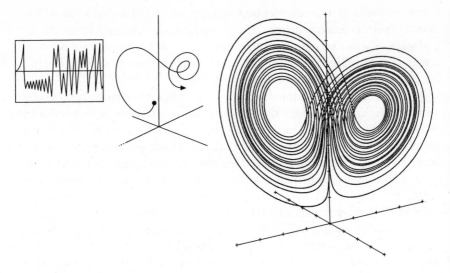

Figure 10.1   Strange attractor.

pattern: the dots circled concentrically a few times, then crossed an axis and circled several times in the other direction. The hidden order inside deterministic chaos had revealed itself. The pattern, which resembles a butterfly, is called a "strange attractor" (figure 10.1).

Later research showed that all chaotic systems, when reduced to a few variables and plotted on phase-space graphs, produce strange attractor patterns; Lorenz's butterfly effect is ubiquitous. It consists of a spaghetti of trajectories, and miniscule shifts in some system's initial conditions may amplify exponentially, as their effects unfold and lead to a different trajectory. But within limits. So the weather in Boston will never feature a monsoon, or a month without rain.

Predicting final outcomes – or indeed anything beyond the very short-term – becomes impossible. Chaos incorporates elements of chance, but it is not random disorder. Rather, chaos theory tries to understand the behavior of systems that do not unfold over time in a linearly predictable manner. When viewed as a whole, these systems manifest definite patterns and structures. However, because the evolution of a chaotic system is so hugely complex, and so prone to perturbation by contingent factors, it is impossible to discern its underlying pattern – its attractor – by looking at a single small event at a single point in time. At no single point can future directions be predicted from past history.

So it is with the emergence of new species in evolutionary change, with changes in the political and social domain, and in grammar. Change is not random, but we are dealing with contingent systems, and we offer retrospective explanations, not predictions. Grammatical change is highly contingent – chaotic in the technical sense. Linguists can offer satisfying explanations of changes in some instances, but there is no reason to expect to find a predictive theory of change, offering long-term, linear predictions.

The emergence of a grammar in a child is sensitive to the initial conditions of the primary linguistic data. If those data shift a little, changing the distribution of the cues, there may be significant consequences for the abstract system. A new system may be triggered, which generates a very different set of sentences and structures, as we have seen. There is nothing principled to be said about why the cues should shift a little; those shifts often represent chance, contingent factors.

If language acquisition is driven by the goal of converging on a grammar which generates the set of *sentences* to which a child is exposed (what I called input matching in chapter 6), one would find linear accounts for change. The scale of the changes in the primary data would be consistent with the scale of changes in the output of the grammar; one would find gradual change pervasively. However, this is not what happens.

Children scan their environment for abstract cues. Contingent changes in the distribution of those cues may trigger a grammar which generates significantly different sentences and structures. Change is not random, but it is unpredictable, a function of contingent changes in the distribution of cues.

Not only does cue-based acquisition provide a productive view of grammatical change; it also facilitates a plausible view of grammar acquisition and variation. It avoids severe feasibility problems, which arise if acquisition proceeds by evaluating the capacity of grammars to generate sets of sentences. If UG provides binary parameters of variation, then 11 parameters generate 4,096 grammars, and 32 generate 8–9 billion grammars. The child eliminates grammars which fail to generate the sentences encountered. If we assume 30–40 structural parameters, and if children converge on a grammar by, say, age seven, then this means that they eliminate grammars at a fantastic rate, several grammars each second on average.

As if this problem is not enough, it is by no means clear that parameters can be kept down to 30–40. If there are only 30–40 structural parameters, then they must look very different from present proposals. We have seen some quite small-scale parameters, particularly in chapter 7. They are well-motivated, and they enable us to understand clusters of changes, but they may be manifested by single lexical items. Also, a single issue of the journal *Linguistic Inquiry* may contain 30–40 proposed parameters. It will take a major rethinking of grammar variation to yield an adequately flexible system with just 30–40 parameters.

Cue-based acquisition finesses these feasibility problems. We are free to postulate 100 or 200 cues, if that is what analyses of different grammars require. That would not raise comparable feasibility problems for the child learner. Our child would not be evaluating quadrillions of grammars against sets of sentences, rejecting hundreds every waking second. Instead, the child would be scanning her environment for the 100 or 200 cues. That task may raise difficulties that we do not now understand, but it does not raise the particular, devastating feasibility problems of input-matching parametric systems.

This does not mean, of course, that we are free to postulate a vast number of cues. We do not want cues to become so fine-grained that they become equivalent to superficial "differences" among languages. Such proliferation might run out of control and sacrifice explanatory force. And one day we may need to think about neurological limits.

Jean-Pierre Changeux (1983) discussed the simplicity of the genome and the complexity of the brain. The genome is limited in the richness of information that it can carry, dramatically so when compared to the extreme diversity and complexity of the anatomy of the brain. The total quantity of chromosomal DNA limits the maximum number of genes. Estimates of the maximum number of structural genes are still very approximate, but in the mouse it seems to be around 150,000. If we ask how the total DNA content per cell nucleus has evolved from bacteria to man, we find that there is a real increase from bacteria to mice: the egg of the fruit fly contains 24 times more DNA than E. coli, and the mouse 25 times more than the fruit fly. Correspondingly, the nervous system of the fruit fly contains about 100,000 neurons, and that of the mouse fifty to sixty times more. However, when we pass from the mouse to humans, we encounter a paradox: the number of cerebral cells jumps from five to six million to several tens of billions; the level of organization and performance of the brain increases spectacularly, while the total quantity of DNA in the nucleus of the fertilized egg does not change significantly. Within 10 percent, it is the same in mouse, cow, chimpanzee, and human, pointing to a remarkable nonlinearity between the DNA content and the complexity of the brain. The paradox is quite striking when one looks at humans: 200,000 or even a million genes are very few compared with the number of synapses in the human brain, or even the number of different types of neurons in the cerebral cortex.

The significance of this is unclear, because we don't have the faintest idea of how much change is needed for a chimpanzee's brain to have the capacity of a human brain. Perhaps very little. There is no simple relationship between the complexity of the genome and that of the central nervous system. Complexity may emerge through *epigenetic* development, particularly in the case of the human brain, which grows enormously *after* birth. Until such epigenetic theories are developed, we should ensure that our cues do not proliferate arbitrarily. However, we do not need to keep them below 30 through fear of the feasibility problems faced by input-matching theories of acquisition.

Our cue-based theory of acquisition allows us to develop an appropriately contingent analysis of grammatical change. That analysis is consistent with more recent chaotic, nonpredictive views of science. So historical linguists are akin to weather forecasters. Despite the popular abuse they are subjected to, forecasters are scientists. They cannot predict weather accurately more than a few days in advance, sometimes less, but they don't need to in order to be scientists. They can explain retrospectively why particular weather patterns developed, on the basis of their scientific principles.

Speaking of weather, I should mention a frequently cited metaphor due to Jerzy Kuryłowicz. Kuryłowicz thought of change as a rainstorm, and he observed that historical linguists could not predict when it would rain, but they should have a good enough conception of the gutters to predict where the rain would go when it fell. On the view sketched here, we cannot predict which cues will change in their distribution and how; that is a contingent, unpredictable matter. We do not know where Kuryłowicz's rain will go. We know only that the new system will fall within the channels prescribed by UG, and that the grammar changes will be a function of which cues trigger the new system.

10.2 History as an Epiphenomenon

There were enormous political changes in England in the seventeenth century, culminating in the Civil War of 1642–51 and the Glorious Revolution of 1688–9. We can ask whether this truly amounted to a revolution. If so, a revolution of what kind? Lawrence Stone (1992) distinguished four approaches to this question.

The *Whig* historians (Macaulay, Trevelyan, Margaret Judson) saw these events as resulting from the struggle of the propertied classes for freedom of speech, for restriction of the power to tax to an elected parliament, and for a curtailment of the tyrannical powers of the monarchs. It resulted in victory for an oligarchy of property owners, which was extended in the nineteenth and twentieth centuries to the middle and working classes and to women.

The *social* historians (R. H. Tawney, Christopher Hill) saw class war, a rise of bourgeois capitalists, who were seeking a larger participation in national affairs and in the protection of their own property rights. The key historical forces were economic, demographic, and social, and these historians paid little attention to the high politics, court/parliament disputes, or legal, and constitutional issues.

Both these models were challenged in the 1970s by the *revisionists* (Geoffrey Elton, Conrad Russell, Kevin Sharpe). The revisionists saw the Civil War and the Glorious Revolution as fortuitous accidents, unrelated to fundamental political and social processes; they rejected all long-term structural causes and concentrated just on personal and factional accidents in high politics (the political personality of the king, etc.); there were no major trends leading to civil war and revolution.

In the 1980s the *counter-revisionists* argued that it was only in the context of ideological conflicts over law, liberty, foreign policy, and religion that the "accidental" high politics of the revisionists made any sense. The counter-revisionists showed that copies of key political documents (including parliamentary debates) circulated widely among gentry, yeomen, and leading citizens, even though there is not much documentary evidence for debates on the topics examined by the Whig historians. But that doesn't mean that the debates did not take place; after all, if punishment for talking about liberty was loss of ears or life imprisonment, one cannot deduce consensus from silence in the documents.

Historians continue to debate what happened in the seventeenth century, and they are constantly reinterpreting the old data and discovering new data. They are well aware that "innocent, unbiased observation is a myth" (in the much-quoted words of Sir Peter Medawar). Some have distinguished the global perspective of the parachutist from the focused concerns of the truffle hunter, and have argued that good history needs the best of both perspectives, as well as several more perspectives that lie between these two extremes. In adopting these perspectives, social/political/economic historians (with the exception, perhaps, of dogmatic Marxists) do not seek principled explanations for what they are describing; rather, they seek to cast light on why events happened, what influenced them, and how they are related to each other.

What about biological history, evolution? Evolutionary biology also deals in contingencies. There were once a few simple organisms, but it is not the case that time brought a steady increase in diversity and complexity, leading inevitably to an intelligent, tool-using, talking animal – us. There are mathematical laws at work, like the scaling laws discussed in section 9.2; but the mathematical laws hold of organisms, not of history. Virtually nothing in the history of life was inevitable. If we could replay the whole evolution of animals, "there is no guarantee – indeed, no likelihood – that the result would be the same" (John Maynard Smith 1992). Would intelligent beings reappear? Hopping marsupials and ink-squirting cephalopods? The contingency of evolution depends partly on the random nature of genetic mutation and partly on the fact that mutations have different effects, and those effects may be amplified.

> Thus a chance change in a single molecule can, if present in a fertilized egg, alter the nature of the individual that develops: natural selection can then amplify a change in an individual to a change in a whole population. This amplification of quantum events, combined with the unpredictability of the environment, makes it impossible to foretell the longterm future, although it may still be possible to explain evolution in retrospect. (Smith 1992)

In the replay experiment, we could predict that many animals would evolve eyes, because eyes have in fact evolved many times in many kinds of animals; that some would evolve powered flight, because flight has evolved four times in two phyla (but one cannot be certain, because animals might never have moved out of the oceans onto land). We cannot predict which phyla would survive and inherit the Earth, and it is very unlikely that human beings just like us would evolve in the replay experiment.

Sometimes it is possible to explain unique events – for example, that the extinction of the dinosaurs was caused by a meteorite collision – and this should be decidable eventually beyond reasonable doubt. But evolutionary origins are harder to explain, as is clear to anybody who has followed recent discussions about the origin of language, where the central ideas are untestable (chapter 9).

Evolutionary biology has a theory about the mechanism of change, based on the laws of inheritance, the concept of natural selection, and the theory of population genetics. Therefore it depends on scientific elements, and it can be described as a scientific history in a way that is less true for human, political history. But there is no real basis for determinism, no basis for predicting that under specific circumstances a specific organism will evolve and proliferate. That could change if Stuart Kauffman's program succeeds; but for the moment there is no way to predict what kind of new organism would emerge if we introduced some new environmental element.

In the light of this, what can we say about language history? We have our analogues to the kinds of things I have mentioned about human history and evolutionary history. We certainly have to engage in the kind of interpretation that the seventeenth-century political historians argue about.

And language history is certainly contingent and subject to accidents of environmental influence and idiosyncrasies. After all, the Latin spoken in Barcelona developed into Catalan, and the Latin spoken in Venice eventually became Venetian. In chapters 5–7 we saw several examples of new grammars being triggered by minor changes in experience.

Historians of language are like human historians and evolutionists, in that we are all dealing with contingent histories and trying to offer explanations. That's not bad company to be in; but I want to suggest, immodestly, that historians of language are leaders and can provide a model: at this point, language historians can offer tighter explanations than are available in the other fields. We can even make predictions in certain domains.

Children are exposed from birth to a linguistic environment which, by virtue of their genetic endowment, leads to the emergence in them of a mature system of knowledge, which goes well beyond their childhood experience. A grammar characterizes formally that mature system of linguistic knowledge. If we take that perspective, a theory of grammar may be seen as specifying a set of cues that a child may be exposed to. For each cue, the linguist specifies what kind of linguistic experience would be needed, appealing only to robust, simple experiences available to the normal child, and shows how that cue, once identified, determines aspects of knowledge beyond the experience of the child, the kind of data that one finds in a journal like *Linguistic Inquiry*. Particularly interesting are cases in which a range of linguistic differences can be traced to some single theoretical choice made differently in particular grammars. This is where language change becomes relevant.

Changes in language often take place in clusters: apparently unrelated superficial changes may occur simultaneously or in rapid sequence. Such clusters manifest a single theoretical choice which has been made differently. If so, the singularity of the change can be explained by the appropriately defined theoretical choice. So the principles of UG and the definition of the cues constitute the laws that guide change in grammars, defining the available terrain. Any given phenomenal change is explained if we show, first, that the linguistic environment has changed in such a way that some theoretical choice has been made differently (say, a change in the way that a case is assigned), and, second, that the new phenomenon (perhaps a new meaning for some verb) must be the way that it is because of some principle of the theory and the new case assignment.

What we cannot explain, in general, is why the linguistic environment should have changed in the first place. Environmental changes are often due to what I have called "chance" factors, effects of borrowing, changes in the frequency of forms, stylistic innovations, which spread through a community and, where we are lucky, are documented by variation studies. Changes of this type need not reflect changes in grammars. But with a theory of language acquisition which defines the range of theoretical choices available to the child and specifies how the child may make those choices, one can predict that a child will converge on a certain grammar when exposed to certain environmental elements. This is where prediction is possible, in principle.

Earlier, I poured cold water on dreams that one day, given a good description of a language at a certain point in time, we will be able to predict the future course of its history. That would involve having some principled basis for predicting that a certain set of primary linguistic data would change in some precise fashion (1). No such principled basis is available.

1   $PLD_x \rightarrow PLD_y$

The comparable dream of a syntactician is that there may be a principled basis for predicting which grammar will emerge on exposure to some specific triggering experience (2).

2   $PLD_x \rightarrow Grammar_x$

This seems to me to be a realizable dream – in fact, the goal of theoreticians. It should be possible to specify the cues needed and to show what kinds of experiences express the cues robustly enough to trigger the relevant grammar.

We have an interplay of chance and necessity, and appropriately so; changes are due to "chance" in the sense that contingent factors influence a child's PLD and make the triggering experience somewhat different from what the child's parent was exposed to. Necessity factors, the principles of UG and the cues, define the range of available options for the new grammar. The historian's explanations are based on the acquisition theory that our synchronic colleagues have devised, and in some cases our explanations are quite tight and satisfying (chapters 5–7). There are no principles of history, and, in this sense, history is an epiphenomenon.

We linguistic historians are dependent on our synchronic colleagues. This dependence is quite virtuous and productive, and it takes us out of a potentially vicious circle. One can visualize different formulations of the theory of grammar, and those formulations may differ in terms of which historical changes they explain and which changes they attribute to chance changes in the environment. Chance changes and necessary changes do not come labeled as such, although there are some guidelines (e.g. changes in relatively exotic structures like embedded binding domains or changes manifested by the obsolescence of certain structures or changes which take place rapidly and "catastrophically" are likely to reflect new parameter settings; chapter 4 offered a partial typology of grammatical/nongrammatical changes). Not knowing in advance whether a change is due to chance or to necessity factors might entail a problem of indeterminacy if, like most historians, we define ourselves as historians and confine our attention to historical changes, being concerned only with theories explaining historical phenomena. But we can avoid this indeterminacy problem by seeking a theory of grammar in collaboration with our synchronic colleagues; such a theory accounts for how the grammar of *any* natural language is attained under normal childhood experience – an enormously strict empirical demand.

This point has been made before. In 1960 Henry Hoenigswald's important book on change and reconstruction had an eloquent footnote:

> Distinguished diachronic work can be done, and was of course done from 1800 on, on the basis of conventional or implicit synchronic formulations. But much time and effort could have been saved if historical theory had been built on more explicit synchronic foundations. At any rate, the champions of a "synthesis" of historical and descriptive work underemphasize an important point: the two are not independent, and any historical statement contains, avowedly or otherwise, at least two synchronic statements – one for each of two or more stages – already. (Hoenigswald 1960: 3)

Lest this paints a picture of a dependent field wherein historians will be forever subject to the whims of the synchronic theoreticians, let us also understand that historians have much to teach their colleagues. Syntacticians are embarrassingly silent on what it takes to set the parameters which they define. What makes historical studies so interesting is that one can sometimes identify cases where grammars change at some stage in the history of the language. If we are lucky, we can then identify changes taking place in the language just prior to the emergence of the new grammar. In that case, if our records are good, we are in a position to identify just what it took to trigger the new grammar. In fact, it seems to me that we can learn more about the nature of the triggering experience from language change than in any other way. This is no small claim, because unless syntacticians start identifying how their parameters get set by children, somebody is going to call their bluff and show that the emperor has no clothes.

On this view, we have a scientific approach to language change. The scientific elements are, first, the principles and cues of UG, which define how phenomena may cluster in diachronic change, and, second, the theory of acquisition, which specifies how cues are identified.

At this stage, the theory is quite embryonic; but it is rich enough to afford the explanations offered in chapters 5–7. The physicist John Wheeler says insightfully that, as the island of our knowledge grows, so does the shore of our ignorance. I have used a cue-based theory of acquisition and shown how it affords an appropriate view of historical change in grammars. Making language acquisition sensitive to a search for abstract grammatical elements seems to be the right *kind* of theory. However, a cue-based theory of acquisition raises new questions and shows us that there are more things that we don't know. In particular, I appealed to a technical definition of the *expression* of cues, in terms of sequences of words which must be analyzed in such a fashion that the cue is manifested. Given the range of options allowed by UG, there is work to be done in characterizing what it means to say that an utterance *must* be analyzed in some fashion.

Nonetheless, we have an approach to history which is significantly more scientific in its ability to explain changes than that of human historians, evolutionists, and linguists who are too historicist and nonpsychological in their diachronic analyses. The political historian and the evolutionist have no analogue to UG, which is equivalently rich in limiting the range of options as change takes place. I believe that the explanations for grammatical changes offered in chapters 5–7 are tighter and richer than the explanations that an evolutionist can offer for the emergence of a new species. The evolutionist's analogue to UG is the set of laws which determine the structure of organisms; the scaling laws discussed in chapter 9 are one example. The political historian's analogue would be a theory of possible political organizations. These theories do not connect with the facts of structural change as tightly as our theory of UG. Again, Kauffman's program could change this. Until then, work on grammatical change is a model for work in other fields which deal with contingent change.

Gould (1991a) reported that Harvard had divided the sciences according to procedural style, not conventional discipline – that is, not into physical and biological, but into "experimental-predictive" and "historical." The division should not be too strict. Linguists have tried that experiment for too long, segregating historical studies into an aging ghetto, often at the end of the department corridor. An appropriate union, however, can work some small wonders ... and give us a claim to a scientific approach to history – in fact, a preeminent claim.

It is hopelessly too ambitious to seek a classical, Newtonian-style theory of language change, predicting changes over the long-term. We can say nothing about distant end results of language change; but we can offer interesting explanations of changes as they take place, in the fashion of a weather forecaster.

A recent rendition of the *Odyssey* had the blind prophet Teiresias telling Odysseus that the journey is the destination:

> You are a clever man, Odysseus of Ithaca, but not a very wise one. You keep your eyes on your home. You do not see that it is the journey itself which makes up your life. Only when you understand this will you understand the meaning of wisdom.

Similarly, linguists will become wise when they realize that there are no historical laws to predict the future, long-term development of languages, but that, with the right kind of theory of variation and acquisition, we can understand particular changes and explain them, as they happen.

Notes

1 Newton's major discovery was that the universe is *not* a machine, much to his dismay and everybody else's. So the tradition is misleading in treating Aristotle and Newton alike.
2 Friedrich 1975; Lehmann 1974; and Miller 1975, respectively.

References

Allan, W. S. 1988: "Lightfoot noch einmal." *Diachronica* 4: 1–28.

Allen, C. 1986: "Reconsidering the history of *like*." *Journal of Linguistics* 22.2: 375–409.

—— 1995: *Case Marking and Reanalysis*. Oxford: Clarendon Press.

—— 1997: "Investigating the origins of the 'group genitive' in English." *Transactions of the Philological Society* 95.1: 111–31.

Andersen, H. 1973: "Abductive and deductive change." *Language* 49.4: 765–93.

Anderson, J. M. 1986: "A note on Old English impersonals." *Journal of Linguistics* 22.1: 167–77.

Anderson, S. R. 1978: "Syllables, segments and the Northwest Caucasian languages." In A. Bell and J. Hooper (eds), *Syllables and Segments*, New York: North Holland Publishing.

—— 1979: "On the subsequent development of the 'standard theory' in phonology." In D. Dinnsen (ed.), *Current Approaches to Phonological Theory*, Bloomington: Indiana University Press.

—— 1992: *A-morphous Morphology*. Cambridge: Cambridge University Press.

Aoun, J. 1985: *A Grammar of Anaphora*. Cambridge, Mass.: MIT Press.

——, N. Hornstein, D. Lightfoot and A. Weinberg 1987: "Two types of locality." *Linguistic Inquiry* 18: 537–77.

Arnold, M. D. 1995: "Case, Periphrastic DO, and the Loss of Verb Movement in English" (Ph.D. dissertation, University of Maryland).

Aronoff, M. 1976: *Word Formation in Generative Grammar*. Linguistic Inquiry Monograph, 1. Cambridge, Mass.: MIT Press.

Baker, M. 1996: *The Polysynthesis Parameter*. Oxford: Oxford University Press.

Barkow, J., L. Cosmides, and J. Tooby 1992: *The Adapted Mind: evolutionary psychology and the generation of culture*. Oxford: Oxford University Press.

Bates, E. A. and J. L. Elman 1996: "Learning rediscovered." *Science* 274: 1849–50.

Battye, A. and I. G. Roberts (eds) 1995: *Clause Structure and Language Change*. Oxford: Oxford University Press.

Bauer, B. 1995: *The Emergence and Development of SVO Patterning in Latin and French*. Oxford: Oxford University Press.

Belletti, A. and L. Rizzi 1988: "Psych-verbs and theta-theory." *Natural Language and Linguistic Theory* 6.3: 291–352.

Berlin, I. 1996: *The Sense of Reality: studies in ideas and their history*. London: Chatto & Windus.

Berwick, R. C. 1985: *The Acquisition of Syntactic Knowledge*. Cambridge, Mass.: MIT Press.

Besten, H. den 1983: "On the interaction of root transformations and lexical deletive rules." In W. Abraham (ed.), *On the Formal Syntax of the Westgermania*, Amsterdam: Benjamins.

Bickerton, D. 1984: "The language bioprogram hypothesis." *Behavioral and Brain Sciences* 7: 173–221.

—— 1998: "How to acquire language without positive evidence: what acquisitionists can learn from creoles." In DeGraff (ed.).

Blake, B. 1994: *Case*. Cambridge: Cambridge University Press.

Bloomfield, L. 1933: *Language*. New York: Holt.

Bomhard, A. 1990: "A survey of the comparative phonology of the so-called 'Nostratic' languages." In P. Baldi (ed.), *Linguistic Change and Reconstruction Methodology*, Berlin: Mouton de Gruyter.

Brandon, R. and N. Hornstein 1986: "From icons to symbols: some speculations on the origins of language." *Biology and Philosophy* 1: 169–89.

Brugmann, K. 1918: *Verschiedenheiten der Satzgestaltung nach Massgabe der seelischen Grundfunktionen in den indogermanischen Sprachen*. Leipzig: Teubner.

—— 1925: *Die Syntax des einfachen Satzes im Indogermanischen*. Berlin: de Gruyter.

Brugmann, K. and B. Delbrück 1886–1900: *Grundiss der vergleichenden Grammatik der indogermanischen Sprache*, 5 vols. Strassburg: Trübner.

Bruyn, A. 1995: *Grammaticalization in Creoles: the development of determiners and relative clauses in Sranan*. Studies in Language and Language Use, 21. Dordrecht: ICG Printing.

Carden, G. and W. A. Stewart 1988: "Binding theory, bioprogram and creolization: evidence from Haitian creole." *Journal of Pidgin and Creole Languages* 3: 1–67.

Casti, J. L. 1994: *Complexification: explaining a paradoxical world through the science of surprise*. New York: HarperCollins.

Changeux, J.-P. 1983: *L'Homme neuronal*. Paris: Fayard.

Chomsky, N. 1965: *Aspects of the Theory of Syntax*. Cambridge, Mass.: MIT Press.

—— 1975: *The Logical Structure of Linguistic Theory*. New York: Plenum.

—— 1977: *Essays on Form and Interpretation*. New York: Elsevier North Holland.

—— 1981: *Lectures on Government and Binding*. Dordrecht: Foris.

—— 1986: *Knowledge of Language: its nature, origin and use*. New York: Praeger.

—— 1995: *The Minimalist Program*. Cambridge, Mass.: MIT Press.

Chung, S. 1978: *Case Marking and Grammatical Relations in Polynesian*. Austin: University of Texas Press.

Clark, R. 1992: "The selection of syntactic knowledge." *Language Acquisition* 2: 83–149.

Clark, R. and I. G. Roberts 1993: "A computational model of language learnability and language change." *Linguistic Inquiry* 24: 299–345.

Cohen, G. A. 1978: *Karl Marx's Theory of History: a defence*. Princeton: Princeton University Press.

Comrie, B. 1978: "Ergativity." In W. P. Lehmann (ed.), *Syntactic typology*, Hassocks: Harvester Press.

Crain, S. 1991: "Language acquisition in the absence of experience." *Behavioral and Brain Sciences* 14: 597–612.

Crain, S. and R. Thornton 1998: *Investigations in Universal Grammar: a guide to experiments on the acquisition of syntax and semantics*. Cambridge, Mass.: MIT Press.

Darwin, C. 1874: *The Descent of Man*, 2nd edn. New York: D. Appleton, 1889.

Davies, A. M. 1998: *Nineteenth-Century Linguistics. History of Linguistics*, ed. G. Lepschy, vol. 4. London: Longman.

Dawkins, R. 1976: *The Selfish Gene*. Oxford: Oxford University Press.

—— 1995: *River out of Eden: a Darwinian view of life*. New York: Basic Books.

DeGraff, M. (ed.) 1998: *Language Creation and Change: creolization, diachrony and development*. Cambridge, Mass.: MIT Press.

Denison, D. 1989: "Auxiliary and impersonal in Old English." *Folia Linguistica Historica* 9.1: 139–66.

—— 1990: "The OE impersonals revived." In S. Adamson, V. Law, N. Vincent, and S. Wright (eds), *Papers from the Fifth International Conference on English Historical Linguistics*, Amsterdam: Benjamins.

—— 1993: *English Historical Syntax*. London: Longman.

Dennett, D. 1995: *Darwin's Dangerous Idea: evolution and the meaning of life*. New York: Simon & Schuster.

Dixon, R. M. W. 1994: *Ergativity*. Cambridge: Cambridge University Press.

Dobzhansky, T. 1970: *Genetics of the Evolutionary Process*. New York: Columbia University Press.

Dresher, E. 1998: "Charting the learning path: cues to parameter setting." *Linguistic Inquiry* 29.

Dresher, E. and J. Kaye 1990: "A computational learning model for metrical phonology." *Cognition* 34: 137–95.

Dyson, F. 1979: *Disturbing the Universe*. New York: Basic Books.

Ekwall, E. 1943: *Studies on the Genitive of Groups in English*. Lund: Gleerup.

Eldredge, N. and S. J. Gould 1972: "Punctuated equilibria: an alternative to phyletic gradualism." In T. J. M. Schopf (ed.), *Models of Paleobiology*, San Francisco: Freeman, Cooper.

Ellegård, A. 1953: *The Auxiliary DO: the establishment and regulation of its use in English*. Stockholm: Almqvist & Wiksell.

Elster, J. 1993: *Political Psychology*. Cambridge: Cambridge University Press.

Engdahl, E. 1985: "Parasitic gaps, resumptive pronouns, and subject extractions." *Linguistics* 23: 3–44.

Evers, A. and J. van Kampen 1995: "*Do*-insertion and LF in child language." In J. Don, B. Schouten, and W. Zonneveld (eds), *OTS Yearbook*, Utrecht: University of Utrecht.

Fikkert, P. 1994: "On the Acquisition of Prosodic Structure" (Ph.D. dissertation, University of Leiden).

—— 1995: "Models of acquisition: how to acquire stress." In J. Beckman (ed.), *Proceedings of NELS 25*, GLSA, University of Massachusetts,

Fischer, O. C. M. 1997: "On the status of grammaticalization and the diachronic dimension in explanation." *Transactions of the Philological Society* 95.2: 149–87.

Fodor, J. A. 1997: "Do we have it in us?" *Times Literary Supplement*, May 16.

Fodor, J. D. 1998: "Unambiguous triggers." *Linguistic Inquiry* 29.1: 1–36.

Fontana, J. M. 1993: "Phrase Structure and the Syntax of Clitics in the History of Spanish" (Ph.D. dissertation, University of Pennsylvania).

Friedrich, P. 1975: *Proto-Indo-European Syntax*. Journal of Indo-European Studies monograph, 1. Butte, Mont.

Fries, C. 1940: "On the development of the structural use of word-order in Modern English." *Language* 16: 199–208.

Fukuyama, F. 1992: *The End of History and the Last Man*. New York: Free Press.

Gardner, M. 1996: "How not to talk about mathematics." In *The Night is Large: collected essays 1938–1995*, New York: St Martin's Press.

Garrod, H. W. 1928: "Jane Austin: a depreciation." *Transactions of the Royal Society of Literature* 8: 21–40.

Gibson, E. and K. Wexler 1994: "Triggers." *Linguistic Inquiry* 25.3: 407–54.

Goldin-Meadow, S. and C. Mylander 1990: "Beyond the input given: the child's role in the acquisition of language." *Language* 66: 323–55.

Gopnik, M. 1990: "Feature blindness: a case study." *Language Acquisition* 1.2: 139–64.

Gopnik, M. and M. Crago 1991: "Familial aggregation of a developmental language disorder." *Cognition* 39: 1–50.

Gould, S. J. 1985: "A clock of evolution." *Natural History*, April: 12–25.

—— 1991a: *Bully for Brontosaurus*. New York: Norton.

—— 1991b: "Exaptation: a crucial tool for an evolutionary psychology." *Journal of Social Issues* 47.3: 43–65.

—— 1997: "Evolution: the pleasures of pluralism." *New York Review of Books*, June 26.

Gould, S. J. and R. C. Lewontin 1979: "The spandrels of San Marco and the Panglossian paradigm: a critique of the adaptationist programme." *Proceedings of the Royal Society of London*, B, 205: 581–98.

Graffi, G. 1995: "Old debates and current problems: *Völkerpsychologie* and the question of the individual and the social in language." In L. Formigari and D. Gambarara (eds), *Historical Roots of Linguistic Theories*, Amsterdam: Benjamins.

Grassmann, H. 1863: "Über die Aspiraten und ihr gleichzeitiges Vorhandensein im An- und Auslaute der Wurzeln." *Zeitschrift für vergleichende Sprachforschung auf dem Gebiete des Deutschen, Griechischen und Lateinischen* 12.2: 81–138.

Greenberg, J. H. 1966: "Some universals of grammar with particular reference to the order of meaningful elements." In J. H. Greenberg (ed.), *Universals of Language*, Cambridge, Mass.: MIT Press.

Grimm, J. 1822: *Deutsche Grammatik*. Gütersloh: C. Bertelmann.

—— 1848: *Geschichte der deutschen Sprache*, vol. 1. Leipzig: Weidmannsche Buchhandlung.

Hale, K. 1983: "Warlpiri and the grammar of non-configurational languages." *Natural Language and Linguistic Theory* 1: 5–47.

Halle, M. 1970: "Is Kabardian a vowel-less language?" *Foundations of Language* 6: 95–103.

Harris, A. 1980: "On the loss of a rule of syntax." In E. Traugott, R. Lebrun, and S. Shepherd (eds), *Papers from the Fourth International Conference on Historical Linguistics*, Amsterdam: Benjamins.

—— 1985: *Diachronic Syntax: the Kartvelian case*. Syntax and Semantics, 18. New York: Academic Press.

—— (forthcoming): "Cross-linguistic perspectives on syntactic change." In Janda and Joseph (eds).

Harris, A. and L. Campbell 1995: *Historical Syntax in Cross-Linguistic Perspective*. Cambridge: Cambridge University Press.

Hausmann, R. 1974: "The development of periphrastic *do* in English." In J. Anderson & C. Jones (eds), *Historical Linguistics*, Amsterdam: North Holland.

Hockett, C. F. 1965: "Sound change." *Language* 41: 185–204.

Hoenigswald, H. 1960: *Language Change and Linguistic Reconstruction*. Chicago: University of Chicago Press.

—— 1963: "On the history of the comparative method." *Anthropological Linguistics* 5: 1–11.

—— 1978: "The *annus mirabilis* 1876 and posterity." *Transactions of the Philological Society*: 17–35.

Hogg, R. 1992: "Phonology and morphology." In R. Hogg (ed.), *The Cambridge History of the English Language*, vol. 1: *The Beginnings to 1066*, Cambridge: Cambridge University Press.

Holmberg, A. 1986: "Word Order and Syntactic Features in the Scandinavian Languages and English" (Ph.D. dissertation, University of Stockholm).

Hopper, P. and E. Traugott 1993: *Grammaticalization*. Cambridge: Cambridge University Press.

Horgan, J. 1996: *The End of Science: facing the limits of knowledge in the twilight of the scientific age*. Reading, Mass.: Addison-Wesley.

Hornstein N. and D. Lightfoot 1987: "Predication and PRO." *Language* 63.1: 23–52.

—— 1991: "On the nature of lexical government." In R. Freidin (ed.), *Principles and Parameters in Comparative Grammar*, Cambridge, Mass.: MIT Press.

Hubel, D. 1978: "Vision and the brain." *Bulletin of the American Academy of Arts and Sciences* 31.7: 28.

Hubel, D. and T. Wiesel 1962: "Receptive fields, binocular interaction and functional architecture in the cat's visual cortex." *Journal of Physiology* 160: 106–54.

Hyams, N. 1986: *Language Acquisition and the Theory of Parameters*. Dordrecht: Reidel.

—— 1996: "The underspecification of functional categories in early grammar." In H. Clahsen (ed.), *Generative Perspectives on Language Acquisition*, Amsterdam: Benjamins.

Iatridou, S. 1990: "About Agr(P)." *Linguistic Inquiry* 21: 551–77.

Janda, R. and B. Joseph (eds) (forthcoming): *Handbook of Historical Linguistics*. Oxford: Blackwell.

Jerison, H. J. 1976: "Paleoneurology and the evolution of mind." *Scientific American* 234.1: 90–101.

Jespersen, O. 1909: *Progress in Language*, 2nd edn. London: Swan Sonnenschein.

—— 1909–49: *A Modern English Grammar on Historical Principles*, 7 vols. London: Allen & Unwin.

—— 1922: *Language, its Nature, Development and Origin*. London: Allen & Unwin.

Johnson, K. 1997: "Head movement, word order and inflection" (MS, University of Massachusetts).

Kauffman, S. 1991: "Antichaos and adaptation." *Scientific American*, August: 78–84.

—— 1995: *At Home in the Universe: the search for laws of self-organization and complexity*. Oxford: Oxford University Press.

Kayne, R. S. 1994: *The Antisymmetry of Syntax*. Cambridge, Mass.: MIT Press.

Keenan, E. L. 1994: "Creating Anaphors: an historical study of the English reflexive pronouns" (MS, UCLA).

Kegl, J., A. Senghas, and M. Coppola 1998: "Creation through contact: sign language emergence and sign language change in Nicaragua." In DeGraff (ed.).

Kemenade A. van 1987: *Syntactic Case and Morphological Case in the History of English*. Dordrecht: Foris.

Kemenade, A. and N. Vincent (eds) 1997: *Parameters of Morphosyntactic Change*. Cambridge: Cambridge University Press.

Keyser, S. J. and W. O'Neil 1985: *Rule Generalization and Optionality in Language Change*. Dordrecht: Foris.

Kiparsky, P. 1995: "Indo-European origins of Germanic syntax." In Battye and Roberts (eds).

—— 1996: "The shift to head-initial VP in Germanic." In H. Thrainsson, S. Epstein, and S. Peters (eds), *Studies in Comparative Germanic Syntax*, vol. 2, Dordrecht: Kluwer.

—— 1997: "The rise of positional licensing in Germanic." In van Kemenade and Vincent (eds).

Kirschner, G. 1957: "Recent American influence on standard English: the syntactical sphere." *Zeitschrift für Anglistik und Amerikanistik* 5: 29–42.

Klima, E. 1964: "Relatedness between grammatical systems." *Language* 40.1: 1–20.

Kouwenberg, S. 1992: "From OV to VO: linguistic negotiation in the development of Berbice Dutch Creole." *Lingua* 88: 263–99.

Kroch, A. 1989: "Reflexes of grammar in patterns of language change." *Language Variation and Change* 1: 199–244.

—— 1994: "Morphosyntactic variation." In K. Beals et al. (eds), *Papers from the 30th Regional Meeting of the Chicago Linguistics Society: parasession on variation and linguistic theory*, Chicago: Chicago Linguistics Society.

Kroch, A. and A. Taylor 1997: "The syntax of verb movement in Middle English: dialect variation and language contact." In van Kemenade and Vincent (eds).

Kuipers, A. H. 1960: *Phoneme and Morpheme in Kabardian*. The Hague: Mouton.

Labov, W. 1994: *Principles of Linguistic Change*. Oxford: Blackwell.

Lachter, J. and T. Bever 1988: "The relation between linguistic structure and associative theories of language learning: a constructive critique of some connectionist learning models." In S. Pinker and J. Mehler (eds), *Connections and Symbols* (*Cognition*, special issue), Cambridge, Mass.: MIT Press.

Lakoff, R. T. 1972: "Another look at drift." In R. P. Stockwell and R. Macauley (eds), *Linguistic Change and Generative Theory*, Bloomington: Indiana University Press.

Lasnik, H. 1976: "Notes on coreference." *Linguistic Analysis* 2.1: 1–22.

—— 1995: "Verbal Morphology: *Syntactic Structures* meets the Minimalist Program" (MS, University of Connecticut). (Repr. in H. Lasnik, *Minimalist Analysis*, Oxford: Blackwell, 1999.)

Lass, R. 1980: *On Explaining Linguistic Change*. Cambridge: Cambridge University Press.

—— 1990: "How to do things with junk: exaptation in language evolution." *Journal of Linguistics* 26.1: 79–102.

—— 1997: *Historical Linguistics and Language Change*. Cambridge: Cambridge University Press.

Lehmann, W. P. 1967: *A Reader in Nineteenth-Century Historical Indo-European Linguistics*. Bloomington: Indiana University Press.

—— 1974: *Proto-Indo-European Syntax*. Austin: University of Texas Press.

Levinson, S. 1991: "Pragmatic reduction of the binding conditions revisited." *Journal of Linguistics* 27.1: 107–61.

Lewontin, R. C. 1995 "Genes, environment, and organisms." In R. B. Silvers (ed.), *Hidden Histories of Science*, New York: A New York Review Book.

Li, C. N. and S. Thompson 1976: "Subject and topic: a new typology of language." In C. N. Li (ed.), *Subject and Topic*, New York: Academic Press.

Lieber, R. 1982: "A note on the history of the English auxiliary." *MIT Working Papers in Linguistics* 4: 81–99.

Lightfoot, D. W. 1979: *Principles of Diachronic Syntax*. Cambridge: Cambridge University Press.

—— 1987: Review of Keyser and O'Neil 1985. *Language* 63.1: 151–4.

—— 1989: "The child's trigger experience: degree-0 learnability." *Behavioral and Brain Sciences* 12.2: 321–34.

—— 1991: *How To Set Parameters: arguments from language change.* Cambridge, Mass.: MIT Press.

—— 1993: "Why UG needs a learning theory: triggering verb movement." In C. Jones (ed.), *Historical Linguistics: problems and perspectives,* London: Longman, 190–214. (Repr. in Battye and Roberts (eds).)

—— 1994: "Degree-0 learnability." In B. Lust, G. Hermon and J. Kornfilt (eds), *Syntactic Theory and First Language Acquisition: crosslinguistic perspectives,* vol. 2: *Binding dependency and learnability,* Hillsdale, NJ: Erlbaum.

—— 1995: "Grammars for people." *Journal of Linguistics* 31: 393–9.

—— 1996: Review of Bauer 1995. *Language* 72.1: 156–9.

—— 1997a: "Catastrophic change and learning theory." *Lingua* 100 (50th anniversary issue): 171–92.

—— 1997b: "Shifting triggers and diachronic reanalyses." In van Kemenade and Vincent (eds).

Lightfoot, D. W. and N. Hornstein (eds) 1994: *Verb Movement.* Cambridge: Cambridge University Press.

Longobardi, G. 1994: "Reference and proper names: a theory of N-movement in syntax and logical form." *Linguistic Inquiry* 25.4: 609–65.

—— 1996: "Formal Syntax and Etymology: the history of French *chez*" (MS, Università de Venezia).

MacWhinney, B. and E. A. Bates (eds) 1990: *The Cross-linguistic Study of Sentence Processing.* Cambridge: Cambridge University Press.

Marcus, G. 1997: "Can connectionism save constructionism?" (MS, University of Massachusetts).

McCawley, N. 1976: "From OE/ME 'impersonals' to 'personal' constructions: what is a 'subject-less' S?" In S. Steever, C. Walker, and S. Mufwene (eds), *Diachronic Syntax,* Chicago: Chicago Linguistic Society.

Meillet, A. 1937: *Introduction à l'étude comparative des langues indo-européennes.* Paris: Hachette.

Miller, D. G. 1975: "Indo-European: VSO, SOV, SVO, or all three?" *Lingua* 37: 31–52.

Mitchell, B. 1985: *Old English Syntax.* Oxford: Oxford University Press.

Monod, J. 1972: *Chance and Necessity.* London: Collins.

Mossé, F. 1938: "Histoire de la forme périphrastique 'être + participe présent' en germanique." In *Collection linguistique de la Société Linguistique de Paris,* Paris: Klincksieck, 42–3.

Mustanoja, T. 1960: *A Middle English Syntax.* Helsinki: Société Néophilologique.

Newmeyer, F. 1991: "Functional explanation in linguistics and the origin of language." *Language and Communication* 11: 3–28.

Newport, E. L. 1998: "Reduced input in the acquisition of signed languages: contributions to the study of creolization." In DeGraff (ed.).

Newport, E. L., H. Gleitman and L. R. Gleitman 1977: "Mother, I'd rather do it myself: some effects and non-effects of maternal speech style." In Snow and Ferguson (eds).

Niyogi, P. and R. C. Berwick 1995: "The Logical Problem of Language Change" (MIT, A. I. Memo No. 1516).

—— 1997 "A dynamical systems model of language change." *Linguistics and Philosophy* (special issue on the mathematics of language).

Nunnally, T. 1985: "The Syntax of the Genitive in Old, Middle, and Early Modern English" (Ph.D. dissertation, University of Georgia).

O'Neil, W. 1978: "The evolution of the Germanic inflectional systems: a study in the causes of language change." *Orbis* 27.2: 248–85.

Osthoff, H. and K. Brugmann 1878: *Vorwort Morphologische Untersuchungen auf dem Gebiete der indogermanischen Sprachen*, vol. 1. Leipzig: S. Hirzel.

Otani, K. and J. Whitman 1991: "V-raising and VP-ellipsis." *Linguistic Inquiry* 22: 345–58.

Passy, P. 1891: *Étude sur les changements phonétiques et leurs caractères généraux.* Paris: Firmin-Didot.

Paul, H. 1877: "Die Vocale der Flexions- und Ableitungssilben in den ältesten germanischen Dialecten." *Beiträge zur Geschichte der deutschen Sprache und Literatur* 4: 314–475.

—— 1891: *Principles of the History of Language*, trans. from the 2nd edn of the original German by H. A. Strong. London: Longmans, Green & Co.

Pearce, E. 1990: *Parameters in Old French Syntax*. Dordrecht: Kluwer.

Pedersen, H. 1931: *The Discovery of Language: linguistic science in the nineteenth century*. Bloomington: Indiana University Press.

Piattelli-Palmarini, M. 1986: "The rise of selective theories: a case study and some lessons from immunology." In W. Demopoulos and A. Marras (eds), *Language Learning and Concept Acquisition: foundational issues*, Norwood, NJ: Ablex.

—— 1989: "Evolution, selection, and cognition: from 'learning' to parameter setting in biology and the study of language." *Cognition* 31: 1–44.

Pinker, S. 1994: *The Language Instinct: how the mind creates language*. New York: William Morrow.

Pinker, S. and P. Bloom 1990: "Natural language and natural selection." *Behavioral and Brain Sciences* 13: 707–84.

Pinker, S. and A. S. Prince 1988: "On language and connectionism: analysis of a parallel distributed processing model of language acquisition." *Cognition* 28: 73–193.

Pintzuk, S. 1991: "Phrase Structures in Competition: variation and change in Old English word order" (Ph.D. dissertation, University of Pennsylvania).

Platzack, C. 1986: "Comp, Infl, and Germanic word order." In L. Hellan and K. Koch Christensen (eds), *Topics in Scandinavian Syntax*, Dordrecht: Reidel.

Platzack, C. and A. Holmberg 1989: "The role of AGR and finiteness." *Working Papers in Scandinavian Syntax* 43: 51–76.

Popper, K. R. 1957: *The Poverty of Historicism*. London: Routledge & Kegan Paul.

Premack, D. 1980: "Representational capacity and accessibility of knowledge: the case of chimpanzees." In M. Piattelli-Palmarini (ed.), *Language learning: the debate between Jean Piaget and Noam Chomsky*, London: Routledge & Kegan Paul.

—— 1990: "Words: what are they, and do animals have them?" *Cognition* 37.3: 197–212.

Premack, D. and G. Woodruff 1978: "Chimpanzee problem-solving: a test for comprehension." *Science* 202 (Nov. 3): 532–5.

Quirk, R. and C. L. Wrenn 1955: *An Old English Grammar*. London: Methuen.

Radford, A. 1997: *Syntactic Theory and the Structure of English: a minimalist approach*. Cambridge: Cambridge University Press.

Rask, R. 1818: *Undersøgelse om det gamle Nordiske eller Islandske Sprogs Oprindelse*. Copenhagen: Gyldendalske Boghandlings Forlag.

Richards, B. J. 1990: *Language Development and Individual Differences: a study of auxiliary verb learning*. Cambridge: Cambridge University Press.

Ringe, D. A. 1995: "'Nostratic' and the factor of chance." *Diachronica* 12.1: 55–74.

Rizzi, L. 1990: *Relativized Minimality*. Cambridge, Mass.: MIT Press.

Roberts, I. G. 1985: "Agreement patterns and the development of the English modal auxiliaries." *Natural Language and Linguistic Theory* 3: 21–58.

—— 1993a: "A formal account of grammaticalization in the history of Romance futures." *Folia Linguistica Historica* 13: 219–58.

—— 1993b: *Verbs and Diachronic Syntax*. Dordrecht: Kluwer.

—— 1994: "Two types of head movement in Romance." In Lightfoot and Hornstein, (eds).

—— 1998: "Verb movement and markedness." In DeGraff (ed.).

Robins, R. H. 1967: *A Short History of Linguistics*. London: Longman.

Rohrbacher, B. 1994: "The Germanic VO Languages and the Full Paradigm: a theory of V to I raising" (Ph.D. dissertation, University of Massachusetts).

Sampson, G. 1980: *Schools of Linguistics: competition and evolution*. London: Hutchinson.

Santorini, B. 1992: "Variation and change in Yiddish subordinate clause word order." *Natural Language and Linguistic Theory* 10.4: 595–640.

—— 1993: "The rate of phrase structure change in the history of Yiddish." *Journal of Language Variation and Change* 5: 257–83.

Sapir, E. 1921: *Language*. New York: Harcourt.

—— 1929: "The status of linguistics as a science." *Language* 5: 207–14.

Schleicher, A. 1848: *Über die Bedeutung der Sprache für die Naturgeschichte des Menschen*. Weimar: Hermann Böhlau.

—— 1861–2: *Compendium der vergleichenden Grammatik der indogermanischen Sprachen*. Weimar: Hermann Böhlau.

—— 1863: *Die darwinische Theorie und die Sprachwissenschaft*. Weimar: Hermann Böhlau.

Shlonsky, U. 1988: "Complementizer-cliticization in Hebrew and the ECP." *Natural Language and Linguistic Theory* 6.2: 191–206.

Sievers, E. 1876: *Grundzüge der Lautphysiologie*. Leipzig: Breitkopf & Härtel.

Smith, J. M. 1992: "Taking a chance on evolution." *New York Review of Books*, May 14.

Smith, N. S. H., I. Robertson, and K. Williamson 1987: "The Ijo element in Berbice Dutch." *Language and Society* 16: 49–90.

Snow, C. 1977: "Mothers' speech research: from input to interaction." In Snow & Ferguson (eds).

Snow, C. and C. Ferguson (eds) 1977: *Talking to Children: language input and acquisition*. Cambridge: Cambridge University Press.

Sperry, R. 1968: "Plasticity of neural maturation." *Developmental Biology Supplement* 2: 306–27.

Sprouse, R. and B. Vance 1998: "An explanation for the loss of null subjects in certain Romance and Germanic languages." In DeGraff (ed.).

Stein, D. 1986: "Syntactic variation and change: the case of *do* in questions in Early Modern English." *Folia Linguistica Historica* 7.1: 121–49.

Stokoe, H. R. 1937: *The Understanding of Syntax*. London: Heinemann.

Stone, L. 1992: "The revolution over the revolution." *New York Review of Books*, June 11.

Supalla, S. 1990: "Segmentation of Manually Coded English: problems in the mapping of English in the visual/gestural mode" (Ph.D. dissertation, University of Illinois).

Sweet, H. 1899: *The Practical Study of Languages*. London: Dent.

—— 1900: *The History of Languages*. London: Dent.

Taylor, A. 1990: "Clitics and Configurationality in Ancient Greek" (Ph.D. dissertation, University of Pennsylvania).

—— 1994: "Variation in past tense formation in the history of English." In R. Izvorski et al. (eds), *University of Pennsylvania Working Papers in Linguistics*, vol. 1, 143–59.

Thomason, S. G. and T. Kaufman 1988: *Language Contact, Creolization, and Genetic Linguistics*. Berkeley: University of California Press.

Thompson, D. W. 1961: *On Growth and Form* (Abridged edn, ed. J. T. Bonner). Cambridge: Cambridge University Press.

Thornton, R. 1994: "Children's negative questions: a production/comprehension asymmetry." In J. Fuller, H. Han, and D. Parkinson (eds), *Proceedings of Eastern States Conference on Linguistics 1994*, Ithaca, NY: Cornell University, Department of Linguistics.

—— 1995: "Referentiality and *Wh*-movement in child English: juvenile D-*link*uency." *Language Acquisition* 4: 139–75.

Tieken-Boon van Ostade, I. 1987: *The Auxiliary DO in Eighteenth-Century English: a sociohistorical-linguistic approach*. Dordrecht: Foris.

Traugott, E. 1969: "Toward a grammar of syntactic change." *Lingua* 23: 1–27.

—— 1972: *The History of English Syntax*. New York: Holt, Rinehart and Winston.

—— 1992: "Syntax." In R. M. Hogg (ed.), *The Cambridge History of the English Language*, vol. 1: *The Beginnings to 1066*, Cambridge: Cambridge University Press.

—— (forthcoming): "On the role of constructions in grammaticalization." In Janda and Joseph (eds).

Traugott, E. and H. Smith 1993: "Arguments from language change." *Journal of Linguistics* 29: 431–47.

Tripp, A. 1978: "The psychology of impersonal constructions." *Glossa* 12: 177–89.

Uriagereka, J. 1988: "On Government" (Ph.D. dissertation, University of Connecticut).

—— 1998: *Rhyme and Reason in Human Language: an introductory dialogue to minimalist syntax*. Cambridge, Mass.: MIT Press.

Vance, B. 1995: "On the decline of verb movement to Comp in Old and Middle French." In Battye and Roberts (eds).

Vennemann, T. 1975: "An explanation of drift." In C. N. Li (ed.), *Word Order and Word Order Change*, Austin: University of Texas Press.

Verner, K. 1875: "Eine Ausnahme der ersten Lautverschiebung." *Zeitschrift für vergleichende Sprachforschung auf dem Gebiete der indogermanischen Sprachen* 23.2: 97–130.

Vikner, S. 1994: "Finite verb movement in Scandinavian embedded clauses." In Lightfoot and Hornstein (eds).

Visser, F. T. 1963–73: *An Historical Syntax of the English Language*. Leiden: Brill.

Waldrop, M. M. 1992: *Complexity: the emerging science at the edge of order and chaos*. New York: Simon & Schuster.

Warner, A. R. 1983: Review article on Lightfoot 1979. *Journal of Linguistics* 19: 187–209.

—— 1990: "Reworking the history of English auxiliaries." In S. Adamson, V. Law, N. Vincent, and S. Wright (eds), *Papers from the Fifth International Conference on English Historical Linguistics*, Amsterdam: Benjamins.

—— 1993: *English Auxiliaries: structure and history*. Cambridge: Cambridge University Press.

—— 1995: "Predicting the progressive passive: parametric change within a lexicalist framework." *Language* 71.3: 533–57.

—— 1997: "The structure of parametric change, and V movement in the history of English." In van Kemenade & Vincent (eds).

Watkins, C. 1976: "Toward Proto-Indo-European syntax: problems and pseudoproblems." In S. Stever, C. Walker, and S. Mufwene (eds), *Diachronic Syntax*, Chicago: Chicago Linguistic Society.

Weerman, F. 1993: "Reconsidering the role of parameters and 'peripheral rules' in language change." In *Handbook for the 11th International Conference on Historical Linguistics, UCLA*.

Weinreich, U., W. Labov, and M. I. Herzog 1968: "Empirical foundations for a theory of language change." In W. P. Lehmann and Y. Malkiel (eds), *Directions for historical linguistics: a symposium*, Austin: University of Texas Press, 95–189.

West, G. B., J. H. Brown, and B. J. Enquist 1997: "A general model for the origin of allometric scaling laws in biology." *Science* 276, April 4: 122–6.

Wexler, K. 1994: "Optional infinitives, head movement, and the economy of derivations." In Lightfoot and Hornstein (eds).

Whitney, D. 1875: *The Life and Growth of Language: an outline of linguistic science*. New York: D. Appleton & Co.

Wright, R. 1994: *The Moral Animal: why we are the way we are: the new science of evolutionary psychology*. New York: Random House.

Index